Caring by the Hour

Caring by the Hour

Women, Work, and Organizing at Duke Medical Center

Karen Brodkin Sacks

University of Illinois Press
Urbana and Chicago

©1988 by the Board of Trustees of the University of Illinois
Manufactured in the United States of America
1 2 3 4 5 C P 6 5 4 3 2

This book is printed on acid-free paper.

Library of Congress Cataloging-in-Publication Data

Sacks, Karen.
  Caring by the hour.
  Bibliography: p.
  Includes index.
  1. Duke University. Medical Center—Employees—History.
2. Trade unions—Hospitals—North Carolina—Durham—
Organizing—History. 3. Trade unions—North Carolina—
Durham—Afro-American membership—History. 4. Women in
trade-unions—North Carolina—Durham—History. I. Title.
RA982.D84D847 1988   331.88'1136211'09756563   87-5865
ISBN 0-252-01449-9 (cloth; alk. paper)
ISBN 978-0-252-01449-9 (cloth; alk. paper)
ISBN 0-252-01392-1 (paper; alk. paper)
ISBN 978-0-252-01392-8 (paper; alk. paper)

Contents

Preface

I first met Duke Medical Center workers in 1978, by participating in the last stages of their unionization efforts. In the intervening years this book about their organizing has made its presence felt in most of the work I've done; consequently, it has benefited from many people's contributions. As a result, I have accumulated more debts than the U.S. government.

First and foremost is my debt to Duke Hospital workers, not only union activists, but also some nonunion and even a couple of antiunion workers. This book is written in the tradition of feminist and radical scholarship in that it takes sides and challenges the idea that there is a privileged, objective, and neutral point of view, that observer and observed, analyst and subject are unrelated. I tried to be accountable in research and writing to those with whom I worked. Among other things, this involved sharing my interpretations with activist workers and submitting prepublication drafts for criticism. Each of these activities had its own consequences, and facing them with more or less success has in turn shaped the final work.

To ask those with whom I was working to share in my research was easier and more democratic in theory than it was in practice. Such participation demands more work from people than the most thoughtful interview. It also contains a hidden constraint: that the co-analyst either approach issues guided by my assumptions and questions, or challenge them. This research has been a very significant part of my life for many years, but it holds no such place in the lives of any of the women with

whom I have worked. Those who read and criticized drafts did me a great
and time-consuming favor. But the facts are that for most workers this
project had very low priority, and they hadn't the time for it. In part, this
reflects changed conditions. In 1978, I was part of a joint effort and was
truly accountable to both the hospital union organizing committee and to
a much more widely shared sense of collectivity and collective endeavor
among hospital workers. It was therefore easier to ask for critiques, and
more meaningful to workers to give them. But as that collectivity and its
constituent ties depoliticized, so too did that meaning. Despite these
barriers, Barbara Aaron, Gladys Glenn, and Barbara Parker read some
pretty raw drafts and remained for many years as some of my toughest
and most supportive critics. There are a few other Duke workers whom
I am able to thank by name for their assistance and advice: Jennifer Allen,
Shirley Ellis, Jennie Fish, Michael Gibson, Dorothy Harris, and Mary
Elizabeth Young. Many others, including more very insightful and persis-
tent critics, will have to remain anonymous for a variety of reasons.

Efforts to share my interpretations shed a new light on issues of objectivity. For example, early in the union drive, I offered my perspective on
a controversy about organizing tactics, based, I thought, on what I'd observed. The response from others on the organizing committee was,
roughly, "cut the crap, you have an axe to grind just like the rest of us."
They meant, first, that academic disciplines had no privileged vantage-
point—researchers ground axes too—and second, even among activists
there was neither one perspective nor a privileged perspective. Still,
because decisions had to be made and acted upon, there had to be areas
of agreement and consent, and therefore consistent relativism was not
consistent with participation and could not be consistent with involved
analysis, either. As in activity, analysis also requires commitment.

One of my early efforts to submit a prepublication draft to political
scrutiny sharpened some of the dimensions of what it means to be at once
subjective and accurate. A few months after all union activity died, I
wrote a short analysis based on interviews with several activist data terminal operators (DTOs) about their daily work lives and how oppressive job
conditions were. I gave it to one of the women whom I had interviewed,
who showed it to her friends. Their collective opinion was that it was
one-sided, that it pulled out only the bad things about their jobs, and
that what I'd written was appropriate for a leaflet if, and only if, they were
in the middle of a union battle. As it was, reading a list of grievances in
a time of movement doldrums made her feel "like I must be some kind

of fool to stay here if that's all there is." I reminded her that, in fact, the bad things were all any of them had talked about. She acknowledged that, and decided that I needed to talk to a range of people who had varying views on the work. She and her co-workers gave me a list of some twenty women to get to know, and their perspectives were more complex than were manifest from our shared context.

That incident and subsequent analysis of DTO work sharpened my recognition of the complexity of presenting something as seemingly simple as "a workers' perspective." I did get very different perspectives from different people, and I got still others from what I saw rather than from anything anyone said. In the diversity and even in some of the conflicting views, a fuller picture emerged, one that spoke to both the grievances and the rewards, and hence spoke as well to some of the reasons that DTOs fought to improve their conditions as well as why they stayed. I took this analysis back to as many of the forty or so DTOs I interviewed and could persuade to read it. The reactions, agreements, and disagreements of the five to ten who did read it varied on particulars, but they all recognized themselves collectively and in their diversity, and they acknowledged that the analysis was accurate in a way that was meaningful to them.

I had a somewhat different experience with my first-draft analysis of the second union drive and its failure. I thought I had written an analysis supportive of activists' efforts. But that is decidedly not the way the three women activists to whom I first submitted it read it. They were all quite angry. One wanted to me to take her out of the book (I did); the other two fortunately made the effort to do a full and persuasive critique and remained as very significant critics. Much of the book's strength comes as a result of our confrontations and their contributions.

Still, the favorable interpretations, like the unfavorable ones, are my responsibility in two ways. First, although I wanted to present workers' perspectives, I tried to do so in a way that highlights and accentuates the understandings that foster change. That is the underlying research question: What does it take to bring about change in the form of successful organizing, women's leadership, democratic process, and material improvements for workers? What then are the differences between "accurate" views and "inaccurate" ones? Is it only that the latter highlighted those understandings too much, or highlighted the wrong ones? I don't think so. Rather, I think that to analyze perspectives with transformative potential requires seeing them in the context of their limitations and their constraints. That means presenting many perspectives and forces, but it also means organizing them in a focused way. I do not know if I have succeeded in doing this consistently, but that is the kind of accuracy or objectivity I have tried to achieve. For it to be successful, workers must recognize it as meaningful, although they do not have to agree with my weightings or conclusions. That tension indicates that bias inheres in the act of analysis and in interaction.

Second, in the process of writing this book, I have also learned a great deal from academic colleagues and members of Durham's activist community. At Duke and UNC, Leah Wise, Jack Preiss, Sid Nathans, James Gifford, Leon Fink, and the staff of the Duke University Archives generously shared their knowledge and unpublished materials about the history of Durham and its movements. Barbara Taylor, my research assistant, conducted indispensable research and interviews with food and housekeeping workers. Dolores Burke and Marietta Whitted provided me with valuable information on Duke's affirmative action efforts. Gladys Glenn let me read her files and scrapbooks; the *NC Anvil* opened its archives to me; and Deborah Swanner of the North Central Legal Assistance Project helped me through the maze of court documents and made public documents of the U.S. District Court available to me.

Ann Bookman, Louise Lamphere, Sandra Morgen, Phyllis Palmer, Naomi Quinn, Nate Raymond, Roberta Spalter-Roth, Carol Stack, Soon Young Yoon, and Kate Porter Young all read and critiqued parts of the manuscript. Ann Kahl and Deborah Klein at the Bureau of Labor Statistics provided valuable information. As the book took on more and more a historical flavor, Eileen Boris, Alice Kessler-Harris, Jacquelyn Hall, Carol Lasser, Barbara Melosh, Ruth Milkman, and Anne Scott all wrestled through the whole manuscript; they helped turn it right side out thematically and made sure that it told the story chronologically. Naomi Quinn, Carol Stack, and Kate Porter Young have all provided my North Carolina homes away from home, sounding-boards, and support for years. Far from least, Benjamin and Daniel Sacks have been very gracious about sharing most of their teenage years with this book and all the moves that it brought with it.

Research support was provided by a National Institute for Mental Health postdoctoral fellowship at Duke's Center for the Study of the Family and the State and by a National Science Foundation research grant in anthropology. The Duke Anthropology Department gave me both collegial and institutional support for the duration of this project. The Business and Professional Women's Foundation provided leave and research support. At Oberlin College's Mudd Library, Kerry Langan, Cynthia Comer, and Allison Gould located hard-to-find sources. At the University of Illinois Press, my editor Carole Appel provided support throughout, and Mary Giles greatly improved my prose. Various parts of the book gained a great deal from presentation and discussion at the Berkshire Women's History Conference, the Pembroke Seminar on Women and Work, the Max Planck Institut-Maison des Sciences de L'Homme Conference on Family: Emotion and Material Interest, the American Anthropological Association, Sociologists for Women and Society, Manchester University's Anthropology Department, and the Women's Seminar at Cambridge University.

Introduction

This book is about how clerical, service, and technical workers almost succeeded in unionizing Duke University Medical Center. The story's beginnings lie in the convergence of the civil rights movement and the industrialization of health-care work. At Duke, the confluence sparked black service workers to unionize. Women's everyday work culture and black women's social networks are at the story's center, because they provided the organizational structure and direction for more than a decade of struggle. This story emerges from a combination of historical narrative and descriptions of everyday work life.

Duke University and its Medical Center stand at the center of many lives. Monument to one of the nation's wealthiest families, the university is the largest employer in Durham, with an hourly work force larger than the population of many a North Carolina town; the medical center's acreage would more than cover the downtown areas of most small towns. Duke has shaped Durham's geography as well as put its stamp on both the town's political economy and the social relations of its one hundred thousand residents.

By 1983, more than 9,000 people worked in the medical center, including a faculty of almost 900 M.D.s and Ph.D.s, 900 salaried administrators, almost 700 interns, residents and fellows, and almost 500 medical students. Together with some 1,200 registered nurses (most of whom were hourly workers in this medical center), they are part of the background of this book. Clearly "significant others" in the world of hospital workers, they will appear only as they impinge on the lives of service, clerical, and technical workers.[1]

Soap operas and scholars seem to agree that hospital workers are doctors
and nurses. There are no television shows and hardly any research about
the work lives of ward clerks, housekeepers, aides, secretaries, and food
service workers.[2] Still, behind Duke University Medical Center's white
men and women in white is an army of black and white, primarily women,
in yellow, blue, and green who are responsible for more patient care than
meets the eye, and who also cook, clean, and keep the records of everyone's work and health. Their fund of experience is often the key to putting
the Humpty Dumpty of hospital specialization together again. This daily
work, and the work cultures Duke workers have created from their experiences, have been the wellsprings of more than a decade of union and civil
rights efforts in Durham. This book is about these workers' contributions
to health and history.

In 1978, I set out to study how women organized and exercised leadership at a grass-roots level. To do this, I participated in the then-ongoing
union drive and also interviewed workers about their past unionization
efforts. But participation and interviewing yielded contradictory impres-
sions. Participation in the 1978–79 union drive and observing women's
daily work lives in subsequent years taught me a great deal about why
that drive did not succeed. Yet interviews and research about Duke workers' efforts for the previous fifteen years left an equally strong sense of the
considerable grass-roots strength and unity involved in sustaining unionization efforts for so long and coming within a hairsbreadth of victory in
1976. As an anthropologist, my first instincts were to base my analysis on
what I observed, and hence it centered on the events of 1978–79. That
analysis was about failure and weakness, although I was not fully comfortable with it, not least because it contradicted things people told me in
interviews about the past. I passed from discomfort to distress when
several workers who read that early draft told me, with justice, that it was
a fairly negative distortion of their experiences. In this instance, I think
that the method of participant observation itself necessarily highlighted
the negative and filtered out the positive: The fact that workers lost the
1979 election indicated that the weaknesses did indeed predominate, and
such an analysis needed to reflect that. An ethnographer might well have
to chronicle a winning fight to do justice to resistance and strength.

Still, interviews and the historical record of Duke workers' efforts contained much to contradict the evidence from participant observation. As
Duke expanded in the 1960s and 70s, these workers seemed to be produc-
ing a commodity—"care"—under conditions long familiar on assembly

lines. Black workers experienced the worst of this new-style industrial efficiency and the old-style paternalistic racism. Heartened by the civil rights movement, they began to organize and to encourage white workers to join them. They fought against Durham's largest employer, unabashedly antiunion and one of the more powerful institutions in a state known for its hostility to unions. To have *persisted* against those odds for over a decade surely must have taken a great deal of organizational strength and shared convictions.

A different picture emerged when I put the insights of participant observation from 1978 to 1984 together with those that came from looking at the past and saw them in relationship to one another. It was less a catalog of strong and weak points and more a descriptive analysis of how and where political activism is embedded in, and flowers from, everyday interpersonal and social experiences. Briefly, the story is as follows: For most of its history the movement at Duke was rooted locally. Its leaders were black workers, and its sustaining core was black women, with critical participation from several networks of white workers, especially women. These efforts rested on an internal structure of women's work groups and community and family networks. Although it sometimes looked as if workers simply followed articulate and popular leaders, leadership came at least as much from collectivities of women as from articulate speakers. The collective leadership of black women's work-based networks was the organizational strength and sustaining force of the movement. When those networks mobilized, the movement lived and grew; when they depoliticized or demobilized, the movement died, and unionization died with it. The historical analysis of unionization focuses on the *conditions* under which women's social networks did and did not become active politically; the participant observation and interviews focus on the *process* by which they did so. The heartening aspect of the synthesis is that it indicates that the seeds of activism seem to be preserved, even if they stay dormant, in the stuff of daily work culture. And that stuff, at least in women's workplaces, seems to include a familistic idiom of resistance. That is, women used family-derived values about adulthood, work, and respect to assert and legitimate their positive evaluation of their own skill and worth in opposition to the hospital's denigration of them.

The enduring paradox of participating and observing was that everyday people doing ordinary tasks in more or less the same way, day in and day out, made things change. In the process, the actors made and remade themselves. It was hard for me to capture on paper these relationships between routine and change; it was like trying to paint a portrait of a flower blooming. The wellsprings for change lie in people's tasks and interactions—but these are multileveled, and their quality and texture are seldom confrontational or radical. If one sits and watches people's work lives, even where they are most arduous and oppressive, it is rare to see anyone openly challenging the status quo. But confront they do. To understand how workers make things *change* requires putting the day-to-day analysis back in the stream of historical analysis, asking how the social alternatives may have changed, trying to capture some of the archeology of workers' cultures.

Research and Methodology Issues

In the fall of 1978 I attended a union open-house for workers and supporters, introduced myself to workers and the campaign director from the Washington, D.C. office of the American Federation of State, County and Municipal Employees (AFSCME), and talked at length with him and with several members of the organizing committee about the possibility of working on the campaign and pursuing my research. They were glad to have additional support. Some were interested in my research, others were not but thought that it was at least harmless. Between November 1978 and the election in February 1979, I worked as a volunteer member of the organizing committee. Afterward, through 1980, and then part-time between May 1982 and October 1984, I observed people work, interviewed them about their work and families past and present, and conducted historical research. The project raises two sets of methodological issues that call for some discussion. The first has to do with combining history and ethnography; the second stems from combining political involvement in the union drive with research.

History and Ethnography. What was originally meant to be a simple description of women's work culture and activism turned into a history of Duke workers' organizing efforts in spite of my intention. During the drive, I was frustrated because I did not find the kinds of work cultures and networks I had expected. After the drive ended, my efforts to understand the nature of women's activism kept leading away from the present and into the past, and away from women and gender issues toward issues of race and class. Workers told me about national and local events that had taken place more than a decade earlier as if they had happened yesterday. Organizers referred to strikes and big demonstrations at Duke in an indeterminate past. Many of them seemed to know of and to take heart in a golden age of activism, when they won real victories and when unity happened almost spontaneously—or as one woman later put it, "We didn't have a a bit of trouble; they just had confidence I guess."

As I became involved in the living histories by which different participants analyzed their actions, I saw that women's work culture and social networks had indeed functioned (and still did) in a collective and oppositional way, but that it would take a study of the historical context of unionization to make that clear. Addressing the historical questions about the success and failure of unionization in turn shed further light on how race and gender structured the lives of Duke workers and shaped the ties and values around which they organized.

The resulting analysis is an odd mixture of history and ethnography, and it draws on methods from both. It also departs from standard third-person narrative and analysis in several places. I have used the first person either to highlight information gathered in later years and applied to earlier times, or where my participation was part of the interaction.

The combination of history and ethnography presents its own problems, because history and ethnography are different disciplines governed by different criteria of evidence and different notions of what constitutes a satisfactory explanation. In this study, the disciplines clashed over time sequences and over the issue of specificity versus anonymity.

Time: Ethnographic Present versus Historical Sequence. As an anthropologist, I expected to be able to learn about and to describe the structure of women's activism during the particular period of time that I conducted participant observation research, what anthropologists call the "ethnographic present." As historical change loomed larger, not only in scope, but also as a major subject itself, I abandoned the idea of trying to establish an ethnographic present and let this become an analysis of change, and necessarily a historical one.

This presented some problems with sequence, because I was simultaneously observing work and social networks as they were structured between 1978 and 1984 and interviewing workers about earlier organizing roughly during the years 1974–79. Barbara Taylor, my research assistant, and I did almost all of the workplace observation and interviews after the union campaign ended in 1979. In some jobs, there seem to have been few changes in the time between unionization efforts and interviews, whereas

I lack clear information about the earlier years of other jobs. When what I observed between 1979 and 1984 seemed to be basically similar to things or events between 1974 and 1979—judging from conversations and interviews with those workers as well as from written information about earlier years—I have used those observations to illuminate the historical narrative of the earlier years. Some of the work-based social networks described are reconstructed from interviews about the relevant historical period, but some of the general descriptions come from observation and interviews done later. Some of the enthnography's persuasiveness rests on the extent to which the analysis of work in the present illuminates processes that seem to have operated in the past.

The medical center itself also changed in important ways during this research. In 1980, Duke opened a whole new hospital, transforming work loads, staffing, where people worked, and their patterns of social interaction. Too, cutbacks in federal funding deepened progressively in the early eighties; increasingly rigid specialization and heightened educational criteria decreased workers' mobility; and the introduction of new rules for Medicaid and Medicare reimbursement in 1983 radically changed how all hospitals operate, not just Duke. In addition, the national economic and political climate worsened. Workers and unionists became more beleaguered and had fewer resources available to them. Black workers faced the dismantling of painfully built affirmative action programs and the closing down of economic and educational opportunities.

In talking with the same people over several years, I learned anew that such changes affect how people see their past and present, what they are willing to do as well as the outcomes of their actions. The rise and decline of organizing itself has had a significant impact on the decisions and priorities of the women I have come to know. The time period in which I interviewed or observed people shaped their interpretations of both the present and the past. For example, my observations of people's daily work gave me a sense of some of their "invisible" work and skills without which the hospital could not function. These skills were not invisible to those who exercise them—although they were not fully visible, either. The women with whom I talked had different views of their work, ranging from agreement with the Duke administration's low evaluation of it to persuasive cases for its key administrative or care-giving nature. Sometimes, the same person expressed both views at different times.

The same women acted and saw themselves differently at different points in this period. Some women who seemed apolitical or to be looking for individual upward mobility in the 1980s were militant organizers not that long before. As gains won in union drives were lost, the wider social horizons and possibilities that animated workers in earlier years shrank. How women saw their work and their relationships to others played a big part in their individual and collective definitions of rights, notions of fairness, and their willingness to act. Some of these changes were more easily learned from watching people work and discussing their work with them, whereas others were sharper when the focus was historical.

I am not sure that I would have understood many of the complexities of historical events had I not combined history with participation and observation Ethnography's usefulness here is in its *interaction* with history. Likewise, the historical narrative derives much of its meaning from the way ethnography fleshes out the richness of daily life. Observations from the present inform and illuminate interviews and documents about the past, and those interviews in turn give new perspectives to the observations.

The interaction of historical change and daily life is a close one in another way. On the one hand, economic and political changes at the national level have helped bring about these particular losses. On the other hand, Duke workers' actions have also made for real changes in the patterns of racial and sexual job segregation and in pay and working conditions for many workers, and these improvements will no doubt influence the likelihood and ways of organizing in the future. Duke has been undoing workers' gains in the years since the movement quieted down. This shows the fragility of workers' victories, but it also indicates that the process of organizing can itself produce real gains.

Specifity and Anonymity. For historians, general truth is inseparable from the historical and social particulars of the case. For anthropologists and social scientists generally, reality and truth lie in principles validated by repetition and replication. Therefore, some particulars can be omitted or changed provided essential principles or generalizations are retained. Anthropologists frequently change particulars in order to protect the identities of people with whom they work. This usually requires using pseudonyms, and traditionally it has meant disguising the location of the study. This may have presented few practical problems in the past for ethnographies of daily life in small communities in lands with which the readers are unfamiliar. It presented great problems in this study, where the particular historical context is what gives meaning to the explanation of social process on the one hand, and gives away the place on the other. Historian friends who read earlier anonymous versions of the manuscript found that it lacked substance because real institutions and places were not identified. Social process cannot be abstracted from real historical time and space. Workers who read it also thought that it would make more interesting reading if Duke were identified.

Disguising individual people was never an issue. I have invented pseudonyms for all the workers, except for public figures, Oliver Harvey and Howard Fuller, described from publicly accessible, written sources. However, because some workers may recognize some others, as may some administrators or supervisors, I have also concealed or omitted things that might be troublesome or harmful to people. I have shown the draft manuscript to as many workers as possible. Also, at the request of specific individuals and on my own initiative, I have deliberately obscured some events and descriptions. I think I have maintained the essential accuracy despite the distorted packaging.

At a practical level, disciplinary clashes revolved around whether or not to try to make the city and the institution anonymous. If authenticity lies in the historical specifics of Duke and Durham, then trying to disguise them would turn the analysis into a novel. Among other considerations, I would not be able to give credit where it was due, as well as where scholarly footnoting practices require it be given. Primary sources and some published ones are dead giveaways. So too are key elements of the narrative itself that involve things that cannot be changed without changing the meaning of the analysis. Various anthropologist friends suggested compromises, for example, eliminating footnotes and putting the sources in a a bibliographical essay along with other sources that point to other sites, thereby taking out some of the particulars. Others suggested that the institutional disguise needs only to be a formality to satisfy disciplinary conventions, because Duke workers and administrators would be able to identify the institution under any circumstances.

If I could identify the institution and protect individuals, were there *any* reasons to avoid identifying the city and institution? The only reason that I could find was a bad one. Anonymity and the protection it seemed to offer would make it difficult for workers, historians, and social scientists at Duke and elsewhere in the area to comment on and criticize this work. There are many such people who have lived through the events described and who know a great deal more than I do. They have shared their work and ideas with me, but they may well disagree with what I have written. A decision to maintain institutional anonymity would have the ironic consequence of forestalling some of the most potentially involved and informed political and scholarly dialogue.

Subjects and Subjectivity. This is a study of how workers organized within Duke Medical Center, but it is not a study of Duke Medical Center. The distinction is important. Its subject is pro-union workers. I tried to develop an interpretation from workers' perspectives, one that was recognizable and reasonable to them, and one that also answered my questions about how they organized. Workers, even pro-union ones (and I am weak on workers hostile to unionization), were not all alike; they had different jobs, families, social ties, histories, hopes, and attitudes, as well as races and genders. My central task was to address some of that complexity. Management's interpretations were not a necessary part of this endeavor, although they were certainly one pole of a polarized union drive situation.

More political considerations informed my initial decision not to request medical center sponsorship or permission to conduct my research; it was the only possible decision at the time. I couldn't straddle the fence in the polarized situation of a union drive, nor did I want to try. Still, most of the research continued long after the drive ended. For most of that time, through 1984, there was no union effort, and the hard pro- and antiunion lines that were so apparent earlier dissolved with the passage of time. It probably would have been possible in later years to arrange institutional sponsorship without being thought disloyal.

I did not do so because I had already become committed methodologically to a focus on workers, their work, and work cultures. As a participant-observer in the union drive, I knew that I influenced what I observed, but I also became very aware of how those with whom I worked and to whom I was obligated shaped my observations and interpretations. Mutual influence and obligations are defining characteristics of social relationships. For a researcher, one of the greatest gifts is information and interpretation. As every anthropologist knows, gifts carry obligations. As I shifted my balance from activism to research, I became increasingly aware of the need to be reasonably consistent in choosing to whom I would become obligated, and thus who would be likely to shape the interpretations. For this reason, I declined an AFSCME offer to become a paid organizer during the union drive. I felt that being on the AFSCME payroll would have obliged me to behave somewhat differently than I wanted to, and I was afraid of trying to think one way while I was acting another.

I was far more reluctant to take on obligations to Duke, even to ask individual administrators connected with the medical center for information. There was clearly much to learn from them, and some would have been willing to share useful information difficult to learn in other ways. I did not pursue such possibilities for fear of informal and unknown obligations that the gift of information might carry. Instead, it seemed that the most ethical and least conflict-ridden course was to forgo both institutional sponsorship and management information. This decision means that there are gaps in the study that result from a lack of information one can only gain, or best gain, from management.

Although there was a certain seat-of-the-pants aspect to this methodology, I think that many researchers confront similar issues. More researchers are working close to home, and many who write about workers, women, and minorities do so out of political and social commitment. Especially in women's studies and social history, there has been a remarkable flowering of working-class-centered scholarship and black feminism, both of which challenge many areas of received wisdom. Issues of agency, subjectivity, and objectivity have long been live ones among radical, black, and third-world Marxist and feminist social scientists. And it seems that anthropologists and historians who do such work are becoming enamoured with each other's disciplines and discoveries. I see this study as part of, and contributor to, those efforts in politics, content, and method.

The book has three parts, each of which combines ethnographic analysis and historical narrative in various proportions. In Part 1 (chapters 1–2), I set out the social context and the historical background for medical center organizing. The players are described in chapter 1, which traces Duke's growth as a major medical institution and the concomitant growth and transformations of its work force. It describes the flavor of work and the institution's changing place in Durham. Chapter 2 locates the beginnings of hospital worker militance in the convergence of the black freedom movement and the industrialization of health-care work. This chapter deals with the successful unionization efforts by black service workers at Duke University from 1965–72 that set the stage for hospital organizing. Part 2 (chapters 3–6) is about the structure and history of black women's places in medical center unionization. Chapter 3 analyzes patterns of racial segregation in clerical jobs and explores the relationship between race, working conditions, and opportunities for black and white women. It links these to different work cultures and patterns of public militance among black and white women. This sets the stage for chapter 4, a historical analysis of the near-successful 1974–76 drive to extend the benefits of unionization to workers in the medical center. Chapter 5 focuses on women's workplace networks, work cultures, and leadership structures to show why that drive was as successful as it was. It also deals with what happened to destroy women's leadership, and hence to contribute to defeat. Chapter 6 returns to historical analysis to describe the failure of the second union drive and to relate it to the continuing lack of mobilization of women's work-based leadership.

Part 3 (chapters 7–8) deals with the erosion and changes that Duke workers see in their work lives since 1979 in the context of national changes in health-care funding and policies. These changes suggest that future organizers are likely to confront a different and differently divided work force. In chapter 7, I examine work-force attrition in food services and cleaning work, and in chapter 8 the negative impact of professionalization and upgrading on black and white working-class technicians, practical nurses, and clerical workers. Chapter 9 is a summary and conclusion.

NOTES

1. Calculated from EEO/AA Report, Sept. 1983.
2. Fox, 1985.

I

Background to Unionization

Health care is one of the nation's largest and most highly differentiated industries, as well as one of the most important employers of women. It is an exemplary industry of the so-called postindustrial service economy. What happens in health care has been and will continue to be very important for shaping the chances of women and minority men in the work force. With almost eight million workers in 1983, it employed one in thirteen American workers, four out of five of whom were women, and one in four of whom was a minority worker. One out of every seven working women is employed in health care. At Duke, four out of five hourly workers are women, and about 45 percent are black. This part of the book will trace the growth of Duke University's medical complex, the evolution of its work force from objects of charity to an underpaid sector of the industrial working class, and the beginnings of protest among black workers.

From the late 1950s to the mid-70s, there was a sharp growth in labor militancy in hospitals across the nation, Duke included. The militancy was fueled by two sets of larger changes. The first had to do with the transformation of hospital work itself. Although the division of labor in hospital work rests heavily on industrial principles, the product, medical and emotional care, is often quite intangible, but has very concrete accounting and costs. Many hospital workers experience the health industry as an oxymoron, as they literally care by the hour. Workers began to feel that their work was growing more factorylike in its separation of conception and direction from execution, increasing intensification of supervision, substitution of less for more skilled labor, and introduction of new technologies to substitute for more expensive human labor power.

The second contributing factor to hospital unionization was the rise of the civil rights and black freedom movements. These movements attacked the patterns of racial segregation that placed minority workers at the bottom of municipal service and hospital jobs. In the late 1950s and the 1960s, it was primarily black, Hispanic, and women workers in expanding major urban medical complexes in the North who initiated a national wave of hospital and public worker unionization by refusing to stay in their abysmally paid places. Their struggle was soon taken up by southern workers. These union drives of the 1960s consciously joined the issues of workers' rights to those of civil rights. They injected issues of class and economic justice into the civil rights movement, forced the labor movement to deal with racial justice, and laid the groundwork for later efforts by women to force labor unions to deal with gender equity. Although southern efforts, including those at Duke, had only mixed success if measured in terms of winning union representation, they underlined health care's emergence as a major industry in America. More significantly, they made black workers, and black women especially, very visible as key actors in a reawakening of working-class activism. The labor movement became aware of race and racism in these years, and the black freedom movement became aware of issues of class, but neither movement dealt with issues of gender and both thought of workers as gender-neutral. So too did workers at Duke; there was no public recognition either of discrimination against women, or of the key roles that they played in organizing and leading. Informally, women and men recognized women's militancy and leadership, although they were not made political issues—a theme that will be treated in Part 2.

1

Duke Medical Center and Its Workers

Modern medical centers and health-care unions both have their roots in the social organization of nineteenth-century hospitals as charity institutions. Sustained by donations from wealthy merchants and industrialists, nineteenth-century hospitals were devoted to caring for the bodies and souls of society's unfortunates, be they patients or hospital workers. Although Duke Medical Center was built in the twentieth century, its impetus also lay in the Duke family's charity and Christian stewardship. Like other large hospitals, its pattern of growth was shaped by the twentieth-century partnership between the rising captains of industry and the emerging medical elite.

Nineteenth-century hospital superintendants did not acknowledge the existence of workers—nurses, aides and clerical, food and cleaning support staff—as a clear category or set of social relationships. One was either a dispenser of charity, as with trustees and doctors, or a recipient of it. Patients in nineteenth-century hospitals were often expected to clean, wash, cook, and nurse each other, and the line between patient and worker was perhaps less clear than their commonality. Both were regarded as beings in need of moral (and sometimes medical) uplift and for whom work was a part of redemption. The result was that hospital workers were treated as casual laborers, or in the case of nurses, unpaid and transient apprentices, objects of paternalism in how and how much they were compensated, as well as in their daily and long-term treatment.

That same philosophy governed both the care of poor patients and employee relations well into the twentieth century, long after hospitals had begun to become more businesslike in their organization and more scientific in their practice of medicine. As a result, by the 1930s, hospitals were becoming contradictory places to work. These contradictions in employee relations persisted for some time, but did not become apparent or explosive until after hospitals had further expanded, specialized, and rationalized their employee functions and relations during the prosperous 1950s and 1960s. This chapter analyzes the contradictory forces of paternalism and industrial rationality at Duke Medical Center.

Good Works and Cigarettes

Created by the Duke family in the nineteenth-century tradition of good works, the Duke Hospital and Medical School complex became a southern instance of the marriage between the emerging industrial and medical elites. Washington Duke and his sons began their career processing pipe tobacco. In 1874, they opened a factory in Durham, then a growing tobacco town, and to better compete with the already-established producers of Bull Durham tobacco, began to produce a newer product, cigarettes. The combination of northern capital, cigarette-rolling machinery, advertising, and "reorganization to make cheaper and more efficient use of labor" helped Duke gain control of cigarette manufacturing in Durham by 1887.[1]

In 1890, Washington Duke's son, James B. Duke, already resident in New York, initiated a consolidation of the existing big tobacco companies and became president of the resulting American Tobacco Company. Although that company was broken up by a 1911 Supreme Court decision against it for illegal restraint of trade, the Court allowed a reduced-in-size American Tobacco Company to remain under Duke control. That company alone produced more than one-third of all cigarettes in the United States.[2] The Dukes' success at popularizing cigarette smoking and organizing the industry along the lines of an industrial monopoly made them an early and major industrial force of the post–Civil War New South. When they subsequently invested in hoisery and textile mills in Durham and the surrounding area, they also became one of its wealthiest families. The enduring capstone of the family fortune, however, was secured in the Southern Power Company, later called Duke Power.

In keeping with the Dukes' place in the nation's industrial ruling class, much of the family fortune not used to create more wealth went into caring for the bodies and souls of the less fortunate through the traditional routes of building schools, hospitals, and churches. Like John D. Rockefeller, whose funding of medicine he emulated, James B. Duke seems to have preferred a businesslike approach to his philanthropy.[3]

The Duke Endowment, which he established in 1924, became one of the South's largest private foundations. It financed Duke Hospital and Medical School, which in turn became a part of the transformation of Duke-financed Trinity College into Duke University. In its turn, according to a contemporary observer, Duke University was intended to nurture and protect monopoly capitalism in general. As B. D. MacNeill, journalist and associate of James B. Duke, paraphrased the latter's explanation: "Public thinking and public attitudes toward private business . . . are determined primarily by lawyers who dominate government; by preachers who dominate religion; by doctors who dominate life and death. Duke University would have the outstanding medical school of the South, and hard by would be a great school of theology and another of law. It was simple enough. Here were the sources of public opinion. The University would take care of them. So with the Endowment."[4]

Duke Hospital and Medical School were also part of the nation's emerging medical-industrial elite. Duke Univeristy's first president, William Preston Few, the son of a physician and a Harvard graduate, was well-connected to the nation's major academic circles and to the cohort that historian Richard Brown has called "Rockefeller medicine men." He was a friend of Simon Flexner, head of the Rockefeller Institute, and through him maintained close relations with John D. Rockefeller's General Education Board, the funding institution set up to restructure medical education. Few developed the medical school project in close cooperation with both the General Education Board and Abraham Flexner, hoping for both board and Duke family support. However, when Duke committed $6 million to the venture, the board refused to fund the school, in part because they feared Duke would have more control than they. However, Duke was wealthy enough to proceed without Rockefeller funding.[5]

The result was a hospital-medical school complex that operated from the outset at the most advanced standards of American medicine of the time. In 1930, it had 156 beds, 46 medical faculty, 9 interns and residents, 70 medical students, 30 nurses, and 31 nonmedical staff. The bulk of its medical and administrative staffs were recruited directly from Johns Hopkins. Still, like other hospitals with longer histories, Duke's initial organization combined the businesslike science of medical administrators with nineteenth-century traditions of medical charity. It sought to provide some form of affordable care for poor people, whom doctors in any case needed as "teaching material." But it also exerted great pressure on all patients—even the poorest—to pay *some* portion of their hospital care. Duke worked in a variety of ways to encourage the North Carolina state and county governments to commit tax revenues to cover the remainder of poor patients' fees. It developed large outpatient clinics designed in part for the poor, and in part as a response to widespread depression-caused poverty. These clinics were intended to operate cheaply by accommodating many patients each day in a small space, and who would be attended by medical students, interns, and residents.[6]

Duke Hospital opened its doors to a poor state in the middle of the country's worst depression in modern times. Despite the fact that both the hospital and medical school were relatively well-subsidized by the Duke Endowment and by fees received by its clinical teaching staff from private patients, they soon found themselves in the same quandry as hospitals across the nation in facing massive problems; people were unable to pay their medical bills and asked to be taken as charity patients. Although the right of the poor and indigent to free hospital care was still widely accepted in the 1920s and 30s, the number of charity patients across the country mushroomed beyond hospitals' capacities or desires to handle them.

A variety of experimental health insurance plans, many of which ultimately coalesced into Blue Cross, were important in helping medicine to survive these lean years.[7] One such plan developed spontaneously at Duke when the hospital began a form of prepaid health insurance, patterned after a prepayment health plan offered by several nearby textile plants. Although Duke's plan was originally intended for farmers and wage earners, it turned out to be priced beyond their means. Instead, it attracted a white middle-class and professional clientele. In this respect it was quite similar to most health insurance plans before World War II. At Duke, only one in four white patients, and one in twenty-five black patients, were able to pay their hospital bills in full. Consequently, the hospital started two less-expensive plans in 1936, a ward care plan for poor whites and a cheaper plan that had fewer benefits for blacks.[8]

Throughout the nation, the Great Depression exacerbated the contradictoriness of modern hospital-based medicine as the tradition of free care for the poor clashed with rising costs of a medicine shaped by a nascent scientific and entrepreneurial medical establishment. In its effort to increase revenues, Duke soon eliminated both free care and its sliding scale for doctors' fees and insisted that patients pay in advance. However, these changes drove away large numbers of clients, many of whom had paid for their care, as well as clinic patients, who were the source of

medical student practice. Although Duke backed down from these measures, it successfully instituted a system whereby patients were required
to raise half the cost of their care from their county of residence or from
friends and to pay before treatment.[9] It is testimony to the power of Duke
Hospital that, in a poor state hard-hit by the depression, it was able to
make a significant assault on the concept of free medical care for the poor,
and to institute the principle that tax monies be used to pay fees at a
private hospital. All of this has now become commonplace throughout the
nation, but Duke was among the pioneers in these practices.

Industrializing Health Care: Financing the Duke Empire

Medicine grew explosively after World War II, and in the process
completed its transformation nationally and at Duke from a craft of general, office-based physicians to an industrial system of hospital-based specialists centered in university complexes for teaching and medical research.
Federal funds fueled most of the metamorphosis, although it was initiated
by social security, unionized workers' struggles for employer-paid private
health insurance, and hospitals' own efforts during the depression. Immediately after World War II, the number of unionized workers who
successfully bargained and went on strike for employer contributions to
health insurance coverage under union agreements expanded significantly, and so did the scope of their coverage.[10] By the early 1950s, unionized workers, then more than one-third of the work force, had won significant access to employer-paid health insurance.[11]

Federal funding for the nascent health industry began with the Hill-
Burton Act of 1946, which provided grants and loans to states, particularly
those with relatively few hospital beds, to build hospitals in communities
lacking them. The passage of Medicaid and Medicare in 1965 came about
largely as a result of popular pressure and urban rebelliousness and
significantly expanded the portion of the populace with access to health
coverage. As a result of all these programs, by 1975, the federal government was paying almost 40 percent of the total cost of the nation's health
care, which by the end of 1984 was 11 percent of the GNP. Medicare and
Medicaid alone paid for 27 percent.[12] Still, in 1984 there were twenty-five
million people who had no health insurance at all.[13]

Duke Medical Center began a major expansion of its physical plant
immediately after the war, building new facilities for teaching, patient
care, and research. Between 1948 and 1960, these included several addi-
tions to the original hospital, a medical research building, a new dormi-

tory for nursing students, a new clinic building, a gerontology building, as well as remodeling of the laboratories and medical school building.[14] Although much of the building boom before the 1960s was funded by the Duke Endowment, Duke received more than its share of the federal monies that were beginning to flow into medical building and research.

Federal and private health-care dollars were disproportionately allocated to large, university-based teaching and research hospitals like Duke and have been critical in putting them into a position of dominance in the organization and practice of medicine. Federal funding for medical research and training grew explosively, as the National Institutes of Health (NIH) rapidly replaced corporate philanthropy in sustaining research and clinical faculty based in teaching hospitals. After 1956, NIH began funding the construction of research facilities; and after 1960, it began making grants to institutions for research and research training programs.[15] By 1968, the federal government's share of total medical school expenditures stood at 53 percent, its share of research grants was 33 percent, and that of medical faculty salaries stood at 48.4 percent.[16]

Duke was among the major recipients of these funds. By 1956, it ranked in the top fifth of all medical schools nationally and first in the South in the amount of funding it received from the National Institutes of Health.[17] As early as 1955, research grants alone covered almost the entire cost of running the medical school. Although this was not an unusual state of affairs among medical schools in these years, it was a source of widespread concern at the time because research was the newest leg of the medical tripod and ranked behind teaching and patient care. Wilburt Davison, dean of the medical school, repeatedly warned of the dangers that easy research monies posed to teaching and patient care, "Another great problem which we are facing is the disproportionate amount of funds available to our staff. . . . We are actually reaching the point at which we have more people working on research problems than in teaching the students or taking care of patients."[18] Nevertheless, while Davison wrote what he was to call "a diatribe in 1950 on the imbalance of research and teaching," he did not publish it because "I knew that it would offend many of my friends at Duke and in Washington, and would not, like Peter's finger in the dike, stop the flood of research dollars and soft money."[19]

Davison's predictions were right, for research money continued to pour into the medical center and Duke University. Between 1963 and 1968, total grants rose from $14.2 million to $32 million, while the government share rose from $9.1 million, or 64 percent of the total, to $24.5 million or 76.5 percent of the total.[20] Funding for research elevated its importance and encouraged much of the expansion and development of medical specialization. Medical staff and the number of hospital beds increased rapidly; the number of hospital beds rose from 549 in 1950, to more than 1,000 in 1980; and the number of operating rooms grew from 20 to 32.[21]

Medical specialization was also furthered when between 1965 and 1975, the federal government underwrote a major expansion of health occupation training and education, almost doubling the number of medical students in the nation and increasing funding for basic nursing education and basic allied health programs. These increases changed the shape of the health-care work force significantly, and as significantly, provided minority and working-class women with much greater access to nursing, to emerging health professions, and to new health-based clerical and technical occupations. Many of these programs were funded in community and junior colleges, where working-class and minority students were able to gain access to them in significant numbers.[22] Funding for both research and education stimulated a sharp increase in medical and allied health specialization and expansion, providing the base for the expansion in numbers of workers and numbers of medical, nursing, and technical specializations in the work force.

As a result of both growth and specialization, by the 1960s, large university-based medical complexes centering on a medical school and its rapidly growing hospital often included a dental school, several affiliated hospitals dependent on the medical school for staff, a variety of clinics, doctors' offices, nursing and other allied health schools, research institutes, and special hospitals. Such empires, as they were often called, controlled from one-third to more than three-fourths of all hospital beds in major U.S. cities.[23] Duke is one of those empires, and one of the largest in the South. Exemplary but not unique, Duke is one of the nation's 327 teaching hospital-medical research-tertiary care centers and has come to dominate the economy and geography of Durham.[24]

Duke Medical Center and Durham's Changing Political Economy

A middle-sized North Carolina city by 1981, Durham had a population of about one hundred thousand (with another fifty thousand in the county) and a work force of about eighty-five thousand drawn from a wider area.[25] Most of the workers discussed in this book come from

Durham and its surrounding counties. They work alongside a professional work force that comes to Duke Medical Center from all parts of the United States as well as from other nations, but who are not *of* Durham. Among the workers, it is not uncommon to find families with several members working at the hospital. In some families, men worked in the city's cigarette factories and women worked in the hospital. American Tobacco and Liggett and Myers both have large plants and warehouses in Durham. In 1970, black women worked as private domestic workers, whereas white women worked in the factories. Women of both races worked in health care, although for the city as a whole, there were about twice as many black women as white.[26] By 1980, that picture had changed. Although black women worked as private domestic workers at about twice the rate of white women, only some 4.4 percent of all black women were domestics. Likewise, manufacturing declined; of all employed women in Durham, less than 10 percent worked in manufacturing, whereas about 23 percent were in health care.[27]

Until the last decade, cigarette and textile manufacturing, in both of which the Duke family figured prominently, were Durham's major industries. Both have declined precipitously in recent years. While American Tobacco seems to be holding on, thanks, according to some of its workers, to its low-tar brand, Liggett and Myers had massive layoffs in the late 1970s. The manufacture of generic cigarettes combined with manufacture for an international market seems to be what keeps that plant running, although with few workers.

Textile mills closed down even before tobacco. By 1978, the only mill in operation in Durham was a rug-making mill that was part of Burlington Mills. The mill village has long since been bull-dozed to make way for Duke University's West Campus apartments. Between 1980 and 1983, several L&M warehouses were converted into a very expensive shopping center and New York-style loft condominiums by a group of urban developers associated with Duke University.[28] The rug mill runs at a much reduced scale compared to when it was locally owned as Erwin Mills, and one of its main buildings has been converted into expensive apartments. The clientele for these and other gentrification projects seems in part to be medical and university people, and in part people brought to the area to develop microelectronics and other high tech industries.

Durham used to refer to itself as the Bull City, after the Bull Durham tobacco that first made the town famous. Now it is called (at least by its civic promoters), the City of Medicine. In 1980, some 22 percent of Durham County's labor force, about seventeen thousand people, worked in health care, and the city had five times the national average number of doctors and hospital beds. With a large Veteran's Administration hospital and the large, new Durham County Hospital in addition to the Duke giant, as well as smaller hospitals, extended care facilities, and a host of quasi-medical weight reduction clinics and diet centers, medicine is indeed Durham's major industry.[29]

Promoters replaced Durham's civic symbol of a bull with a caduceus. The change was explicitly intended to transform the class image of Durham from "a blue collar industrial town" to "a white collar professional-scientific community on the move," according to the private committee that organized the successful campaign. Not surprisingly, committee members were among Durham's "business and medical elite." The committee chairman was head of surgery at Durham County Hospital, and Duke Hospital's CEO was a member.[30]

There is an element of grim humor in Duke's rise as a medical complex. The Dukes' original success in popularizing cigarette smoking did more than make them wealthy. It also helped make cigarette smoking a national addiction and cancer a national disease. Much of the huge governmental and popular support for medicine in the postwar decades concentrated on efforts to find cures for cancer and heart disease because the combination of cigarette smoking and industrial carcinogens rapidly made them the nation's major killers after epidemic diseases came under public health and medical control.[31] The National Institutes of Health's budget explosion in the 1950s and 60s marked the fact that taxpayers had replaced corporate philanthropy as the major financier of a high tech research establishment largely devoted to cancer and cardiovascular diseases. At Duke by 1960, federal research and state building funds were underwriting part or all of the construction of new buildings, equipment, and laboratories. Although it is ironic that one of the figures most responsible for today's major health hazards is viewed as a philanthropist and honored with a hospital, it is more ironic still that this hospital became one of the nation's larger medical complexes, much of it built at public expense with research funds for undoing some of the damage caused by cigarettes Duke popularized and from which he profited so handsomely.

Work and Its Changes at Duke

Duke continued to expand throughout the seventies and is still doing so despite an economic chill—although the methods of expansion have changed. From ten buildings in 1960, the complex grew to fifteen in 1970; by the 1980s, it was almost a city in itself. Covering 140 acres, its 24 buildings—including a brand new hospital—sprawl across much of the west side of Durham and include staff in the Veterans Administration Hospital across the street from Duke North, doctors' offices and clinics in the Hilton Hotel adjacent to the Duke campus, extended care facilities, sports and nutrition clinics, an eye center and an affiliated children's hospital down the road, affiliations with the fairly new Durham County Hospital and a variety of other hospitals in the area, as well as a wholly owned outpost hospital in a rural part of the state. Although its nursing school is closed, Duke's Allied Health Department still runs a wide variety of training programs at certification, B.A., and M.A. levels. In addition, the medical center and the university operate their own parking lots and transportation service linking the various sites.

Hospital Space and Time. What used to be referred to as the Hospital in the early sixties is now called simply South. It was built before health care replaced automobiles as the quintessential industry of America's "second industrial revolution," before our economic base was said to have shifted from production to services. These medical center buildings with their appendages, wings, clinics, and never-ending renovations grew haphazardly and unselfconsciously in the halcyon days of medical expansion. Perhaps that is why much of the old hospital lacks the fortresslike perimeters, controlled movements, and functionally segregated spaces of modern factories and modern hospitals. Much of the hospital's inner workings are visible both to public viewing and to movement of people, to socializing, to seeing and to being seen.

As in most hospitals, older buildings at Duke have been modified to house new health-care services. The buildings span a half-century during which health care was undergoing especially rapid changes. The creation of new spaces and the changing uses of old spaces at Duke reflect changes in the nature and divisions of the work process. The layout of the medical center also mediates the nature of contacts and relations among workers, patients, and administrators.

The old hospital's corridors are public space, always crowded with workers, clinic patients, and university students taking shortcuts between campus buildings and parking lots. Until Duke North opened in 1980, they shared the halls and elevators with inpatients in wheelchairs or stretchers being wheeled by attendants to and from the operating and procedure rooms that are among the far-flung processing stations of the health-care assembly line. Even the wards on the upper floors were always full of painters, carpenters, television repairmen, therapists, technicians and medical students, housekeeping and dietary workers, and the ward's nursing, clerical and medical staffs. The hospital was laid out so that one had to travel through at least one ward to get virtually anywhere. As a result, much of the space felt more like an office than a factory.

Despite South's sociable ambience, it takes only a little effort and imagination to see some of the assembly-line aspects of the hospital. Not far off a main hall, and sometimes in the corridor, patients are "stacked" in their wheelchairs and stretchers waiting for an x-ray or some other procedure. Their detachable parts—blood and urine—are transported to laboratories by white-coated technicians or phlebotomists (blood drawers), who bustle through the halls with their racks of tubes. The results of the technicians' work clatters off printers, with luck to be assembled into the patients' medical charts.

Some hospital spaces are like fossil-bearing cliffs in that they display a visible record of some of the changes in Duke's postwar history. Such a mini-Olduvai Gorge is a clinic tucked in a corner of the sub-basement of South for most of its existence. The main waiting room of this clinic is something of a contradiction; it contains strata from different epochs. The institutional-colored paint on its walls was replaced several years ago by an artist who designed a silvery blue and green sky shot with an orange sunrise on one wall and a bright starry night on another. While the walls have been brightened to counteract a factorylike and institutional ambience, the room's inner space still has something of the holding tank character of a standard hospital waiting room. Hard, molded plastic chairs are bolted to the floor in rows. They are almost always full of children and of parents holding babies, trying to feed or diaper them as they wait, often for hours.

During the early 1980s, South, with its patchwork use of space, was eclipsed by the very expensive Duke North, a high-rise, multi-acre stone and glass hospital housing a new emergency room and almost all of the hospital's 1,000-odd beds. Since Duke North's opening, the only bustle in South occurs during the daytime in the pass-through halls on the main floor and in the public and private outpatient clinics—where everyone is dressed. To me, and to many workers with whom I spoke, Duke North felt as closed and cold as South felt public and sociable. In Duke North, almost everything is hidden from public gaze. It is a vertically oriented and much less congested place despite its awesome concentration of high tech medical hardware. The upper floors—at least outside the nursing station vicinity—are usually nearly deserted; each function seems to be encased in its own separate area behind closed doors.

While workers and itinerant anthropologists may prefer the old space for the interactions and mobility it afforded, it was certainly less than ideal for patients. For them, the new building's privacy is a plus. Inpatients do not have to be wheeled through crowded halls with their hospital gowns flapping in the breeze. Too, North has only single rooms; all inpatients now have their own rooms regardless of payment status, mitigating some of the contrast between public and private inpatient statuses.

When the new hospital opened, inpatients and the workers who care for them almost all moved to North, as did the emergency room. The medical school, the clinics, and clinic staffs remained in the old building, although there are also clinics in the new. There are laboratories, kitchens, and housekeeping in both places.

The rhythms of the two buildings reflect their differences and specializations. Inpatient and emergency work run round the clock, and therefore, so does Duke North, whereas the clinics, medical school, and South are primarily on an 8 to 5 schedule. Indeed, outside these hours, many places on the upper floors of the old hospital are positively creepy, and I have been told by several women workers, less than safe for women to walk alone. Even though North runs seven days a week, three shifts a day, there are many fewer workers on evenings, nights, and weekends than on weekdays. While interns and residents are always present, the clinical faculty works days. Thus, clinic appointments, surgery, and diagnostic tests and procedures are not done at night or on weekends unless there is an emergency.

In the old building, one could also see a two-class health-care system fairly clearly. From its beginning, Duke has had separate and unequal facilities for public patients and private, paying ones. A key difference is in physician care. Private patients have their own doctors who are members of the clinical teaching staff, whereas public patients are seen by medical students or interns (who are checked in turn by a resident or staff physician). Public patients have less continuity of physicians' care.

Although money and physicians are essential aspects of the division, there are a variable range of other differences in treatment. Public inpatients used to be housed in separate wards with multiple beds, whereas private patients were on units with private or semiprivate rooms with more amenities. Most of the private clinics have reasonably comfortable waiting rooms with soft chairs; some have free coffee. Public clinics have hard chairs, crowded waiting rooms, and a snack sales area that sells junk food but lacks a proper place to sit and eat.

In the clinics of some services, public and private differences are confined to physician care and billing with its associated, but considerable, paperwork. Here, all patients sit in the same waiting room and check in at the same desk. In one of theses clinics, one set of women registers the public patients, another set registers the private. There are no differences in laboratory and nursing care, but there are real differences in the paperwork, costs, and physician care. Most people don't seem to realize that there is a division of labor, or even that there are different patient statuses, and check in with whomever is free. But the workers pass the clinic cards back and forth so that each registers the type of patient for whom she is responsible. Most of the staff speak of "green sheets" and "white sheets"— the color of the clinic record sheet for private and pubic patients respectively—as often as they do of public or private patients. It is no secret that there are two categories of medical care, but it is not flaunted, and some of the staff seem a little uncomfortable with the division.

Specialization. Mrs. Grace Beecham is an LPN and the most senior nurse I met at Duke. A tall, dark-skinned black woman with salt-and-pepper hair, she has worked twenty-eight years in this hospital, sixteen of them on surgery wards, and she trained Mary Pearce when Mary first came to the clinic. Both women remember nursing before the specialization of the last two decades. "When I first got here it was different," Beecham noted. "We saw sick patients generally. Thursday and Friday were all physicals. In hematology there used to be three or four patients a week; now there's twenty a day. It's the same with all specialties. The big change is to specialties. Back then they took sick people to walk-in. We had drop-in in two treatment rooms off the nursing station—isolation."

Mrs. Sarah Moore's first job at Duke in the early 1960s was as a nurse's maid. She became a patient care assistant (PCA) some time in the midsixties. As she described the clinic where she worked as a maid, her quiet and deliberate manner of speaking conveyed a fatigue born of walking endless hospital corridors and gave a feeling for early years of health-care industrialization. "When I first came I was hired as the maid. When I first came there was only one LPN, one RN, one aide; and I was the maid. That was the nursing staff. I'm not talking about the secretarial staff. There wasn't but two secretaries—the appointment secretary and the one that registered them in. So you can just walk out there now and see how things have grown. And I've been under a spell of head nurses. I don't know how many; I tried to count them up last night.

"Friday morning was well-baby morning. We would see from seventy-five, eighty to a hundred people in a morning. It was not like it is now. Mrs. Hunter [the aide] would weigh them in and I'd put them in the rooms. My poor little legs was about to drop off because each doctor was trying to see how many patients they could see. People don't believe me, but there's books of it in the back if they haven't thrown them out."

Although it may have been hard on the workers, such a clinic had much to recommend it to patients. "Then it was a clinic and you didn't have to pay but fifty cents or a quarter to have the baby checked over. And now," said Mrs. Moore, "you think of how much you have to pay!"

Because new wine is being aged in old bottles, there is no especially neat correspondence between space and its functions. Grace Beecham's clinic was built as a single, general clinic because that is how it once functioned. It still looks like a single clinic, but today, reflecting the growth of medical specialization, it is more than twenty-five separate "clinics"—here, a medical and administrative term rather than a spatial one. A clinic consists of people seeing the same type of medical specialist. On any given half day, there may be from four to more than ten concurrent clinics sharing the same space, each coordinated by a nurse, who may handle two or more clinics on a given day.

Much of the incessant remodeling of the old hospital buildings is reflective of that change to specialties. "Now, they use those treatment rooms for heme [hematology], for bone marrows," Mrs. Beecham continued. "They didn't used to do more than finger sticks in the lab, and the doctors did venipunctures. We had to set up for them and help. Now the phlebotomist can handle it herself." Some space has been remodeled to accommodate the more acute procedures done on an outpatient basis. In one clinic, the nursing staff remodeled a doctors' conference room into a "day hospital" for patients undergoing transfusions and other long procedures. Patients had been previously fitted into scattered places wherever nurses could find space. Having a proper place for such patients eased nurses' work and gave patients and their families more comfort and a modicum of privacy.

Space and time are at a premium—probably always have been—and there are usually competing demands on any given worker and for any given space. In outpatient care, there is ongoing competition between caring for the exotic and the acute on the one hand, and the common cold, the rash, and the upset stomach on the other. Until about 1980, a walk-in clinic was held five days a week in the old Emergency Room (ER) at South to handle the latter, before the ER moved to Duke North. The walk-in clinic was staffed by a senior resident, junior residents, medical students, a nurse, and an aide. Clinic patients could use it at clinic rates and not have to pay the (much) higher ER fee. Because the new ER does not accommodate walk-ins, sick people who use the ER now have to pay a high fee.

With the emphasis on medical specialization, ordinary communicable illnesses become a recurring headache for staffing and space alike. The unpredictability and short-term intensity of such illnesses bring people to the hospital, but physicians can do little beyond diagnosing each case of flu, an activity often at cross-purposes with the practice and training of medical specialists. Nevertheless, walk-ins regularly happen and need to be dealt with, although much of the space where that is done is also needed for specialty care, leaving garden-variety "*sick* sick patients" as orphans of the system.

"When the ER had the walk-in clinic, our clinic could be for specialties. But now, people are discovering that the walk-ins are gone. They call their doctor who tells them to come to the clinic and they'll see them there." Pointing to an examining room, Mary Pearce indicated, "The patient in the next room is Kevin's [the resident responsible for the clinic]; he told them to come in."

"That's what happened Friday," Grace Beecham picked up. "Friday was awful. We had three people with 40 temps [fevers of 40 degrees celsius, or 104 degrees Fahrenheit]. I don't think these doctors are equipped to work with *sick* sick patients. They're specialists in one thing, but not used to general. They have to get lots of consults and have to leave scheduled patients to care for drop-ins." Mary continued, "Friday we were tied up all morning and half the afternoon with one man who they finally figured had the flu. Then a mother in a wheelchair came in with a temp of 40 degrees. They finally got her to the ER where she should've been sent in the first place." Slipping into the standard hospital jargon that describes people as their symptoms, Mary added, "They can't keep bringing temps and rashes in with oncologies who are on chemotherapy [chemotherapy weakens the immune system]."

Hospital Jobs. When the first dean of the medical school, the effective chief of the whole health complex, wrote his memoirs in 1950, he thanked *by name* the three-woman clerical staff as well as the twenty-two-person "maintenance, financial, housekeeping and technical staff" of the hospital.[32] Although he presided over a fairly small space by today's standards, it was adequate then. In 1950, the nursing staff consisted of 141 student nurses; the nursing school, as was common practice, was built to assure a supply of cheap, skilled nursing labor for physicians. Together with some 201 medical faculty and 229 housestaff, they were the traditional care-giving trio in charge of about 524 beds.[33] There were an average of two employees for each inpatient bed.[34]

By 1983, there was more than one RN alone for each of the hospital's more than one thousand beds, and almost one medical faculty member and one administrator *each*, per bed. The twenty-five-person nonmedical support staff had grown to more than five thousand clerical, technical, and service workers.[35] Professionals—technicians, technologists, therapists, and pharmacy workers, together with RNs—have become a larger and increasingly important part of the hourly work force. By 1983, there seemed to be at least one kind of technician and technologist for every substance and electrical wave the human body can emit. Each of these people needs individual space. Other technologists specialize in undetachable body parts such as the lungs, the heart, and circulatory functions, or in radiation procedures and tests. There are respiratory, physical, occupational, and recreational therapists. Some comparable functions had been performed by jacks- and jills-of-all-trades in the 1950s, and some functions did not exist then. The number of supervisors grew apace with specialization and even faster than the number of workers. By the early 1980s, Duke's hourly workers were divided into some three hundred well-defined positions in a complex and integrated organizational and reporting hierarchy.

Between 1969 and 1983, black workers remained between 42 percent and 48 percent of the total hourly work force, but the jobs they held shifted away from service and toward clerical work. Clerical workers grew from less than 33 percent of the 1973 hourly work force to perhaps 38 percent by 1976, and black women's access to these jobs increased significantly. Less than 10 percent of all clericals throughout the university and medical center in 1969 were black, but that percentage grew to about 20 percent in 1973 and to almost 29 percent of all clericals in 1976. Service workers shrank as a percentage of the work force, dropping from almost 40 percent to about 25 percent. Because more than 80 percent of all service workers were black, as this sector shrank, so too did one set of jobs for black workers.[36]

The job a person holds shapes her working day, the people she encounters, and the conditions under which she encounters them. Together with race and gender, it is a lens through which workers view Duke and its changes. By 1976, the earliest year for which full information is available, the work force was in the middle of ongoing change and still more specialization. Nevertheless, a 1976 profile of the jobs, who did them, and how much the workers were paid, can give us a quantitative freeze-frame of a work force at one point in its continual transition and can serve as a basis for subsequent discussions of the rewards and discontents of work at Duke Medical Center.

There were some 4,500 hourly clerical, technical, RN, craft, and service workers, including slightly more than 200 of their direct supervisors in 1976.[37] To these should be added perhaps another 1,600 medical faculty, professionals, and administrators on the salaried payroll, about 97 percent of whom were white (60 percent men, 37 percent women, 2 percent black women, and 1 percent black men).[38]

Duke's hourly work force in 1976 was overwhelmingly female and biracial, and it has remained relatively constant in its racial and gender composition: women make up more than 80 percent. There are about 46 percent white women, 35 percent black women, 11 percent black men, and 8 percent white men. Hourly workers were fairly evenly divided among service, technical, clerical and nursing work, although these sectors themselves were not balanced racially (Table 1).[39] Too, as will become

Table 1. Hourly Workers, 1976

Category	Percent	Percent Black
Service and craft workers	24	85
Technical	24	24
Clerical	30	29
Nursing (RN and LPN)	22	47

Source: Calculated from work-force printouts; excludes supervisors.

clear, there is a great deal of occupational segregation within this already gender-segregated work force.

At one level, the variety of work and the amount of specialization among hourly workers even in 1976 was truly staggering—even without the medical and nursing specializations and the divisions of upper administrative and financial work. If the post-1976 trends can be extended backward, hourly job *titles*, which grew by almost one-third from approximately 265 to 350 in the next seven years, were proliferating faster than the *number* of workers, reflecting the progress of technological specialization at all levels.

Fortunately, much of the specialization seems to have stopped with the title and had little to do with the work itself. For example, I counted twenty different clerk titles in 1976 and thirty-five in 1983. These titles seem more descriptive of where a person works than with what she is likely to do there. Likewise, sometime between 1976 and 1983, even though they worked side by side doing the same things, cooks who cook for the public cafeteria line and those who cook for patients seem to have taken on different job titles. Secretaries who work for clinical faculty are generally called medical secretaries, whereas those working in other offices are usually called secretaries (and paid less). In each case, there are no doubt some significant differences between jobs, but probably there is at least as much variation among people with the same job title. Well over three-quarters of the hourly workers at Duke Medical Center seem to fall into one of less than twenty types of job—if one combines junior and senior, licensed and unlicensed versions of the job (Table 2). These jobs cover the major areas of work in a hospital—inpatient and outpatient care, food and building care, laboratory work, record-keeping, and—last but hardly least, bill collecting. During the course of this study, my access to workers in many jobs—especially in intensive and emergency care and the operating suites—was limited, because I did not enter those areas. I also stayed out of patient rooms, procedure rooms, and examining rooms, and in general, confined myself to public space. Within those constraints, I tried to learn about some jobs in each of the major categories of clerks and secretaries, laboratory and therapy, food and cleaning work, as well as racially segregated and racially integrated jobs. Although I make no claims to comprehensiveness, some sense of coverage was not as impossible a task as the number of job titles might suggest.

Because jobs have been and continue to be segregated by race as well as by gender, black and white women (the vast majority of hourly workers are women) often have different jobs. Almost all the food service workers are black women, and black women and black men together are virtually all the cleaning personnel. Black women in clerical jobs tend to be clerks and ward secretaries, called data terminal operators (DTOs), while most office secretaries are white women. White women are also RNs and technologists (the latter along with white men), and black women are LPNs. Occupational segregation translates into pay differentials as well,

Table 2. Number of Hourly Workers in Selected Kinds of Jobs

Type of Job	1976	1983
Housekeepers	285	341
Food service aides	171	146
Patient care aides	172	156
Clinic receptionists	56	37
Laboratory assistants	51	46
Medical laboratory clerks	23	51
Laboratory technicians	54	39
Cooks	55	129
Medical record clerks	94	67
Data terminal operators (DTO)	175	233
Pharmacy technologists	45	93
Secretaries	566	542
Medical technician/technologists	59	29
Licensed practical nurses	485	517
Radiology technologists	51	50
Research technician/technologists	255	274
Medical technologists	171	234
Staff nurses	463	1106
TOTALS	3231	4090
Total hourly work force (including supervisors)		6652*

Source: Calculated from work-force printouts.

*1983 totals from EEO/AA, Sept. 1983.

with black workers (both men and women) clustered at the lower pay levels, and the relatively few white men toward the top (Table 3).

Table 3. Pay Level by Race and Gender

Pay Level	White Females	Black Females	White Males	Black Males	Total
1	18	408	21	197	644
2	51	93	22	63	299
3	78	136	22	35	271
4	207	260	30	72	569
5	428	74	39	23	564
6	363	312	22	24	721
7	200	126	72	24	422
8	121	32	28	14	195
9	521	69	107	26	723
Total	1987	1510	363	478	4338

Source: Calculated from work-force printouts.

In the late 1950s and early 60s, when activism was beginning to take root in the black community, Durham was still very much a working-class town. Wages were low at Duke and in North Carolina. Until recently, the state ranked fiftieth in wages, and there were few unions.[39] Since the 1950s, North Carolina politicians have been successfully courting new industries. Low wages and right-to-work laws have been among the state's main attractions. North Carolina's political spectrum at the level of state politics was and is fairly narrow—and by comparison to the grass-roots range, it is conservative. Liberals and conservatives have dealt with unions somewhat differently. The textile industry, most recently J. P. Stevens, has a notorious history of overt and brutal resistance to any organizing attempt. In apparent contrast, Duke University, of which Duke Medical Center is a part, presents a liberal face to union opposition. Still, Duke is part of the state's major financial and manufacturing networks through its board members and its politically active president during the 1970s.

The city of Durham, like Duke University, presents itself as liberal. It has long been home to one of the nation's strongest black bourgeoisies; some say the first sit-ins were held here and not in Greensboro. Integration of schools and public places occurred without the major conflicts or violence of other cities.[40] In the late 1960s, Duke prided itself on allowing "responsible" student protest.[41] There is nothing in the nature of Durham's economy that explains this particular style or self-perception. It would appear that the city's liberalism is a relationship more than a stance. It is a relationship between those with power and those without, a relationship of consent—to limit resistance on the part of the powerless and to accept that level of resistance on the part of the powerful. When that consent broke down, as it did occasionally and briefly, so too did Durham's liberalism.

Summary

From its birth, Duke Hospital combined twentieth-century ideals of a mutually reinforcing system of science, education, and industry with nineteenth-century ideals by which wealthy and prominent families validated their social position by dispensing charity and Christian stewardship. Industry, science, and education flourished at Duke and in Durham as they did elsewhere in the prosperous postwar decades. They transformed hospital work and workers' expectations. Clerical and technical job opportunities expanded rapidly as health-care specialization grew.

Black workers were conspicuously absent from this proliferation. Confined largely to cooking and cleaning in the hospital and in Durham, they experienced the worst of prewar paternalism combined with emerging postwar emphasis on productivity. Civil rights and black worker unionization efforts sprang from the contradiction between growing economic opportunities and black workers' exclusion from them. The next chapter will analyze the rise of these movements in Durham and at Duke.

NOTES

1. Janiewski, 1985:69.
2. Ibid.:68–70.
3. Ibid.:36.
4. Quoted in Krause, 1982:7.
5. Gifford, 1972:31, 45.
6. Ibid.:82.
7. Law, 1976.
8. Gifford, 1972:99–102.
9. Ibid.:81–102.
10. Lens, 1949; Lipsitz, 1982; Lichtenstein, 1983; Munts, 1967:85–87.
11. By 1954, twelve million workers and seventeen million dependents had some employer-paid health coverage, and one-quarter of all health insurance came through union bargaining. The total employers' share of workers' health payments in 1945 was 10 percent; by 1950 it was 37 percent; and between 1954 and 1962, it jumped from 47 percent to 70 percent (Starr, 1982:313; Munts, 1967:86).
12. U.S. Department of Health and Human Services, 1982:139; Rich, 1984a.
13. Himmelstein and Woolhandler, 1984:13–14.
14. *President's Report*, 1949–60.
15. Brown, 1979:226; Freyman, 1977:84–85. By 1960, the NIH budget grew to $400 million, and by 1975 it stood at $2.8 billion, or 60 percent of all money from all sources spent on medical research. (This was also the peak percentage of NIH funding of such research.)
16. Freyman, 1977:87.
17. *President's Report*, 1957–58:87.
18. Ibid.:78; see also similar warnings in reports of 1954–55 and 1958–59.
19. Davison, 1972:542.
20. These figures include both the university and the medical center, although a large portion is certainly medical (Knight, 1970:7, 11.).
21. Davison, 1952:4, 9, 54; *Bulletin*, Duke University School of Medicine, appropriate years.
22. Institute of Medicine, 1983; Backup and Molinaro, 1984; Barocci, 1981:110.

23. Starr, 1982:361–62; Bodenheimer et al., 1974; Kotelchuck, 1976; Reverby and Rosner, 1979.

24. Culliton, 1984; Colloton, 1982; Relman, 1984; Anlyan and Elchlepp, 1982.

25. Greater Durham Chamber of Commerce, 1981.

26. U.S. Bureau of the Census, 1972.

27. U.S. Bureau of the Census, 1982, "General Social and Economic Characteristics, North Carolina," Table 122.

28. *Durham Morning Herald*, Jan. 30, 1981, 1.

29. Ibid.

30. Starr, 1982.

31. Davison, 1972:539.

32. Duke University, 1952:4, 54.

33. Ibid.:54.

34. Opportunity Development Center, Sept. 1983 Report.

35. EEO–1 1969 for all campus and medical center; *Caston et al.* v. *Duke University*, Peterson deposition Exhibits A and B for 1973 and 1976 total number of workers by race; *Fuller* v. *Duke University*, Hoffman deposition for composition 1973; my calculations 1976. These sources do not use strictly comparable categories, so can only be as rough guides.

36. My calculations from April 1976 are 4,572 and include RNs; Duke listed 3,983 bi-weekly workers, excluding RNs for Dec. 31, 1976 in *Caston et al.* v. *Duke University*, Exhibit A.

37. These figures are from Sept. 1978, EEO/AA Report.

38. Calculated from April 1976 printout; excludes some 214–34 supervisory jobs; figures rounded; categories are Duke's EEO reporting categories, with modifications regarding nursing.

39. *Durham Morning Herald*, Jan. 14, 1979.

40. Chafe, 1980.

41. Carter, 1968.

2

From Clients to Workers:
The Beginnings of Activism

Hospital service workers were not among the beneficiaries of health-care expansion in the 1950s and 60s. Their experiences more often combined the worst of the old paternalism and the new notions of factory-style efficiency. Hospitals grew visibly more wealthy during these decades. Health costs rose faster than the overall cost of living, and both upper-level staff growth and construction booms took place in full public view—and often with public protest when medical centers bull-dozed working-class neighborhoods that stood in the paths of their expansion. Women and minority hospital workers in particular contrasted such institutional wealth and power with their circumstances. They were among the lowest paid workers in the country; their benefits remained almost nonexistent at a time when employer-paid benefits were becoming commonplace elsewhere in the labor force. Under these conditions, the movement for racial justice struck a particularly responsive chord among minority service workers who were crowded at the very bottom of the expanding industry.

Paternalism continued to govern many hospital employment practices in these decades. Nineteenth-century hospital workers had often been compensated in board and free meals rather than in living wages and modern benefits. They served as all-purpose maids and aides to hospital officials and doctors and were governed by personal command rather than by specific job-related criteria. Payment in kind prevailed in many hospitals until recent history, in some places through World War II. A study of unionization at Montefiore Hospital in New York City found patterns similar to Duke's, where workers were also treated like "dependent members of an extended family."[1] Even nurses, who had managed to gain some recognition as professional workers before the war, were paid poorly and expected to work long hours. Hospital nursing was largely done by student nurses—as it was at Duke—while graduates sought out private duty nursing.[2] Although Duke was built in the twentieth century, it nevertheless inherited these traditions, which were perhaps accentuated by Duke's almost entirely black service work force and by southern practices of segregation.

Hospital paternalism, especially in food and cleaning work, intersected with and was reinforced by the related paternalism that governed the work relations of domestic workers. Through much of the nineteenth and twentieth centuries, working-class women in a variety of circumstances but above all black women in the South, were not housewives in the conventional sense of the word. Although they certainly "kept house," they also earned significant portions of their households' income by their informal and entrepreneurial activities, among which cooking and cleaning for others loomed large. They worked as domestics and did laundry.[3] They washed, cooked, and cleaned, primarily for other women and usually, although not always, in well-to-do households. Racial differences sharpened and were often the idiom for expressing class differences, as when immigrant women worked for native-born, or black women for white. By the 1920s, domestic work had become day work and was identified increasingly with black women in the North as well as the South. White women found new and better employment opportunities opening to them in the growing clerical and sales jobs of the North and in Durham's cigarette and textile factories. The casual labor market was not an economists' abstraction; it was more often concrete—literally an empty lot or a street corner where prospective workers gathered to wait for employers to drive by and hire them for a day's work.[4]

Employers often related "maternalistically" to their domestic workers, stressing charity and uplift more than employment contract.[5] This was similar to the treatment of hospital workers who did similar work. Both in hospitals and in homes of the wealthy, women of color were hired to cook and clean and were expected to be grateful for the opportunity. All strains of racism, sexism, paternalism, and open-ended unending work expectations seem to converge in the cultural traditions that have shaped cooking and cleaning occupations. In some ways, the availability of institutional food and cleaning services appeared to provide an alternative to private domestic work. Despite the low wages and factorylike conditions, such work promised some improvements, not least of which was an escape from the personal denigration and infinitely expandable workloads that came with day work. Many black women must have taken these jobs with this hope. However, Duke food and housekeeping workers found that continuing traditions of paternalism (or maternalism in the case of female supervisors) and arbitrariness adhered to these jobs, and indeed seemed to be attached to their very beings as black workers in a city where virtually all the private domestic workers and most of the institutional food and cleaning workers were black.

The civil rights movement heightened black and Hispanic hospital workers' awareness of the racist dimensions of their situation and catalyzed their activism across the nation. In turn and in time their struggles gave the civil rights movement a visible working-class dimension that had been lacking previously. Led by minority service workers, hospital unionization drives were broadly based parts of a more general struggle for both racial and economic justice. Although most of the established labor unions and the AFL-CIO gave only grudging and belated support, some unions saw this movement as a chance to put some motion back into an otherwise stale and conservative labor "movement." Beginning with Local 1199's drive to organize New York City's Montefiore Hospital in 1958, black and Hispanic workers' activism explicitly linked unionization and civil rights. They were joined by the Service Employees International Union (SEIU) and the American Federation of State, County, and Municipal Employees (AFSCME). Each of these unions emphasized the paternalism and racism, although seldom the sexism, as well as the economic dimensions of hospital treatment and sought to mobilize black community as well as white unionist support for hospital workers.[6] Unionization efforts by Duke University's hospital and campus service workers followed this pattern.

Civil Rights and the Beginnings of Worker Organizing

During World War II, many black Durhamites gained access to somewhat better jobs when the federal government grudgingly supported civil rights efforts in the face of severe labor shortages in many key industries.[7] When the war was over, white women were not the only ones who were told to go back to the kitchen, or who lost union protection. Black men and women also lost many factory jobs they held during the war as the wartime plants that employed them closed, or as their jobs were given to returning white men.[8]

The civil rights movement in Durham had its roots in black people's struggles during and after the war. Oliver Harvey, who for some twenty years was the most prominent and consistent animating force for unionization at Duke, embodies some of the continuities and links between the civil rights generation of the 1940s and 50s and the hospital unionization generation of the 1970s.[9] During the war, he attempted to integrate the separate black and white unions at the Durham Hosiery Mill, but without success.[10] Shortly thereafter, he led a successful fight to integrate the segregated black and white unions at a bottling plant in Durham. His wartime experience convinced him that segregation and racism could be beaten. In 1951, Harvey started work as a janitor at Duke University, where, as he put it, workers "had no voice and no job security. . . . We were treated like subhumans until we started organizing."[11] He found Duke's practice of black workers having to call students "Mr." and "Miss" particularly intolerable. Harvey is reputed to have ended that custom when he confronted a student who objected to being called by his first name. Harvey forced the student to admit the absurdity of the practice and convinced him to help end it.[12] Black workers were not allowed to sit down and eat in any of the cafeterias or dining halls on campus. "It was a segregated institution. You had separate restrooms and separate waiting rooms. Now we cooked the food served in the dining hall and daggone it, can't eat in the dining hall. Black people eat in the kitchen."[13]

By the 1950s in Durham, jobs had become scarce, and black women worked as domestics or did seasonal piece-work in the tobacco stemmeries.[14] But as Duke expanded, many black women found jobs there. Margaret Sims was a contemporary of Oliver Harvey and a longtime activist who worked in housekeeping at the hospital. For some fourteen years, between August and March, she hung tobacco at the American Tobacco Company. She like the work there, not least because the money was relatively good, at least relative to what it became. In two weeks at American, Mrs. Sims recalled, she made $80, as much as she received for a month's work when she started at Duke. Then American Tobacco closed down its hanging room. "Around 58 a lot of jobs closed for black people; the only jobs were laundry, house cleaning, or in the cafe." Margaret Sims applied at Duke on a Wednesday; on Friday she was told to report for work in housekeeping the next morning. Because the only other job she could find at the time was laundry work, she took it. "I didn't think I'd be working at Duke this long."

In Duke and Durham, strict segregation prevailed during the 1950s. Duke Hospital segregated its ward patients, its bathrooms, waiting rooms, and dining halls.[15] Watts Hospital was for whites only until 1964. Lincoln Hospital, built in 1901 by the Duke family, was the only other hospital in town for black people. Mrs. Sims listed some of the forms that segregation took in downtown Durham: bank and store clerks were white; separate entrances and bathrooms at Belks' downtown department store; segregated lunch counters at Rose's and Kresge's; and the requirement that black people ride in the backs of busses and use separate water fountains. She chuckled as she told of her satisfaction when the civil rights movement put an intransigently segregationist Kresge's out of business "right before Christmas."

In 1956, inspired by Rosa Parks and the Montgomery bus boycott and frustrated by inaction on the part of Durham's well-to-do black leadership, Oliver Harvey and Beatrice Noore, also a black worker at Duke, sparked the integration of the city's busses (run by Duke Power Company) by refusing to obey the bus driver's order to give their seats to white students. As Harvey remembered, "So Mrs. Noore and myself, we got off the bus and said, 'We're going to walk to campus and we're going to call the manager of Duke Power when we get there.'" To Harvey's surprise, the students also got off the bus and walked with them in support. The buses in Durham were integrated that year. According to Harvey, the integration was because the NAACP and the Durham Committee on the Affairs of Black People (the voice of Durham's conservative black leadership) began to discuss it. "And the white folks agreed mutually. . . . After the Supreme Court made their decision, then Duke Power, before they were forced to, volunteered [to desegregate]."[16]

Although worker organizing did not really begin to coalesce until the mid-1960s, when it became part of Durham's broad-ranging antipoverty movement, a few black workers at Duke were active from the earliest days of the civil rights movement and sought to expand that movement to include racial justice at the workplace. Oliver Harvey kept up a series of petition campaigns throughout the 1950s for improved working conditions and equal treatment with white workers. By 1959, the voices of Durham workers were beginning to be heard. An editorial in the *Carolina Times*, the newspaper of Durham's black community, titled "Peonage at Duke University" excoriated the university for "disgracefully low wages paid the 225 maids and janitors," and concluded that Duke "was nothing but a bloodsucker when it comes to dealing with its Negro employees." It recommended that "The maids and janitors should form a union and connect themselves with the AFL-CIO for their own welfare and protection."[17]

By 1957, civil rights activists in Durham were beginning to hold demonstrations against segregation in movie theaters, motels, and eating places. In the fall of 1959, as a result of NAACP court action, the Durham schools began to *think* about desegregation.[18] By 1960, civil rights direct action had come to the city, and the years 1960–63 were the peak of civil rights, civil disobedience, and sit-ins. Durham claims to have had the nation's first sit-ins in 1960, initiated by a Hillside High (then Durham's black high school) student group that grew out of a church-sponsored Boy Scout troop.[19] Public desegregation came relatively peacefully and rapidly to Durham.[20] In less than a year, Durham's sit-ins succeeded in integrating the lunch counters and continued to target other forms of public segregation through 1963.[21] By 1963, motels and food services were almost all desegrated, and the city had at least pledged to desegregate its schools. By the early 1960s, too, Duke University also desegregated and admitted its first black undergraduate students. However, desegregation brought little economic improvement to the university's black workers. As Harvey recalled, "We got an increase in salary without a petition in 1960 and 1963. But that was simply because the Movement was going on in Durham."[22]

After 1963, Durham's black community began to focus more sharply on economic justice. Despite a shortage of low-income housing, a combination of urban renewal and expressway construction was threatening to demolish the community of Hayti, one of Durham's most poverty-stricken black neighborhoods. Howard Fuller, a dynamic and politically experienced organizer who became Durham's best-known black community leader, had been hired to help coordinate Operation Breakthrough, the city's antipoverty agency. He recruited black college students to canvass, organized a mothers' club in a poor black housing project, and within a short time four black neighborhoods and a primarily black housing project organized five local councils into an area council in Hayti. Representing some three hundred households, this became a major vehicle for a sustained campaign to demand improved low-income housing. The area councils were also a major base for a wide range of black community issues. When black workers in Durham's public schools held a two-month strike in the fall of 1965, the area councils supported them. By the end of that year, additional area councils had been organized in three more black communities. They formally separated from Operation Breakthrough early in 1966 and were chartered as the United Organizations for Community Improvement (UOCI), with Fuller as overall director. Under UOCI's leadership, 1965 and 1966 were years of major community protest and mass movements in housing, voter registration, education, and community improvement.[23] Black workers at Duke were part of both Operation Breakthrough and the more general movement. Many of the women who became the first black clerical and technical workers at Duke also received their post-high school education and job training in programs sponsored by Operation Breakthrough. Their generation was to become a leading force in medical center unionization in the 1970s.

Howard Fuller was a central figure in shaping and coordinating the black student movement in North Carolina, the movement in Durham's black community, and that among workers at Duke. His initial endorsement for Operation Breakthrough came from Durham's traditional black leadership, and Fuller maintained support from them despite his and the movement's turn to the left in the late sixties. By 1967, Fuller, working for the North Carolina Fund, was organizing and training antipoverty organizers statewide. Their success at grass-roots mobilization and militancy throughout the state called forth a conservative backlash. Fuller and the growing cadre of black student and community organizers were becoming more radical, more critical of capitalism as well as its institutional racism as they encountered deeply entrenched resistance to economic improvement for their black constituents. At this same time, too, black power was taking root among college students, and Fuller was much involved with speaking to and educating black students and community groups. By 1968 and 1969, black student activism was at its height, and Fuller became increasingly embattled by conservative national and local white political forces. In mid-1969, Fuller developed Malcolm X Liberation University as an organizing and educational effort for the black community. It was an institution that tried to link student nationalism, black power, and community organizing. It soon moved to Greensboro and took on Pan-Africanist politics; Fuller changed his name to Owusu Sadaukai. Although Fuller's radicalization at once reflected and channeled the changing political climate in Durham's black community, he and the student organizers he trained remained firmly committed to the economic rights

of working-class black people, and it was from this perspective that
he and his co-workers were to become active in the struggles of Duke
workers.[24]

Service Work. In the late 1950s and early 60s, Duke University's
growth and work-force specialization were not matched by changes in its
attitudes toward black workers. Thus, housekeepers were still given one
"free" meal but had wages deducted to pay for their uniforms. They received no health insurance or other, by then, standard employee benefits
that implied an ongoing commitment on Duke's part as an employer.
Black workers complained to being treated as personal servants. "When
I was a [nurse's] maid," Mrs. Helen Johnstone recalled of her work in the
early 1960s, "our second head nurse, Joan Ashley, she used to run me
everywhere—uptown to get the immunizations and to put them in my
refrigerator. She had me run to the library to return her books for her on
work time."

Black workers chafed at the lack of clear job definitions, at being given
arbitrary work to do by supervisors, at the absence of job mobility and
the lack of black supervisors, at working erratic and arbitrary schedules—
often ten to twelve days without a day off, at the lack of insurance coverage
and other benefits, and at their sub-minimum wages. Take-home wages
of $30–$40 for a two-week pay period were common. After five years at
Duke, in 1964, Margaret Sims was earning $55 for two weeks' work in
housekeeping. When Helen Johnstone came to Duke in the early 1960s,
she was hired as nurses' maid. Despite her title, her work overlapped
considerably with that of the nurses' aides, who were then white. She
described Saturday morning clinics. "At first it would be the nurse and
aide and secretary and me. We would clean and stock the rooms Saturday
mornings. When the patients came in I'd have to stop my stocking and
weigh and take temperatures; and if there was a fever, I'd order a hemo-
globin and carry it up to the lab on the ground floor and have the results
back to the doctor when he got out of conference." Mrs. Johnstone was
expected to do not only her own work, but work that was theoretically
reserved for aides and perhaps even nurses.

Despite her skills and qualifications, the color bar limited Mrs.
Johnstone's opportunities for promotion. "[My head nurse] told me to
apply for the [nurse's] aide job. Ms. Smith there [in the nursing office]
said, 'I'm sure you are qualified for this job, but there are no openings.'
I knew it was because of my race. I had had a nurse's aide course at

Lincoln Hospital and they wouldn't recognize it. They wanted me to take a Duke course. I guess it was because Lincoln was black. But I'd been doing the work. They hired Shirley [who is white], and I trained her.

"I had to take a basic aide course for eight weeks. I went to class four hours in the morning and worked four hours in the hospital. Mr. Hazlett, who worked across the street and was bringing his son to the clinic here, he told me not to leave because I didn't get the job. He said, 'After a while it'll change and you'll get the job.' And it changed, and I'm doing it. I guess it's when they did away with this racial segregation."

Race and the Introduction of Scientific Management

In the 1960s, unionization efforts at Duke included both campus and hospital·workers in a single organization; separate medical center organizing took place later. Thus, when Oliver Harvey began to organize the Duke Employees Benevolent Society among hospital and campus workers early in 1965, it was a continuation of his earlier petition campaigns to end job discrimination throughout the Duke complex. Margaret Sims was among those who were involved from the beginning. As she recalls, "The housekeepers started it all." A cover letter to the petition was addressed "To selected members of the Duke University Community," asked for support for the "large number" of maids and janitors who had signed the petition, and pointed out that maids earned 85 cents an hour and janitors earned between $.90 and $1.05—and that there were no promotions of employees from within. The petition demanded wage increases to meet the then federal minimum of $1.25 per hour in one to two years; time-and-a-half for overtime and holiday work; training and competition for supervisory positions; and notification of vacancies, unemployment insurance, better pensions, sick pay, and disability insurance. There were more than 1,400 employee signatures, black and white, on the petition mailed to Duke's president, Douglas Knight.[25]

Harvey recalled that the university answered their petition by firing nine workers. This sparked a mass meeting, determination to unionize, and a search for a national union with which to affiliate that would not toady to segregationist practices in the South.[26]

At about the same time, and apparently at least partly in response to pressure from black workers, Duke initiated its own survey of its wages and discovered that indeed, more than 1,500 workers earned less than the then federal minimum wage of $1.25, and that Duke paid less than average wages in the area to its clerical, service, and trades workers. Nonacademic workers were paid "23.5% below the Durham average, which was well below the Federal minimum."[27] The results of this survey do not seem to have been shared with Duke workers. The survey may also have been motivated by the fact that new companies were entering the Raleigh-Durham-Chapel Hill region in the 1960s, and by improving job opportunities for residents, were exerting pressure on Duke to improve its wages.[28]

In August 1965, the Duke Employees Benevolent society affiliated with the American Federation of State, County, and Municipal Employees (AFSCME) as Local 77. The local was an active one. Mrs. Sims remembers collecting dues from hospital workers for the Benevolent Society and large meetings in St. Joseph's church.

According to Harvey, Duke continued trying to intimidate workers in the months after the petition drive and after the Benevolent Society became a union. From its beginning, Local 77 took an activist stance in fighting for black people's *rights as workers*. The local was particularly strong in fighting what it called "the plantation system." This phrase covered capricious treatment, personal abuse, and treatment of black workers as unworthy of ongoing commitment from Duke. It came to be a metaphor for all the racism and paternalism in the university's and medical center's treatment of black workers. The local's first newsletter, *We the People*, reported winning an eight-hour day for laundry workers, who had been made to work "as many as 13 hours a day and suffering considerable abuse and mistreatment."[29] The local also took on personal offenses by supervisors. Reporting on an insult of a dining hall worker by her supervisor, the newsletter noted, "The swift action of shop stewards . . . and others resulted in a full apology from the supervisor and the statement that he would 'never do it again.'" Local 77 commented that without a union, workers could only quit or "meekly submit" when they "were insulted, abused or cheated." "Your union stewards were able to show Mrs. M. . . . that the plantation system at Duke has come to an end." They also successfully prevented the university from calling a worker in to work on New Year's Day, which fell right in the middle of his vacation. The worker was out of town and refused to come back. When he returned to work, he was docked a day's pay. As a union officer, he argued his own case, "that vacation time should run consecutively—and won." He received back pay and "established now for everyone that vacation time will not be interrupted."[30]

Shortly after Local 77 was founded, the university fired three house-keeping workers. In response, the fledgling union organized a walkout, held a large meeting, and scheduled a demonstration at the university's Homecoming game the following day to protest the firings publicly. Some two hundred students joined them. On the same day, Duke announced pay raises, insurance, and a grievance procedure, but did not acknowledge the existence of the union or of worker efforts to gain these rights. Duke presented the improvements as voluntary and spontaneous in what was to become a patterned response to worker pressure. Subsequent improvements were announced in 1966, but no formal job descriptions or union recognition were forthcoming, nor was significant sick leave or vacation time awarded.[31]

One faculty supporter of the Benevolent Society petition wrote a separate letter to university president Knight urging him to implement the workers' demands. Speaking no doubt of Harvey, John Strange noted, "One of the janitors at the University, a very close personal friend of mine, is one of the most remarkable and able individuals that I have ever encountered. But because of the fact that he is a Negro, his job opportunities have always been limited including limitations imposed by Duke University."

Knight's response seized on the cooptive potential of promoting an "exceptional Negro" without seeming to recognize the racism inherent in this stereotype: "I wonder if you could tell me the name of your janitor friend. . . . We have been looking hard, honestly and for some time in the hope of finding men who could carry responsible supervisory jobs."[32] Oliver Harvey, on his part, recalls many cooptive offers from the university. "They offered me pretty much whatever I wanted to stop raising sin."[33]

But President Knight's letter continued in a more ominously racist and divisive vein, "We have made very genuine improvement in the minimum salary structure, and intend to continue doing so; but I honestly think that it is far more important both for the University and the region to make certain that salaries continue to rise for more skilled people than those who receive minimum compensation."

He noted as well the significance of the issue, "This, as you can imagine, is not a problem to be resolved casually, since it involves a great many thousand people, and ultimately a great many millions of dollars every year—since there is no point, of course, in making increases which cannot be sustained over a period of years.

"One solution to this problem—and it is one that has already been adopted by most major universities in the Northeast—is the elimination of employees who can work only at a minimum level of effectiveness. I find this a great moral burden, and I know that if we were to move abruptly to increase the salary scale and eliminate those who honestly were not competent to earn $1.10 or $1.25 an hour, we would be hurting individuals and also the community, which would then have to support them."[34]

Knight seems to have believed that many or most black workers were so deficient that they did not deserve to make even the minimum wage, and that Duke was benevolent to let them work at all. From this perspective, organizing could well have seemed the deepest ingratitude, topped only by widespread community and campus support for black workers' rights.

Whether these attitudes figured in the university's decision to hire an "efficiency expert," the Chicago-based Alexander Proudfoot Corporation, is not known. But the attitudes—that many black (and some white) workers were paid more than they were worth, and that this was out of Duke's noblesse oblige—were consistent with subsequent acts, and the message was not lost on black workers or their supporters. Perhaps that is why "the plantation" became an enduring image. The Proudfoot firm claimed they would "reduce operating costs, improve service and patient care, and provide improved management control" that would save the university $1.25 million a year—at a cost of only $368,000 for their services.[35]

Perhaps the loudest and most organized protest against Proudfoot came from the campus maids, who filed grievances charging the university with increasing in their workloads enormously. Informal protests apparently took place as well. One longtime organizer told me, "On campus they had a man stationed in the kitchen timing how fast people were working. He stood behind the door and when the people came out of the kitchen they'd slam the door open—and that soon got rid of him."

Some hospital secretaries remember Proudfoot for eliminating a pneumatic tube system used to send mail and medical records. Proudfoot reputedly redesigned the medical records in such a way that they were too large for the tubes, creating more work for secretaries who subsequently had to get and return charts on foot. One hospital union activist claimed Proudfoot never got far in the hospital. "They were trying to tell people how fast they should work and how many people it took to do the work." She thought that the secretaries stopped them. Whether or not

Proudfoot ever saved Duke money, it is clear that they sparked a great deal of antagonism among workers, worker support by students, and a significant boost to unionization efforts.

The Proudfoot Corporation came down hardest on those who earned least—kitchen workers, maids, and janitors—and who were also the ones fighting to improve conditions for all workers. As a result of Proudfoot's system, one janitor was assigned work that had formerly been done by two and forty-two maids filed grievances, all of which were denied by the university-controlled grievance system. One maid pursued her grievance to the final step with Local 77's assistance and gained a great deal of student support, both for her case and for the union's demand for impartial third-party arbitration of grievances. On three occasions students tried and failed to do the work assigned to the maid; actually none did as much of it as she did. A student-faculty committee interviewed twenty-six maids about the changes in their work with the implementation of Proudfoot-style efficiency. They discovered that these women, who averaged fifty-five years of age, had been given an average 81 percent increase in their workloads.[36] The Women's Student Government Association launched an investigation into the wages paid to black maids who worked in the women's dormitories; other students joined a local campus rally.[37]

Indeed, for much of 1966–67, Local 77 concentrated on a two-pronged effort. They represented individual workers in their grievances, using a university-controlled grievance system they recognized was partial to management, and at the same time they pushed to establish an impartial system and recognition of their union by the university.[38]

Rose Gattis, who became a leader of the hospital drives, was an early activist in Local 77. She remembers those days as an uphill battle. Workers were clear about their needs and grievances; Mrs. Gattis was taking home only $30 a week in wages. Her husband, like Margaret Sims's, worked in the unionized tobacco factory. It was obvious to Rose Gattis that union wages and benefits were far better than those she earned at Duke. Although she saw this as reason enough to push on, other workers whose pay was as paltry as hers feared losing even that. One woman who had been at Duke for twenty-seven years told Gattis to forget about unionizing; she'd only lose her job. Rose Gattis's husband also believed that the Duke complex was just too big to beat. However, her attitude was a growing one among Duke workers, and Gattis herself was becoming more active and would soon go on to chair the organizing committee for medical center unionization in the next decade.

Duke's First Union: 1968–74

Union recognition and the beginnings of sustained efforts to organize hospital workers at Duke have their most direct roots in the events surrounding Martin Luther King's assassination in April 1968, while he was supporting the union drive of black sanitation workers in Memphis. King's assassination called national attention to a working-class turn in the civil rights movement and marked a new stage nationwide in linking issues of race and class, a path upon which Duke workers had embarked more than three years earlier. In Durham as elsewhere, King's murder heightened people's determination to persevere, and the immediate success of their efforts encouraged optimism about significant union progress.

Food service workers, overwhelmingly black women, were an early center of union strength and remained a consistent one. There was widespread support for unionization among hospital food service workers, and some were active members of the fledgling Local 77. Workers in the main kitchen at Duke Hospital had staged a walkout a week *before* King's assassination.[39]

In 1968, food service workers earned well below the minimum wage. One participant in that walkout still remembers her starting wage in the kitchen in the late sixties—75 cents an hour. Another was paid $1.15 an hour as a cook. In 1968, when the federal minimum wage was $1.60 an hour, most dining hall workers earned less than $1.40 an hour. Other service workers earned comparable wages, even allowing for systematic gender inequalities. Maids earned between $1.25 and $1.40, janitors up to $1.65, hospital blue-collar workers earned between $1.15 and $1.40, and most laundry workers were paid less than $1.25. These wages were below those of comparable jobs in the industries beginning to move to the area.[40]

Although wages were the underlying issue, scheduling sparked the walkout. Kitchen workers had been pursuing a collective grievance for some time in order to gain alternate weekends off. Their strike leaflet was quite mild. "We are from the dietetics department. . . . Like everybody else, we want to go to church every Sunday, but we get only one Sunday off each month. We asked to be off 2 Sundays a month, so that we could attend the Sunday services at our churches at least twice monthly. . . . "[41]

Barbara Flowers, an early union activist, recalled that members started to go out on strike three times, but each time someone tipped off the food service manager. One night, activists met at the union office and decided to keep out the cooks and others who began fixing breakfast at 5 a.m. Shirley Rice, another key organizer for more than the next decade, described how pro-union kitchen workers set up their picket lines before the 5 a.m. shift began and persuaded early workers to either join them or to go home. The rest of the cooks who reported to work either walked the picket line or went back home. Mrs. Flowers remembers only four, and Mrs. Rice five or six, kitchen workers who crossed the line by sneaking into the kitchen through the emergency entrance to avoid the pickets.

Except for this handful, it was a solid front; kitchen workers stayed out all day. Barbara Flowers laughed as she described an administrator who came down and told the picketers that they would all be fired if they did not go in to work. Flowers told him he'd have to fire a lot of people. Kitchen workers and other Local 77 activists took shifts picketing the main front and back entrances of the hospital to publicize their action. They also picketed the heating plant where many white male skilled trades workers were centered to carry the union message to this group. "Then we could picket," Margaret Sims noted, "because we didn't have a contract [with a no-strike clause]."

On the third day, the hospital administration came down and negotiated with the striking food service workers. It was a clear victory. Kitchen workers were given alternate weekends off, and they received a minimum wage of $1.25. At least as important in Barbara Flowers's mind was that people felt closer after their walkout. "It was a feeling of we are people and could get what we want." That feeling was to last through the next decade and was particularly strong in departments where black women were concentrated. Indeed, some time later, when kitchen supervisors attempted to have cooks wash their own pots, they spontaneously walked out of the kitchen and sat in the hall. In less than an hour, management backed down.

After everyone returned to work, management tried—without success—to buttonhole individual workers to persuade them to tell who the organizers were. Shirley Rice, who worked in the main kitchen, recalled being confronted by a supervisor who demanded to know why she didn't cross the picket line and work. The supervisor might have had better luck breaking into Fort Knox:

"A girl said for me not to go in there," Mrs. Rice answered. The supervisor asked who "the girl" was. "I never seen her before," was the answer. "She's my co-worker but I said I never seen her. She [the supervisor] says, 'You walk around here taking orders from strangers?' I said 'I'm taking them from you and you're a stranger. I don't know you. . . . I don't know nothing about you.'" Supervisors tried to punish the strikers by having them wash the walls and floors after they returned to work. It didn't dampen their spirits, nor did the harassment last long. Those who crossed the picket lines and worked, however, "had the hardest time when the strike was over."

Encouraged by the success of this walkout, Local 77 began, also before King's murder, to plan for a full-scale strike of kitchen and housekeeping workers on the campus and in the hospital. But with the assassination, there were massive protests in Durham and at Duke as there were throughout the rest of the country. In Durham, there were angry demonstrations downtown to which the city responded by imposing a curfew, arresting numbers of black people, and bringing in almost five hundred National Guardsmen.[42] As Durham and the Duke campus erupted in anger, Local 77 decided to continue with its plan and to seek student and faculty support.

Duke students responded to King's assassination with a sit-in and vigil that focused on a variety of racist practices at the university. They soon added new demands in support of campus workers—that Knight appoint a committee of workers, students, and faculty to make recommendations about union recognition and collective bargaining, and that the university work toward a $1.60 minimum wage for campus workers. When the president refused to meet these demands, the student protest escalated to a massive sit-in of 1,500–2,000 students on the main quadrangle of the campus. This vigil of April 6–11 became largely a support movement for workers and Local 77.[43]

By April 8, when Duke had not yet responded to Local 77's request to raise wages to the federal minimum of $1.60 an hour, workers voted to strike and organized a strike committee composed of campus workers, hospital workers, and a representative of the Duke students' Afro-American Society.[44] Workers voted to demand a $1.60 minimum wage, recognition of Local 77 as their bargaining agent, and establishment of an impartial grievance procedure.

Margaret Sims recalled that they "decided we'd pull the dietetics department out because that's where it would do most good." The resulting strike involved all food service units and shut down the dining halls because most workers stayed out and because campus support for them was widespread. Kitchen workers from the hospital joined the campus people, and, as Shirley Rice remembers, "It was one beautiful sight to see." Some workers sat with the students, while others picketed on the main quad.

The following day, campus maids and janitors, members of Local 77, joined the strike and set up picket lines around classrooms and dormitories. Nonstriking workers and students collected money to feed those on strike, and striking workers remember being "well fed" by their supporters. A strike fund of more than $6,000 was reported to have been collected. Activists also remember supervisors calling them and trying to find out what they were planning in their union meetings. Howard Fuller and others from Durham's black community spoke at rallies of students and workers; Durham's Central Labor Council supported the strike, and about one hundred members of other unions, most of whom were white, walked Local 77 picket lines. The strike lasted thirteen days.[45] For many workers looking back, "That was the good old days."

Students went back to their classes after six days, but the workers held out for more than a week longer. Only at that point did the administration acknowledge "inadequacies in the relationship of the university and its non-academic employees," and offer to raise the minimum wage to $1.60 by July 1 (with intermediate steps in the next months).[46] However, it refused to grant collective bargaining or union recognition. Instead, the administration set up a faculty committee to make recommendations for how to deal with nonacademic workers at the university. Local 77—fearing that the workers were tiring and might soon go back, especially because student support had weakened considerably when the administration raised workers' wages—agreed to call a three-week moratorium to the strike and return to work.[47]

Duke faculty had been divided and ambivalent during the vigil, so it was not surprising that their committee did not recommend collective bargaining. Instead, they proposed, and the administration accepted, an Employees Council of twelve technical and clerical worker representatives and twelve service and maintenance worker representatives who would negotiate with the administration on worker concerns. They also recommended creating the Duke University Employees Advisory Committee (DUERAC), a faculty group that would mediate and arbitrate disputes between workers and the administration.[48]

The more militant workers and their leadership saw this counteroffer of an Employee Council as a "company union" and as divisive of black and white workers, who had been making progress in uniting to press for collective bargaining.[49] Almost as soon as the council was formed, approximately, three hundred white male maintenance workers, most of whom were skilled tradesmen, asked to be separated from the black service

workers. The administration complied immediately.[50] As Oliver Harvey
expressed it, "When they set up the Council they set up the division. . . . It would divide *us*. Duke's main purpose was to kill union interest, because a few white people, especially, and technical and clerical,
women, were all ready to participate with us, 25 or 30 or more. And these
people were influencing more technical and clerical people, women. We
had very few white men who participated with us because of their racial
views."[51] According to Harvey, Local 77 had had some success, part of it
with a white organizer, in attracting about sixty white women clerical
workers despite Duke's attempts to divide the races.[52] But they did not
coalesce into an identifiable or public constituency.[53] In 1968 and 1969,
the movement in Durham and elsewhere in North Carolina was becoming
more militant in tone as black student groups became active on many
campuses and joined their activism to community organizing. In this
context, some black workers became impatient with the lack of progress
toward collective bargaining and union recognition. These differences led
to friction in the prounion ranks.[54]

Local 1199, the national hospital worker union, was invited to Duke by
workers unhappy at the lack of union progress and began a campaign to
unionize workers in the medical center only. Younger workers, especially
young black women in nursing and clerical jobs, seem to have gravitated
toward 1199. They organized a sit-in in the office of a hospital administrator to protest a white doctor's having hit a black worker. The hospital
called the police, who broke up the demonstration and arrested eighteen
people.[55] Local 1199 had made itself a visible force at Duke.

Local 77 was affiliated with AFSCME largely because Duke workers
were too poor to go it alone. That relationship had been and was to remain
consistently rocky, but Local 1199's arrival led to new dimensions of conflict, because the AFSCME-1199 quarrel exacerbated differences among
activist Duke workers.[56]

In the fall of 1970, a National Labor Relations Board (NLRB) ruling
gave workers in private universities the right to form unions and to bargain
collectively, giving workers the potential to force Duke to recognize a
union. Both 1199 and AFSCME were encouraged and hastened toward
representation elections.

Duke maintained its opposition to unions, but pushed for a unit that
included clerical, technical, and maintenance workers as well as service
workers in the hopes, union supporters noted, of bringing in a large block
of white workers believed to be hostile to unions.[57]

Meanwhile, the two internationals apparently came to an agreement behind the backs of the campus and medical center workers that 1199 would organize a bargaining unit made up of hospital service workers only, while AFSCME would organize a unit of campus service workers. As far as Duke workers in Local 77 were concerned, their organizing efforts did not distinguish between service workers in the two locations— they all had the same boss, and Local 77 had been consistently organizing them into one local.

Oliver Harvey remembers that he and Rose Gattis, who worked in a hospital laboratory and chaired the hospital organizing committee, led the local's opposition. He recalled the Gattis was angry because hospital workers were particularly strong supporters of Local 77. "We've got 90 percent of the people who participate with us over there. So this is going to stir those people up and those people are going to hate AFSCME."[58] Local 77 succeeded in preventing the deal made by the two internationals, but then they had to define a bargaining unit that would cover both campus and medical center service workers.

The behavior of the local NLRB officials further impeded worker unity. They delayed from mid-February 1971, the time they were asked to rule on the bargaining unit(s), to mid-November 1971, when they finally announced their decision.[59] Their ruling separated hospital and campus workers. It denied collective bargaining to hospital workers on the grounds that voluntary, or private nonprofit, hospitals were not included under the NLRA at that time, but gave campus service workers the green light to form their own unit. Particularly significant, the NLRB also ruled that service workers on the campus—without clerical, technical, and maintenance workers—were an appropriate bargaining unit. Some four years later, the NLRB would do an about-face with devastating results and rule that medical center service workers were *not* an appropriate bargaining unit without clerical and technical workers (chapter 4). Both rulings threw cold water on the organizing efforts of service workers in the university's hospital, although in different contexts.

Although the ruling denied union representation to hospital workers, it also simultaneously indicated that hospital workers whose work did *not* involve patient care were eligible for union representation. People were initially confused because an industrial model did not apply clearly to the medical center. Oliver Harvey explained, "You're talking about service people. How much time do these people spend with sick people, percentage-wise. If it's over 50 percent, then they're not eligible. Then we got to go by all job classifications, what units ought to be included and why are they eligible. This was a four-day thing. . . . "

Local 1199 and AFSCME seem to have worked inadvertently as a sort of nice cop-nasty cop team. Duke's strategy seemed to be to give a little in order to save a lot: "strategically improving the income and working conditions of the non-academic employees in order to avoid conflicts which might strengthen the unions," as one faculty analyst viewed it.[60]

Hospital and campus workers both wanted a union, and both had been given some NLRB encouragement to pursue the matter. At this point Duke agreed voluntarily to allow medical center housekeeping and laundry workers to join campus housekeeping and food service workers in voting for Local 77 as its bargaining agent. As Oliver Harvey analyzed it, Duke did so in order to avoid continued unionizing pressure in the hospital and the possibility that food and other service workers might succeed in unionizing.[61] Local 77 won the election with a solid victory of 80 percent in late January 1972 for a bargaining unit of more than seven hundred service workers.[62]

Almost immediately, the white male, skilled trades, and maintenance workers who had been written off, at least by university-based union supporters, as antiblack and antiunion, partially reversed themselves and decided to unionize. Duke sociologist Jack Preiss quotes one of their leaders in explaining the decision, "I've got to admit the blacks are right about some things, especially that you can't just take what's handed to you. Duke always said they would take care of us, but I see now that they never gave more than they thought they had to. They could always rely on us to oppose the blacks and the radicals. Well, I don't feel buddies with either of these groups but I'm not going to be a fall guy for the administration, either. We figure if the blacks can get what they want, so can we. I don't mind saying the blacks showed the way and I admire them for it. I don't think we could have taken the lead on our own."[63] Maintenance workers won their election by some 75 percent and became Local 465 of the International Union of Operating Engineers.

There were casualties however. The interunion fighting combined with the NLRB's exclusion of many pro-union workers from union representation left recriminations, divisions, and much bitterness. Some of it was directed at Local 77's leaders, most notably Oliver Harvey, who became alienated, discouraged, and, against the advice of other activists, took the supervisor's job Duke had urged on him for so many years. As expected, this only fed people's feelings of betrayal.[64]

Birth of a New Generation of Black Women Activists. In some ways the division between Local 77 and 1199 may have reflected differences in tactics between older and younger black workers. The latter were among the first black women clericals and nurses to enter the medical center in significant numbers. This cohort, of about 1968–70, benefitted from the freedom movement's success in opening up college admissions, in stimulating government funding for education in medicine, nursing, and allied health programs, and in making them accessible to black students. Many of these women had been activists in high school, thus contributing to their own opportunities. They were a cohort politically experienced beyond their years.

For most of the sixties, black workers had been concentrated in service work and almost excluded from clerical jobs. Only 4 percent of the combined university and medical center clerical staff were black, whereas service workers were about 84 percent black.[65] Before the late 1960s, the DTO job (then called ward clerk) was held primarily by white women. Sometime between 1967 ad 1970 it shifted to become a job held primarily by black women. Verna Clemons, a pioneer black DTO, recalls that when she started in 1969, the white clerks were being promoted to secretarial jobs or to ward clerk supervisors, which at that time were two pay levels higher than ward clerk. Most of her cohort in the DTO training program were from Hillside High School. "All of us came out of high school together—the class of '68 or '67 or '69." In retrospect, "Duke seemed like the logical place to work," and DTO was "the only nice job" if you were black and did not have nursing skills.

The freedom movement and the programs of Operation Breakthrough helped birth this generation of black women activists. Operation Breakthrough combined political education with courses and training for better paying jobs. Many of the health-care training programs black women participated in were federally funded efforts to alleviate personnel shortages as a result of that industry's rapid expansion. As Denise McRae, another DTO, remembers, "Back in the '60s that was the thing. You got your [high school] work-study program and worked for Operation Breakthrough. There was always a social struggle for years and years. I worked for Breakthrough when picketing was the thing and the emphasis was on sticking together."

She also took advantage of Operation Breakthrough classes and "experiences you couldn't get as a poor black person in Durham—sewing, drawing, painting." Operation Breakthrough had a voter registration program and a New Careers Program "for high school graduates who didn't have money to go to college." They paid tuition, books and transportation to the courses that led to certification in various fields, among them LPN and operating room technician. After she graduated high school in 1968, Denise McRae took a ward secretary course at the University of North Carolina for six months and became a ward secretary at Carolina Memorial Hospital before taking her job at Duke.

Although Verna Clemons also came to Duke as a ward secretary, she couldn't take the harassment and stress of the work—nor its low pay, so she soon became a secretary. This was not easy in 1969, when black secretaries were even fewer in number than they were by the latter seventies. There were some 1,684 office workers at Duke in 1969, but less than 10 percent were black.[66] By the end of 1976, almost 29 percent of all medical center clericals were black although the percentage of black secretaries was half that, and the percentages of black administrative and medical secretaries was lower still.[67]

Verna Clemons was the only black secretary in the whole wing where she worked. "At first I didn't have any problems because they ignored me. Then they recognized I existed—and *then* they recognized I'm human." Mrs. Clemons works in a large department for one of the head doctors and for research and clinical fellows as well. By the time I met her, she had worked in the department almost ten years and had been promoted to medical secretary about three years earlier. She has managed to attain this niche as well—where black women are still quite rare. In 1980, only 10 medical secretaries of 186 were black, less than a 1 percent increase over 1976.[68]

Despite Verna Clemons's skill, seniority, and good relations with her doctor, it wasn't easy to get her promotion. When her doctor requested the promotion, the administration denied it on the grounds that Clemons didn't do enough to be considered a medical secretary. Given her workload in handling both clinical appointments and screening calls, keeping patient and departmental files, typing research grant proposals and manuscripts, handling laboratory finances, billings, and statistics, and typing housestaff clinic notes as well as doing a fair amount of informal coordination, this seemed unlikely to both Clemons and her doctor. He rewrote Mrs. Clemons's job description and then the promotion went through, however, she received no wage increase with the promotion. Particularly galling was the fact that a white secretary who started in the department after she did, and whom she trained, now makes more money than Mrs. Clemons does.

Mabel Snead was one of the few black clinic receptionists in a private clinic in 1978.[69] "We're more or less like clinic ward secretaries." When she first started, Snead was one of four black workers in the entire clinic, two of whom were orderlies. She noted that black and white workers get along well interpersonally in her office—"If it wasn't for that, the office would be in a terrible mess"—but she was less happy about overall clinic administration: "it's probably more racist than anywhere else." Snead feels that the administration has held back a number of black workers and hired from outside rather than promote them.

Despite any age and occupational lines of cleavage that may have under-lay the Local 77–1199 conflict, once Local 77 won its election, it maintained a high profile and kept up the pressure on Duke, giving other medical center workers encouragement for unionization as well. In June 1973, some fifty women housekeepers in Local 77 in the hospital walked off their jobs to protest the addition of wet mopping of patient rooms to their regular workload. Women in housekeeping did general cleaning, while men did the wet mopping. Duke claimed that the change was instituted to cut down the number of daily interruptions in patients' rooms. Women, supported by men, stayed out all day and picketed the hospital's main entrance with mops, buckets, and picket signs. They returned to work after a letter of understanding between Duke and the local indicated that women would not mop until the issue had been discussed at a meeting of the parties, and that there would be no disciplinary action taken against the participants.[70] The outcome was that women would not mop.[71]

Summary and Conclusion

Even with the limited bargaining unit, unionization brought many improvements. Margaret Sims recalled that the starting pay for house-keepers went up to $62.50 weekly within a year or two. In campus food services, one early activist in the dining halls remembers the pre-union layoffs of most food-service workers for three months during the summer, when students were not on campus. Some workers also used to work split shifts, where the work covered a twelve-hour period, but they were paid for only eight actual working hours. Other employees worked ten to twelve days without a day off and without overtime pay. Collective bargaining ended the split shifts. Workers in dining halls closed for the summer were no longer laid off automatically. Instead, they gained the option of shifting to another work site. Workers now have health insurance, a credit union, overtime pay, paid sick days, and regular paid holidays. Where black workers used to work under white supervisors only, there is now a majority of black supervisors in both housekeeping and food services. Underlying the specifics though is a fairly basic shift in the way Duke was forced to deal with black workers.

The push to unionize at Duke University had been initiated by black workers of Oliver Harvey's and Margaret Sims's age group. They had been adults during World War II and seen inroads made on segregation then only to experience the contradictions of a decade of postwar segregation, discrimination, and dead-end work. Mrs. Sims worked at the hospital, and Mr. Harvey worked on the campus, but they shared many of the same experiences. Unionization efforts grew naturally from the civil rights movement in Durham and became an integral part of the economic and political movements in the black community. At Duke, black service workers were the ones to initiate and sustain organizing efforts in a unified movement of campus and medical center workers. They introduced white trades, clerical, and technical workers to the possibility of having a union, and white professionals to organizing themselves to reform health-care delivery.

By 1968 too, the first generation of black clerical workers, practical nurses, and technicians was joining the service workers in the medical center work force. These jobs were changing rapidly under the impetus of accelerating specialization and growth. Although there was some racial desegregation of clerical, technical, and nursing work as a result of movement efforts, most jobs remained fairly racially segregated, as with black clerks and white secretaries, black LPNs and white RNs. The trajectory of specific medical center organizing efforts from 1974–79 was influenced heavily by the ways that race and occupation interacted to shape workers' grievances and willingness to act on them. The next four chapters will explore how the dynamics of race, gender, and job interacted within and beyond the hospital to sustain a five-year movement to organize the medical center.

NOTES

1. Fink and Greenberg, 1979:230; see also Denton, 1976:61.
2. Gifford, 1972; Melosh, 1982; Reverby, 1979.
3. Janiewski, 1985; Palmer, 1984; Rollins, 1985.
4. Katzman, 1981; Palmer, 1984.

5. A study by Judith Rollins (1985) uses the term and provides a particularly vivid description and analysis of this relationship. Neither Rollins nor this study discuss differences and similarities between maternalism and paternalism.

6. Hoffius, 1980; Fink and Greenberg, 1979; Denton, 1976:182–227; Foner, 1980:426–28.

7. Anderson, 1981; Honey, 1984; Kessler-Harris, 1982:279.

8. Wise, 1980:39; Jones, 1985:256–68.

9. Wise, 1980. Much of the material in this chapter is drawn from this fine work; see also McConville, 1978.

10. Wise, 1980: 20–32; see also Janiewski, 1985, for a history of race and gender in tobacco unionization in Durham.

11. *Aeolus* Feb. 14, 1979, 10.

12. McConville, 1978:25.

13. Wise, 1980:33–34.

14. Janiewski, 1985.

15. Preiss, n.d.:2.

16. Wise, 1980:54–57.

17. *Carolina Times*, March 21, 1959.

18. Bishop, 1967.

19. Ibid.; Miller, 1976.

20. Miller, 1976, 50; Redburn, 1970:57.

21. *Aeolus*, Feb. 14, 1979:10; Wise, 1980; Bishop, 1967.

22. Wise, 1980:57, see also 60–64, 169.

23. Redburn, 1970:79–94; Wise, 1980:86–88, 137–40; Bishop, 1967.

24. Wise, 1980:136–48.

25. DU Archives, "Employee Union" file; petition with cover letter addressed "To Selected Members of the Duke University Community, Feb. 22, 1965."

26. Wise, 1980:65–70.

27. Aten, 1971.

28. Ibid.

29. *We the People*, March 17, 1966; DU Archives, "Employee Union" file.

30. Ibid.

31. Wise, 1980:84–92; Aten, 1971:3–4

32. DU Archives, Sect. 25, John Strange folder, deposited by John Strange in DU Archives, "Strange to Knight, March 3, 1965"; "Knight to Strange, March 11, 1965."

33. McConville, 1978:26.

34. Knight to Strange.

35. Aten, 1971:5; but see Wise, 1980:92 for a higher estimate.

36. "History of Local 77" in "The Crisis on Our Campus Does Not Appear to Be Over," May 1968, DU Archives, Sect. 25, the Vigil Papers, 1968–70; Wise, 1980:92, 170.

37. Segal honors paper from DU Archives: 9–10.

38. *We the People*, March 7, 1966; Wise, 1980.

39. DU Archives, Sect. 25, leaflet, "We Are from the Dietetics Department," March 28, 1968; Wise, 1980:84.

40. Leaflet, "Why Local 77"; DU Archives, Sect.25, Vigil Papers.

41. Vigil Papers, Feb. 28, 1968.

42. *Duke Chronicle*, April 8, 1968.

43. This was the high point of student activism here; materials focusing on student and faculty activities include Carter, 1968; Preiss, n.d.; in DU Archives: Vigil file, David Henderson journal, Segal honors paper, special issue of *Duke Chronicle*, April 29, 1968.

44. DU Archives, Sect.25, leaflet, "All Duke Workers Strike Meeting", April 8; *Duke Chronicle*, April 9, 1968.

45. Aten, 1971:15; *Duke Chronicle*, April 10, 18, 19; Preiss, n.d.:8–9; Wise, 1980:107.

46. Henderson journal, app. 1, item 18; *Duke Chronicle*, April 22, 1968.

47. *Duke Chronicle*, April 22, 1968.

48. Preiss, n.d.:9–10, 62.

49. Wise, 1980; McConville, 1978:28.

50. Preiss, n.d.:74, f/21, f/26; DU Archives, Sect. 25: "Duke Hospital and Labor," *Praxis* position paper, n.d.:9; unpublished leaflet.

51. Wise, 1980:110.

52. Ibid.:81–82.

53. Preiss, n.d.:74.

54. Ibid.:63, 68.

55. DU Archives, 1199 folder; Preiss, n.d.:68–69. This was the only incident of civil disobedience I encountered in records and recollections of more than a decade of organizing efforts, but 1199 never really dug into Durham, and it left almost no mark on subsequent events.

56. Wise, 1980:133.

57. Ibid.:74–75, 82; DU Archives, the President's Letter, Oct. 26, 1970; 1199D folder.

58. Wise, 1980:150–52.

59. Whitney, Wayne, "NLRB Gets Hospital Union Case," *Duke Chronicle*, Feb. 18, 1971; Wise, 1980:156.

60. Preiss, n.d.:69.

61. Wise, 1980:155–56.

62. Unreferenced newspaper clipping, Local 77 files, folder "1970–1973"; Wise, 1980:156.

63. Preiss: f/26.

64. Wise, 1980:160.

65. Preiss, n.d.:f1 for 1966; EEO Employer Information Report EEO-1 Duke University 1969.

66. EEO, Employer Information Report EEO-1, pt. 2, sect. G.

67. *Caston et al.* v. *Duke University*, Peterson Deposition, Exhibit B, "Active Biweekly Clerical Employees as of December 31, 1976," hereafter Exhibit B.

68. Exhibit B.

69. This seems to have changed since then.

70. *Durham Sun*, June 18, 1973, sect. B; *Durham Morning Herald*, June 19, 1973.

71. Report of trip to Winston-Salem NLRB, July 3, 1973, Local 77 files of meeting minutes.

II

Organizing the Hospital

In the nation as a whole, hospital unionization success peaked in 1974–75, but solid efforts continued nationally throughout the decade. After 1975, the struggle was an uphill one. Between 1974 and 1979, unions won less than one-half of all union elections—a significant drop from the peak 62.5 percent of 1974–75 wins. There was less activity in the South and in right-to-work states in general, and less success as well.[1] Where the political climate through the early seventies nationally and at Duke had been very supportive of unionization, this attitude changed as the economy slumped and as activism declined on the campus and in Durham's black community. Although students and the black community continued to be supportive of the drive, the level of activism between 1974 and 1976 was certainly lower than it had been in earlier years.

The NLRB's role was perhaps reflective of, as well as contributor to, a shift to the right in national policy. In mid-1974, the board extended collective bargaining to workers in private, nonprofit hospitals. By late 1975 though, the bargaining unit that the NLRB created for the Duke election added clerical and technical workers to what had been a service worker drive, thus creating a unit with about equal numbers of black and white workers. This mid-stream change severely undercut the chances of a union victory. At least as significant, the board's 1975 decision contradicted its 1971 decision. The timing and method of integration differed significantly from the integration black workers and white women had tried to build in the latter sixties, where both organized together from the outset. There had been promising but embryonic ties between black service workers and white women clericals in the late sixties, but these were undercut when Duke separated clerical and technical workers from service workers on the Employee Council. In retrospect, unionists had been caught in a catch-22 situation. Unionists responded to this setback by building a service union, Local 77, and sought to extend it to all medical center service workers, almost all of whom were black. In 1975, white workers were suddenly asked to vote for or against what unofficial gossip and racist sentiment termed a "black union," and moreover, one that represented workers at the bottom of the class and status hierarchy. It was not an easy situation in which to build unity across racial lines.

Still, changes in racial hiring patterns by the mid-1970s, especially in clerical work, seemed to be favorable for building an integrated effort. Although DTOs were the most visible black women clericals, there were significant numbers of clerks and a small scattering of black secretaries. In addition, the 485 LPNs, more than four out of five of whom where black and who constituted one-half of all nurses in 1976, gave black women a highly visible presence in nursing. Black women were also gaining a small presence as technicians and technologists as well as among RNs. Chapter 3 will examine the work and racial composition of important clerical jobs in relationship to the development of an oppositional work culture and pro-union sentiment.

Union organizers at Duke seem to have begun from the premise that even if the political tide was turning, progress against it was possible with some new tactics. Massed demonstrations and confrontations were rare in the hospital drive; there were no sit-ins or strikes. Instead, this campaign relied on maintaining a solid infrastructure among hospital workers and on persistence—in leaflet wars, in fighting workers' grievances, and in enrolling people in the union. But it was neither a timid nor a narrow campaign. Unionization was still presented as part of a larger struggle for social justice, one that linked workplace and community issues as well as issues of race and class, although not gender. These dimensions of radicalism were an important part of the union's appeal to workers. Chapter 4 is about the structure and conduct of the organizing campaign, and the changing political climate in which it took place.

Unfortunately in the months preceding the election, some of the campaign's most vocal spokespeople came to be on opposing sides of a political conflict about how to be radical, and how radical to be. This was part of a much wider pattern of political infighting on the left, which some believe was itself produced by recession and repression and their combined chilling effects on activism. The consequences were disastrous for the immediate and long-term success of hospital unionization at Duke. Chapter 5 will build on the discussion of work organization and work culture begun in chapter 3 and analyze how black women politicized their workplace networks. It describes the political idiom of these networks and the leadership of centerwomen, or the women who held the networks together. The structure of effective leadership of the union drive lay in the interaction of centerwomen and the more visible male public spokesmen. Faction-fighting destroyed that infrastructure and leadership and led women workers to depoliticize their networks. This was a large part of the reason for the first drive's failure. Chapter 6 will deal with why the second drive, from 1976–79, failed despite its efforts to undo the damage of factionalism. It had to contend with deteriorating political and economic conditions and the participation of union-busting consultants, all of which made organizing even more difficult. But there were additional internal problems that resulted from the end of the first drive. Organizers in the second drive were unable and reluctant to mobilize and repoliticize women's workplace networks, some of whose centers sat the drive out, while others joined as individuals but were reluctant to exercise the kind of leadership they had taken in earlier years. As a result, this drive was conducted "from above," with a strong International presence and strategy that did not involve workers.

NOTE

1. Denton, 1976:228–31.

3

Work and Race, Work Culture and Collective Action

The activities of food, cleaning, and patient-care service workers in the medical center showed a visible and militant tradition of resistance both to exploitative working conditions and to racially discriminatory treatment in their work lives. Black workers have consistently been the center of union strength at Duke, in large part because of the strong links between unionization and the movement for racial justice. The material basis for those links lay in the structured segregation of jobs such that black workers were concentrated at the bottom of the pay scale in all or largely black jobs or departments. In medical center organizing, this affected black women especially because they were crowded in dietary services as aides, clerks, and data terminal operators (DTOs). Unionists saw grievances about the organization of work as linked to those about racial discrimination: black workers were in the worst jobs because they were black, and those jobs were organized as oppressively as they were because the workers in them were black.

What about white workers? There were white workers on the organizing committee and an indeterminate amount of pro-union feeling among white workers. There was a history of union sentiment that reached back to the sixties among white women clerical workers, and there was also a largely white male skilled trades union, stimulated by the success of Local 77. Unionists worked consistently to build strength across racial lines by pointing out the similarities in pay and treatment between white and black workers. Perhaps the bulk of their leaflets dealt with wages and working condition issues shared by workers of both races. After all, there was not much of a dollar difference in the wage levels of cooks, DTOs, and secretaries, and the benefits of all workers were widely regarded as inadequate.

Unionists had to contend with patterns of racially segregated jobs throughout their efforts to organize the medical center. Jobs held by black workers and those held by white workers tended to be organized differently, and the kinds of work cultures that developed from those organizations also differed. By *work culture*, I mean the understandings and values about work and workplace social relations that co-workers share and reinforce among themselves. These understandings were sometimes oppositional toward management and sometimes not; they sometimes supported resistance to management and other times reinforced consent to the status quo.[1] Work culture at the hospital did not develop in a straightforward way from the organization of the work itself. Instead, the racial and gender composition of the specific job and the fact of occupational segregation in the work force as a whole seemed to shape the way in which workers experienced their job and the work cultures they did and did not develop.

This chapter focuses on the work and work cultures of clerical workers, who were growing in numbers, and who were key to the success or failure of unionization. The first part examines the work of DTOs, a visibly discontented and pro-union group of women, most of whom were black. The second part of the chapter examines secretaries and clinic receptionists, neither of whom appeared publicly to be pro-union or consistently angry about their working conditions. Still, the administrative and coordinating skills demanded in all these jobs were central to the smooth functioning of a highly specialized bureaucracy, but were not recognized by the hospital in word or in pay. Although DTOs and secretaries performed similar work, they did so under different conditions and social relations. DTOs and secretaries did not have the same perceptions about their work, nor did they have the same traditions of collective militance. To a great extent, this was because DTOs were black and secretaries were white, and because DTOs and secretaries did not have the same opportunities for promotion and transfer. The third part of the chapter describes work on a racially integrated clerical assembly line in the medical records department. Although medical records clerks were clerical workers, their jobs, working conditions, and grievances were much like those that food and cleaning-service workers protested in the mid-sixties. In medical records, factorylike working conditions and intense supervision did generate an oppositional work culture even across racial lines, but medical records clerks were reluctant to express or act on their discontent publicly, largely for fear of opening racial divisions.

DTOs: Coordinating and Flak-Catching

Hospital wards are intimidating places for the uninitiated. Most ambulatory patients, visitors, and workers, hoping to find a person to guide them, gravitate toward the large, counterlike desk somewhere in the middle of the hall: the nursing station or ward desk. Sooner or later, everyone who has business on the ward will be there—for a while. I did most of my ward observation in South, before Duke North opened. The desk there was permanently staffed, usually by two DTOs whose job it was to coordinate and organize patient-care information, orders, and tests for all patients on the ward. Since the move to North, I have usually seen only one secretary on a desk, with a floater to fill in when things get too busy. DTOs tell me that this practice has indeed been the norm for years, and they are less than pleased with it.

In one hour with Denise Thompson, I got some indication of the range of invisible skills that DTOs need to exercise. A gregarious black woman not yet thirty, Denise had been working at Duke for about ten years. During that time, she had thought about taking other jobs and was active in efforts to improve wages and work life at the hospital, but mainly she enjoys her work and the people she meets. Until the new hospital opened, Denise worked days on a small ward. She was supposed to be one of two DTOs, although I often saw her alone or with a trainee.

The morning that I interviewed her, Denise's partner was working elsewhere because they were short-staffed, and her new trainee was sitting with her books on her lap, watching the activity. It was very busy, too much so for anyone to pay much attention to the trainee. Denise was on the telephone most of the time—actually on two telephones—as well as paging nurses and aides on the intercom to go to one or another patient's room. As a woman in a nightgown and robe walked by the desk, Denise hailed her to ask if she'd brought her chart back from the test she'd just had. She hadn't, and apologized with some embarrassment. Denise told her not to worry, that she'd telephone down and have the chart sent up.

At the same time, a man about to be discharged stopped at the desk to pick up the return clinic appointment and prescriptions that his doctor was supposed to have given him. After some searching, because this was the first Denise had heard of it, she found them at the desk. She suggested that the man wait in the back room for a bit because the intern was supposed to talk with him before discharge. The man pointed out that both his doctor and the intern had walked by him twice and waved without stopping. Denise paged the intern to have him come up as he was supposed to do.

The intercom buzzed. A patient wanted a nurse to come to her room to open a can of soda. This is a private ward. Denise rolled her eyes, turned to an LPN at the desk, and said, "Would you?" The nurse answered "No," but went anyway.

I felt conspicuously idle, when Denise took advantage of a break in the action to ask me what kind of work I did when I wasn't hanging around the desk. I told her that was my work. "Oh," she replied deadpan, "Nothing."

According to hospital management's official job description, Denise's job involves no patient contact and certainly no medical background. At Duke, as at other hospitals around the country, hers is an entry-level job requiring only a high school education and is defined as routine chart keeping, scheduling, and verifying supplies. A standardized job description requires ward clerks to be able "to carry out repetitive operations under specific instructions and in accordance with established procedures."[2] In reality, Denise's job, like that of many other so-called unskilled hospital jobs, requires a great variety of invisible skills.

DTOs are linchpins of inpatient care. They convey care plans and orders, the doctors' ideas about what a patient needs, to the nurses, laboratory personnel, and people from the dietary department who put various parts of the plans into practice. They link the wards or units where patients "live" to the technicians, therapists, aides, and dietary workers who take an active role in a particular aspect of their care. DTOs have to mesh the schedules of many people, often with diplomacy and some firmness.

There are two aspects of DTOs' work. They coordinate and organize the records of medical care, and they coordinate the actual people who give this care. These two aspects require different kinds of skills, and successful DTOs need both. The job is much more demanding mentally and complex than one would guess either from its job description or pay.

In the hospital, there is no planning for treatment without a record of what has already been done to the patient by a variety of people who may never see each other. Every real act has its paper or computer counterpart. DTOs keep these records for all patients on their ward or unit. They also communicate with all hospital personnel who perform services for these patients and handle the scheduling.

Much of their work involves using video data terminals to enter patient information and doctors' orders into a computerized medical record. Each communication can produce multiple copies of a printout of the transactions. These copies can be printed out where the information needs to go. Requisitions for tests, for example, are printed in the relevant laboratories. DTOs keep a copy of all printouts to keep track of all their work. This is, literally, the paper image of inpatient hospital care. A DTO coordinates the record keeping for all patients on her ward and is responsible for seeing to it that all tests are ordered and that results are entered, for arranging transport for patients, for scheduling procedures with laboratories and various specialists, and in general acting as traffic police for everyone's schedules.

The other half of the job relates to people. Almost all the DTOs I spoke to agree that they are "the nerve center of the ward," and that the job "is a real mental strain." Sally Hughes put it more forcefully, "To be honest and truthful, DTOs run Duke Hospital." As I listened to DTOs describe what they do, and as I watched them do it, I began to realize that they were not only clerical or data processing workers, but that they were also administrators, and that this aspect of the job produced most of the stress. When Beverly Jones elaborated on the tension of the job, people were largely the cause: "Ten people talking to you at once, the phone is ringing and the teletype is jammed. Doctors talking to you like you're supposed to know everything."

DTOs orchestrate the activities of specialists of all levels of the medical center hierarchy, but they do so in a context that is conducive to stress and conflicts. Administrators, with their high pay, status, and formal authority, have an easier time telling people what needs to be done than do DTOs. But DTOs, with no authority, low pay, and low status in the hospital's chain of command, have to do a significant amount of such work. There is plenty of talk about teamwork and the "Duke family" by hospital administration, but there is no recognition that health-care teamwork encompassing many departments needs on-the-spot coordinating. So far as I can tell, that job falls to DTOs, who have to do it without bossing or ordering because some personnel—particularly doctors—would not take such treatment well.

Even though their job description claims that DTOs have no patient contact and no direct role in patient care, in reality they play an important role as informal intermediaries between patients and the mass of specialists charged with different facets of their care.

It is often the DTOs as well as the nurses who organize parties for patients' birthdays or discharges. Perhaps because they have no formal role in patient care, DTOs are often the primary people that think about hospital patients as people with human needs for conversation, rest, and cheer.

This is also true when it comes to scheduling tests or procedures. Doctors might ask that a particular patient be scheduled for a number of tests. Tanya Wilkins explained that she has several things to consider when she does so. First, she needs to know how long each test is likely to take. A liver scan, for example, can take a patient off the floor for up to three hours. Some departments are known for cancelling a patient's test if they are not on the floor when called. Although diplomacy may help in stalling for some time, it is better not to schedule too closely. Second, and more important, doctors seldom consider whether or how much a particular test or series of tests can fatigue a sick person, or how tiring being wheeled around a large, crowded hospital can be. Wilkins tries not to schedule anyone for more than two or three procedures in a day because most of her patients are exhausted by that time. DTOs often need to exercise their judgment in order to mesh doctors' plans for treating an illness with the state of a sick person's constitution at any given time.

Teaching is another unrecognized and unrewarded job that DTOs perform. At Duke, as at other teaching hospitals, primary care and responsibility for each patient is given to first-year interns, who are supervised more or less closely by a resident and an attending physician. The workloads of DTOs shoot up each July when new interns come on the job. Until early July, the interns were medical students, and the duties of an intern are new to them. They do not know many of the hospital's procedures, nor do they know their way around the hospital. Some tests and procedures can only be scheduled by interns, who often do not know they have to do their own scheduling. New interns also have to be taught to write out reasons for procedures that they want DTOs to schedule. In that case, teaching often consists of paging the intern, which is time-consuming.

Robert Harris, a male DTO, noted matter-of-factly, "New interns are indoctrinated to get all they can from the DTOs." One of Sally Hughes's biggest frustrations is trying to read doctors' writing and to get them to write legibly. "If you can't read it, you've got to page them to come up and decipher it before you can do anything with it."

Teaching people who are already overworked, high in the hospital's status hierarchy, and unaware that they are being taught is a difficult and often thankless assignment. Because such teaching is not part of their job description, DTOs get no support from administration, and housestaff do not recognize it as a necessary part of their training and seldom appreciate it, either. Indeed, DTOs often complain about the abusive way that doctors treat them and about how the whole burden of resisting and "straightening them out" falls on their shoulders. Problems are multiplied by the number of interns who have patients on the ward and by the number of doctors involved in the care of each patient.

Mary Larson pointed out that even routine work involves directly coordinating people. The phones ring constantly: "Mostly it's people wanting to know where a patient is and what they've had done. Some things can't be done before others. If a patient needs four tests in one day, I'm on the phone for fifteen minutes getting each department to tell me when they're through so I can have a messenger pick them up and take them to the next place."

DTOs also help coordinate nursing. As they come on duty each shift, nurses get a care plan for each of their patients. In the past, nurses came to the desk to find out what the orders were. Maybe it was the nursing shortage—which was often acute—together with a high turnover rate, but, "Now they expect to be called and told." Beverly says that she does this even though she really hasn't the time and resents the extra work, because, "It's a pain to have the doctor asking if the test is done, and to have to say you don't know [because the nurses hasn't picked up her orders]. I'd rather initiate the procedure by calling the nurse and telling her."

I have often watched nurses, housestaff, and medical students ask, while standing by a telephone, a DTO to telephone someone for information. They continued to stand by the telephone during the conversation to clarify their question to the DTO in response to a query she relayed from the party on the line, and to wait for the answer from the DTO when she got off the telephone. Patricia King sighed and agreed that both doctors and nurses often interrupted her work to ask her to do something for them that they were quite able to do for themselves. "To keep peace a lot of time I go ahead and make the phone call." Too, some doctors write their orders piecemeal, "and that keeps us hopping."

There are concrete skills involved in coordinating and maintaining coop-

eration from people whose jobs and places in the hospital's hierarchy of
power and prestige often put them in conflict while forcing them to work
as a team. For the most part, DTOs learn these skills from each other and
in their own families, and they share them among themselves informally
along lines of friendship, work socializing, and on-the-job training.

DTOs have to deal with two kinds of perennial problems. The first is
the interpersonal problem of maintaining working relationships with
higher-ups who belittle DTOs at the same time that they have to re-
socialize those higher-ups to the realities of what a DTO actually does.
The second problem is the institutional problem of low pay, grievances
over scheduling, staffing, and other working conditions, and of the low
esteem in which Duke holds DTOs. The institutional situation, of course,
encourages abusive behavior from doctors, supervisors, and nurses. DTOs
have been fighting on both the interpersonal and the institutional fronts,
but in different ways.

The interpersonal battles sometimes seem like a series of unconscious
catch-22s. Offensive behavior from doctors, supervisors, administrators,
and nurses seems to come from an unspoken belief in their high prestige
relative to DTOs and from an institutional view that DTOs just do routine
paper-pushing. To be successful, however, DTOs have to get those whom
they coordinate, especially doctors and some RNs, to stop acting as if they
were commissioned officers ordering enlistees and to start behaving like
part of a team. The catch is that many of the "officers" they coordinate do
not know that there *are* coordinators, or that coordination and teamwork
with so-called nonprofessionals is really how health care happens. Instead,
they tend to equate teamwork with their giving orders. As Helen Lynch
observed, "They don't think the DTO position is important til they don't
have one; then they run on like a chicken with its head cut off."

Jane Wilson spoke for many DTOs. "Their attitudes are really, really
nasty. You have to count to fifty. Sometimes I just walk away. I don't like
being yelled at. I'm an adult; I'm grown. If you can't speak to me without
yelling, don't speak to me at all. Often they yell about something the
DTOs don't know about. It's the really big ones that think you're, excuse
the expression, shit. What they're saying is that they think you're ignorant;
and they never apologize when they accuse you wrongly. They don't try
to learn your name; they call us 'hey you.' Very few say 'good morning.'
It takes everything I have to keep this job."

For some doctors, tantrums and loud abuse are an automatic response
to anything short of instant compliance; they act as though they had a
right to yell without regard for anyone's feelings, and feel no obligiation

to apologize when they are wrong. Some doctors are racially prejudiced, and some DTOs felt that this was why doctors disregarded their feelings and were blind to their capabilities. DTOs regard the kind of behavior that Jane Wilson described, as well as less-offensive acts like asking them to make calls that the doctor or nurse could make just as easily, as ways of pulling rank. Doctors and others use their high status to belittle DTOs, to reinforce managerial and institutional views of their "worth" in the hospital ranking system and of their capabilities as both workers and adults.

Institutional ranking systems and interpersonal rank-pulling are inextricably bound to racist attitudes and institutionally racist patterns of job allocation. With very few exceptions, doctors and RNs are white; most DTOs and LPNs are black. Several women discussed their frustrations with racist staff. One DTO, who was the only black person on her ward at the time, told of a group of white doctors who referred to black people by a variety of derogatory names. When she objected, they just laughed at her. She said that it was hard to confront a group of doctors, and harder still being the only black person on that ward. Another woman wrote up a doctor for calling a black patient a "subhuman animal." She got no results from the hospital administration, but she wasn't surprised. The consensus was that DTOs had no help from management in stopping racist behavior; they were on their own and had to help each other.

In part because the formal education of professionals and management in general leaves them ignorant or misinformed about social relations, or "manners," and about the people they work with, and in part because DTOs are so in the center of activity that everyone comes to them, the burden of initiating on-the-job remedial training in social relations falls to them. Duke's formal rules and medical education both encourage rank-pulling and hierarchy, but the nitty-gritty of medical care needs to be carried out by a different set of behavioral rules. Although most DTOs dislike snobbishness and arrogance, I do not think they are making a fundamental challenge to the existence of the formal hierarchy. Instead, they are telling doctors and others that insisting on the privileges (real and imagined) of rank can make it almost impossible to solve problems and resolve conflicts such that people can continue working together. Almost all DTOs indicated that they had to set these ground rules. This is a concrete skill that takes time to learn. In general, senior DTOs said that they had good relations with doctors, that they had learned to elicit "teamwork" behavior with a minimum of conflict over the issue. However, younger ones, or newer ones like Jane Wilson had more difficulties. It

takes time to learn those skills, and experienced DTOs are angry that
Duke does not recognize that fact.

Racial Discrimination and Occupational Segregation

Although it is true that black women have made significant gains in
access to clerical work, new occupational patterns have reproduced racial
segregation in new areas. DTOs see their job as a prime example, easy
for black women to get and hard for them to get out of. It is one of the
few clerical jobs that requires weekend work and night work, and it is a
high-pressure job, sorely underrated and underpaid. Black women in
dietetics and housekeeping have made similar statements about job segregation. They have done more than complain. In 1975, a black woman in
housekeeping initiated a class action suit arguing that black workers, despite their qualifications, were assigned to "jobs which are disproportionately black and that these predominantly black jobs are generally the
lowest paying jobs, with the least opportunity for advancement."[3] In 1980,
after filing individual EEOC complaints against Duke, three black women
clerical workers, two of whom were DTOs, attempted to join this case,
which was still pending at the time. When their motions to do so were
denied, they, together with two other black women DTOs, filed a class
action suit on behalf of black clerical workers against racial discrimination
in promotion and transfer opportunities at Duke.[4]

Public records of the case give a more detailed account of the frustrations encountered by black women trying to move up—or even out—of
their "places" in Duke's occupational hierarchy. Three of the women were
college graduates and two had completed three years of college when
they were first hired at Duke between 1972 and 1978. The work history
summaries and supporting documentation of the four women who were
DTOs show them being steered into DTO work with promises of promotion and locked into it by denials of their attempts at promotion or transfer
to other clerical jobs. These black women were more than qualified in
education and in experience—as subsequent events indicated—for such
promotions. One woman with a B.A. sought a job in social work and was
told that there were no openings and encouraged to apply for a DTO job.
She was told that after six months she could transfer to a better job, one
more appropriate to her interests and background. Her attempts to transfer to clinic interviewer and patient processor jobs were frustrated, and
she soon quit Duke. A second woman, with three years of college and

work experience in interviewing, claims, counseling mental patients, and as a teacher's aide was hired as a ward clerk (pre-DTO) but told she could move up. Although she completed her B.A. and began graduate work, she was turned down for what seemed to be five jobs that went to whites; she was not promoted until after the class action suit was filed. The third woman arrived at Duke with a B.A. in education; her husband was a graduate student at Duke. She was told that the only openings available were DTO or grounds work, that if she got into the system she could move up. She too was turned down in favor of white applicants for a variety of better paying clerical positions. She was also unable to transfer to other clerical jobs at her present pay level that had weekday and non-rotating hours. Only after she joined the class action suit was she promoted. The fourth woman, also with a B.A., applied for a variety of clerical jobs but had a difficult time even getting an interview. She too was told that she could apply for promotion or transfer from her DTO job after six months, but she had the same experiences as her co-plaintiffs, being rejected for both promotions and transfers in favor of white applicants, some hired from outside (despite the policy of promotion from within) and some with manifestly less experience or other qualifications. And, coincidentally, she too was promoted only after she joined the class action.[5]

The earlier suit seems to have merged with the later; neither ever came to trial, and the clerical suit was settled out of court.[6] However, the public records provide statistical and anecdotal evidence in support of black workers' claims. Most striking is the available data from the earlier suit dealing with pay differentials between 1973 and 1977. Plaintiffs' records indicate they provided the court with seven boxes of computer printouts listing "the dollar amount of each black employee's loss based on discrimination, by comparing for each for the years 1973–77, how much each employee should have made, given his or her education, level and seniority, with what he or she in fact earned."[7] The plaintiffs calculated that the 3,661 black workers then at Duke lost more than $19.8 million in five years because of discrimination.[8]

Secretaries and Receptionists: Putting Humpty Dumpty Together Again

Like DTOs, secretaries and receptionists bridge a bureaucratic chasm in a system made up of specialists, each of whom is responsible for a specific task at a specific station on the health-care assembly line. They have to coordinate the passage of patients and their records through the system, as well as coordinate staff involved in care. Their work too depends heavily on their exercise of know-how, a wide range of unacknowledged, undervalued, and uncompensated skills. They grease the bureaucracy's wheels by coordinating the interactions of many different types of health-care workers at many different levels in the hierarchy. Among professionals, coordination seems to be managed by interdepartmental teams of specialists who confer on a structured and regular basis. However, a great deal of interaction between professionals and nonprofessionals also requires coordination, although no one has responsibility for it. Despite the fact that it is neither acknowledged nor compensated, secretaries, receptionists, DTOs, and nursing staff often exercise that responsibility, in part because it is expected of them and in part because the consequences of not exercising it affect them directly.

Clinic receptionists under a variety of titles link the clinic to the rest of the hospital and direct traffic within the clinic. The registration desk is also the nursing station, the busiest place in the clinic. The desk has two sides; one faces the patients and the waiting room and is the clerical side. It has all the forms for registering public and private patients, for finding laboratory fees, taking and making telephone calls, and handling all clinic pages. The other side is where nurses and doctors congregate to ask about patients, supplies, and broken telephones, as well as to check clinic assignments, patient arrivals, and the whereabouts of patients and staff. Anita Martell and Barbara Smallwood are expected to be aware of all these things. Much of their job is to mediate between staff and patients and to try somehow to coordinate everyone's movements.

Martell has been at Duke for more than fifteen years, and Smallwood for two. Their job is critical to clinic functioning, and their desk, like ward desks, must be covered at all times. Much of their work is to direct traffic—both routine traffic, such as transferring calls and paging people on the intercom, and nonroutine. Dotty Morrison, a "jack-of-all-trades" secretary whose main job is to type the dictation of all the clinic residents, covers for Anita when she is on break or out sick. Louise Webb, who works with patient insurance and finances, covers for Barbara and sometimes for Anita. Front desk coverage is part of their job requirement. Although she likes contact with patients, Dotty dislikes the stress involved in coordinating: "It's too much pressure. There are four phones ringing; someone's always behind you who's not supposed to be there; someone's using your phone or asking something when you're trying to do a bunch of things and your mind's preoccupied." Her comment is much like Beverly Jones's for the wards.

Nevertheless, much of the clinic's ability to function and to provide a sense of place to its staff are results of successful clerical coordinating. This is part of the reason Dotty Morrison can note that it "is my home. I belong here; we have a good little family. Last Friday there were several out sick, and people shifted around. We coped; we back one another up reasonably well." Although Anita and Barbara are everyone's first contact, clinics have more clerical staff, more clerical functions, and more interdependence among them. Private patients who call for appointments are transferred to their doctor's secretary for specialist appointments, or to the secretary for Dr. Farnsworth, the clinic's head, for general appointments. Public patients are transferred to Sandra Stone, the appointment secretary.

Morrison's main work—when she is not filling in for Anita Martell or Sandra Stone—is typing and compiling patient statistics for the clinic and typing the dictated clinic notes and correspondence of some forty residents and clinical faculty, who together staff the clinics. She has no backup. "If I'm out or behind I have to do my own catch-up."

Barbara and Anita have to exercise considerable judgment and initiative routinely. Much of it has to do with financial and medical matters, areas certainly outside their field of clerical authority. "Sometimes when a patient is sent as private, and they're from out of town, and [their medical problem] is complicated and expensive, you need to stay attuned. For example, in hematology especially, I *know* it's going to be expensive, and I route them to see if there's a sponsored program they qualify for. For example, one man today, started private. We noticed the bills and after a while we routed them to a sponsored program." I asked Barbara Smallwood how she knew who was likely to need and to qualify for sponsored payment of part of their medical bills. "I like people and we get to know them; it's a sort of sixth sense. You both get to know after a while. Anita's real good at it." These dimensions of concern and initiative are not officially recognized in the hospital's division of labor, but they are often critical to clients' treatment and pocketbooks.

Likewise, Anita Martell routinely exercised the kind of nursing judgment that Marsha Ross, the clinic's heard nurse, especially welcomed. A woman arrived for an immunization but without an appointment card; she wasn't listed for an appointment that day. It turned out that when she had been in the previous week she had a cold and couldn't be treated. Her doctor told her to return this week, but had done no follow-through to make sure she would be seen. The woman had taken a day off work to come in. Anita telephoned the doctor's office and put Marsha on to talk with him. Only RNs can take doctors' orders over the telephone. Marsha could thus give the shot right away, and the woman would not have to wait several hours until the clinic began. Here too, Anita's and Marsha's shared concern and creative use of protocol helped a patient left in limbo by her doctor.

Barbara and Anita have also developed a background in the contents and costs of various kinds of labwork and find themselves watching out for patients in ways that doctors might not. "We order the lab tests the doctors write; but if I think there's a mistake we need to check on it. For example, where they order a sodium, potassium, and creatinine, it costs $23, when they can order a chem 7, which includes all those for $20. We usually ask the doctors about that. A lot of times medical students don't know. Or in July when we get new doctors, where they're used to doing things a different way, we need to keep up til they learn how its done." In this system, doctors order and prescribe, but their training seldom informs them of absolute or relative costs. Indeed, looking out for patients' pocketbooks is no one's special responsibility. Fortunately, Anita and Barabara are among those who take it upon themselves to do so.

As is the case for the wards, nursing, clerical, and medical work are interdependent, but no adequate channels exist for coordinating them; the same is true in outpatient care. In both places, nurses, especially head nurses, often try to fill the breach. One clinic head nurse described nursing as "the director of the band" for this reason. But the power of dynamics of the hospital can make this effort oppressive, as it was for DTOs. Where a nurse may see a task that needs doing and try to assign it, she may have no authority to do so; those to whom she assigns it may have no authority to make the decision demanded, but they do it.

For example, Carol Brandon, the head nurse in another clinic, is pushing beyond the limit of her authority because she believes that the staff's separation needs to be breached for the clinic to work well. "I'm trying to get a situation where secretaries and nursing staff can pick up some responsibilities [outside their assigned areas]. For example, a client was sent to allergy clinic and someone [a doctor] decided they needed to order a theophilin level. But no one asked when he last took that medication. The test will tell you nothing because he hadn't taken any medication for six months."

I asked whether that wasn't the *doctor's* responsibility. Carol agreed that it was, but seemed less inclined to pursue a strategy for making doctors more responsible than to pursue one that protected patients from their errors. She knows that picking up such medical errors is not part of the receptionists' jobs, but much of the clinic's smoothness depended on the fact that they had a fair amount of de facto medical knowledge, and she wanted them to exercise it—which they usually did.

Clinic clerical and nursing staffs overlapped in many areas, and between them were often called on to patch up the holes that are inevitable in a clinic of specialists, part-timers, and rotators, where more emphasis is placed on teaching about specific problems than on delivering health care to people. The latter job falls more to front line clerical and nursing staffs than to doctors, whose presence is too episodic and whose perspective is necessarily too fragmented. To a great extent clericals and nurses, like DTOs, have to coordinate housestaff and physicians over whom they have no authority.

Unlike DTOs and secretary-receptionists, few hospital visitors have any contact with most office secretaries, who are scattered in ones and twos throughout the medical center in departmental and faculty offices where they are a kind of glue within and between different parts of the medical center. In 1976, there were more secretaries—about 566, including 364 secretaries, 96 medical secretaries, and 106 administrative secretaries— than anyone else on the hourly payroll, including RNs.[9] Their jobs vary enormously—both from job to job and in the variety of tasks for which each secretary is responsible. Administrative secretaries have some formal supervisory authority over other workers. The medical center usually requires medical secretaries to have formal training in medical terminology, although most hospital secretaries gain this in the course of their work. Medical secretaries for the most part work for clinical faculty, who also have private practices in the hospital. Medical and administrative secretaries are paid a little more than regular secretaries. I could find no clear practical distinctions in the work of these three classifications.

For example, Sara Johnstone is a white medical secretary, even though her work is probably more administrative than medical because she spends most of her time coordinating a small clinic—primarily its medical and professional staff. In addition, she makes appointments, unlocks gridlock in everyone's schedules, finds missing charts and strayed staff, and oversees the proper release of medical information. "They kind of introduce me to people who come around as 'she runs the place.'"

"Keeping pleasant relations among staff I consider a very important part of my job. It's a way of handling people and getting done what you want done and make them feel really good about themselves. We had a secretary without typing or English skills for the job; but she could do lots of things—file, answer the phone. Appreciating her as a person and being interested in her as a person, I think that's probably the first thing before you can deal with anybody."

Secretaries come from a wide variety of backgrounds. It would not be strange to find a two-woman office where one woman's family work history went from sharecropping to mill work to secretary in two or three generations while the other's went from several generations of professionals and Seven Sisters college attendance to marrying a medical student and working as a secretary. Despite the class diversity, less than 8 percent of all secretaries were black in 1976: There were 36 black secretaries, 4 black administrative secretaries, and 3 black medical secretaries.[10]

Like their counterparts in the clinics and on the wards, many office secretaries also staff the clerical front lines and need to exercise the same kinds of coordinating skills, as well as similar kinds of medical, financial, and interpersonal judgment—all without the authority to do so.

I first became aware of these dimensions of the job when I observed in Susannah Hughes's office. Especially after ward observation, work in this one-woman office seemed very dull. I had very little to report after watching Susannah type dictation and answer the telephone for several hours. She pointed out that her work was duller for me than for her, because she knew the callers, both the hospital staff she had to deal with and her doctor's patients, whom she also came to know. Susannah told me about one woman whom she has come to know from the telephone because the woman has tried to see a doctor at Duke. She is from a rural area and thinks her doctor, the only local one, is not taking proper care of her. Protocol at Duke requires that the woman have a referral from her physician before she can be seen at Duke, however she is afraid to ask her doctor because he is "mean enough" to refuse to treat her again should he find out she went to Duke. "I'm working on it. I'll find a way to get her seen if it's the last thing I do," said Hughes.

Although medical secretaries are supposed to make appointments, they are certainly not supposed to diagnose. Nevertheless, the two are not entirely separable, and a certain amount of screening is a routine part of many medical secretaries' work. Verna Clemons is among the handful of black medical secretaries, and one of very few who have been medical secretaries for more than a few years. She described what is involved in setting up an appointment. First, it is necessary to know whether a prospective patient needs your department. If not, you need to know where to refer them. "I've even made appointments for them; I feel sorry for them when they say 'I've been trying for three days.' I know how frustrating it is." Before Verna makes an appointment, therefore, she asks for the person's symptoms. "I've learned that if they're sick they'll say what their symptoms are; if they won't say, the doctor won't call them back [without any notes on what is wrong]." Verna stressed the need for judgment; "You got to listen or you'll wind up with a whole page of notes of nothing."

She feels that most of the time the doctors accept her judgment of what is needed for a particular patient in regard to an appointment and to scheduling studies that seem indicated from telephone symptoms. She has also developed working relationships with many patients' local physicians because she is responsible for forwarding this information to them. Likewise, she is in close telephone touch with people in a variety of other clinics and has come to know them, too. "You wind up increasing your patient load by running your mouth." Nevertheless, the clinic is the "fun side": it "makes you feel like you're doing something worthwhile."

As work is now organized, doctors or administrators often cannot (even if they wanted to) fully control the work of their secretaries. Secretaries are often the only people with a full overview of the organization of a department or office and all the networks and contacts radiating from it. As a result, their bosses often rely on them to make a wide variety of work and administrative decisions. They cannot be easily replaced if they do not train their successors.

Many doctors and administrators (although not all) recognize that their secretaries are the the best judges of how to do their work and so grant them the autonomy to do it. They let them work their own hours, do not watch the clock closely, and let their secretaries decide how they want to do the work because the employers recognize that they don't know how to do the jobs themselves—nor do they want to learn. When Verna Clemons was interviewed, her doctor said he wanted someone he didn't have to stand over. Verna's response was "good, I hate to be stood over." Melissa Allen, an administrative secretary in another department, can work flexible hours and can bring her daughter to work on school holidays. Louise

Riggs, medical secretary for a busy doctor, and her office-mate informally coordinate taking days or time off to take care of their family responsibilities. Their doctors all allow them to control their own clocks so long
as their work is done. Private secretaries' relationships to doctors is very
different from that of DTOs, or even clinic secretaries.

Probably the best protection of secretarial autonomy has been the fact
that bosses have their own work to do. In this respect, secretaries differ
from many other clerical workers who are supervised by someone whose
only work is to watch them and monitor their output. Thus, doctors,
researchers, and many administrators have certain things for which they
want their secretary to take full responsibility. If these are done, most
bosses are relatively indifferent about whether the secretary *could* do
more, either because there is not more to do or because they must work
more in order to create more work for the secretary. They also want their
own secretary because this is the easiest way for them to guarantee not
only that their work is done, but also that responsibility is delegated—that
is, that much of the load is taken off them. An additional aspect, although
one I did not explore, is surely the status of having one's own secretary.

Secretaries are formally supervised by a unit administrator. Although
these are seldom around and have very little contact on a day-to-day basis,
they are important for determining a secretary's pay and raises and can
undercut doctors' efforts at raises and promotions for their secretaries.
Vivian Pettiford, a medical secretary for a busy department chairman after
having worked for a lower ranking doctor, believed that the primary thing
that determined a secretary's pay was the clout her particular boss wielded
in the hospital bureaucracy. As was discussed chapter 3, Verna Clemons's
promotion recommendation from her boss was rejected by unit administration. She was ultimately promoted to medical secretary because her
boss made the effort to rewrite her job description, and even then, she
received no increase in pay. This structure makes secretaries dependent
on their particular bosses to run interference for them, something not all
doctors were equally willing or able to do. Nor were all doctor-secretary
relationships good ones.

Melissa Allen at first enjoyed the autonomy and variety of being personal secretary (although that was not her title) to a prestigious faculty
physician of a large department. She loved arranging his business and
vacation travel and helping to plan the redecoration of his house. It was
certainly better than straight typing, and she saw nothing demeaning in
the personal service aspect of the work. When I spoke to her two years

later, it was precisely this aspect of the job that had become particularly oppressive. "My boss is dependent on me"; he thought that Melissa was an "extension of him," and even called her at home. He got furious when, before she went home to the West Coast for her vacation, she took all of her family's telephone numbers out of the computer. She was afraid that he'd call her while she was on vacation. He did try, and wrote her an angry letter for trying to elude him. Melissa took a demotion of sorts just to get away and switched from being an eminent doctor's secretary to working for two ordinary faculty clinicians. When I saw her a year later, she had become a militant feminist and very aware that as a secretary she was at the mercy of her boss's personal whims. She had seen one secretary fired on a slim pretext that her job was no longer funded and watched the faculty hire a replacement by playing musical chairs with titles. She was angry too at the way that the computer system was being used against clerical workers. The faculty didn't know how to operate it and felt no great need either to learn or to get staff training and a decent manual for its multiple uses. The faculty assumed that computers meant instant turn-around time and multiple edits on their manuscripts. They pressured secretaries to turn out drafts and didn't realize that there were too few printers and that the system was outmoded. Melissa's major complaint about computers is shared by secretaries throughout Duke: There is "no time to learn and work on the job, [and the] manual's written for the computer, not for us."

Workloads are also a major source of irritation for secretaries. This is the other side to the coin from doctors having their own work to do, and therefore, not interfering with secretarial autonomy. Secretaries' work is determined by what the boss assigns, and some bosses expect miracles. Susannah Hughes was an administrative secretary for a doctor who was also a departmental chairman. As an administrative secretary, she was responsible for seeing to it that all other secretaries and typists in the office did their work. What wasn't done fell on her shoulders. If anyone was out, Susannah shifted people around to cover and caught the flak when they didn't like what she did. She also had to mediate when people fought with each other, as they often did under pressure of too much work. She did not like the supervisory aspect of being an administrative secretary; it seemed to be extra responsibility with no real authority. She received the aggravation but wasn't given the authority to resolve conflicts. She was not the only administrative secretary to dislike this aspect of the job—or to express a disinclination to go into supervisory jobs in general.

One secretary, given a clerical supervisory job against her will, was told to take it or quit. She quickly found another job and quit.

Susannah's particular doctor didn't see why he should have an extra secretary to handle his patient load and saw no reason why Susannah couldn't do that along with administering all the departmental and house-staff paperwork. He also refused to take Susannah's recommendations about hiring more staff or firing people who didn't do any work. She exercised the traditional secretarial remedy: She kept tuned to the secretarial vacancies that are always opening up in the huge medical center and transferred when she found a job with a doctor whom she liked better.

In addition to discussing their particular grievances with one another, secretaries also shared their recognition that the skills and scope of their jobs were unacknowledged and unappreciated, certainly in their pay and all too often in their day-to-day treatment. Vivian Pettiford likened the skill of her work to that of an electrician, the significant contrast being that electricians get paid for their skills whereas secretaries don't. That is perhaps the central dimension of secretarial work culture, and it is one that secretaries are aware of and share with one another. Its most public, organized, and visible expression though is in wall hangings. One in particular sums up a variety of understandings: "I have a responsible position. If anything goes wrong I'm responsible." In many offices, secretaries and clerks have filled the walls around their desks with hand-made, photocopied, and store-bought statements about their working conditions. Secretarial culture (really office worker culture) is a written one, but action to remedy shared grievances seemed to be overwhelmingly individual and to take the form of finding another and more congenial boss. Some analysts have predicted that bureaucratic administrations may use computers to "break the doctor secretary relationship," as one secretary put it, in order to heighten clerical output. However, such an action might well remove a buffer against secretarial rebellion.

The Paper Chase: Medical Records

In the basement of the medical center, food and cleaning work have long been subjected to factorylike pacing and supervision. Also in the basement, literally and symbolically, is a clerical back office assembly line in the filing unit of the medical records department. The overriding impression that emerged from conversations and interviews with filing clerks is that they felt watched and driven. Although dietary and housekeeping workers had a long tradition of visible and militant work culture in which these grievances were an important ingredient, medical records clerks have no such tradition, although they do complain to each other. In this case however, that sharing seemed to prevent the very resistance it urged. Indeed, no one with whom I spoke, including pro-union clerks themselves, felt they knew the extent of union strength in this unit. This section explores some of the ways that complaining can mask feelings and retard rather than sustain resistance. Most of the explanation lies in the particular dynamics of medical records work at Duke, but back office clerical work has a history of its own that includes traditions of race and gender typing, and these traditions have influenced the work organization and the gender and racial composition of filing clerks at Duke.

Office work has a very different class and racial history from that of cooking and cleaning, and a different status and racial idiom adheres to it. With the introduction of typewriters in the late nineteenth century, office work became not just women's work, but work for white, native-born women.[11] In the 1960s and early 70s, black and other racial minority women began to gain access to clerical jobs, but they did so at a time when the jobs were subdividing into "front" and "back" office work. As early as 1956, C. Wright Mills used the metaphor of "The Enormous File" in *White Collar* to describe the postwar division and de-skilling of office work with the establishment of back office jobs: separate typing and transcription pools, filing clerks, and office machine operators. Almost twenty years later, Harry Braverman used the metaphor of a paperwork assembly line for this work. It is hard to say to what extent minority women's success in breaking the clerical barrier fostered the subdivision (and new patterns of racial segregation), and to what extent these new occupational patterns encourged minority women's access to clerical jobs. It is safe to say that they reinforced one another. As at Duke, with white secretaries in front offices, these jobs in general desegrated more slowly than back offices.[12] Workers in the filing unit in Duke's medical records department might well believe that Mills and Braverman developed their metaphors by watching them work. Most clerks in the filing unit, both black and white, are women. They do not like their jobs, and they seem to leave as fast as they can.

There is a chart or medical record for every person, dead or alive, who is or has been a hospital or clinic patient in the half-century that Duke Hospital has been in existence. Whenever you come to Duke, your chart follows you on your rounds from hospital bed or clinic to laboratory to x-ray. It records all symptoms, diagnoses, laboratory tests, medications, and operations. It is busy even when it is not following you around. Researchers want it coded in a standardized way so they can use it in their work; the hospital billing department also wants it as a basis for specifying services in billing patients and insurance carriers.[13] Consequently, medical records are extremely popular. Nomadic, always on the move, charts have a life of their own, and thus are often not at home.

Home is the filing unit of the medical records department. Located in a windowless basement and staffed in 1976 by about 94 clerks—42 white and 52 black—and a supervisor, it is the largest unit in this vital department.[14] The good news about filing is that you don't take the work home. Almost everything else seems to be bad news. Although different workers had different complaints, filing is not as popular job. Trying to keep pace with filing charts is like shoveling sand against the tide. Charts, constantly arriving singly or in large batches, are everywhere including the floor. Requests for charts also arrive constantly, by telephone and on slips of paper. Said one very tired clerk, "You can never finish your work, and if you're out, you've got to catch up. People constantly quit and there are always vacancies. There's no one to fill in when you're out."

Clerks are almost as nomadic as the charts. Ella Graham transferred out of the unit after a year. So did more than twenty of the thirty-seven clerks with whom she worked. Most of the long-termers, about ten of them when she was there, were senior clerks. "They're not exactly supervisors, but they can act like supervisors."

There is a system for housing, routing, and tracking thousands of migratory records. At the front counter, receptionists take telephone and hand-delivered requests. There are two messengers. Gerry Richardson delivers charts and picks up requests throughout the hospital on foot. Anna Young handles pick-ups and deliveries to outlying buildings and the warehouse where inactive charts are stored; she uses a mail truck.

Most clerks do filing—all day, every day. The files are divided into sections, with filing clerks responsible for a particular section. They spend their days pulling charts out of their section, keeping a file of the destinations of every outgoing chart, adding loose notes to the proper files, and filing returning charts away again. It is hard to find a sense of accomplishment in all this. Other clerks sort the chaos of incoming charts and requests by section, while still others—too few—are floaters, helping out wherever they are needed. One person is assigned to tracking missing charts and to trouble-shooting in general. Once charts are pulled and checked out, Gerry sorts them by each of the ten clinics and delivers them.

The filing room runs three shifts, twenty-four hours a day. The day shift is by far the busiest and deals with charts needed that day. The evening and night shifts pull charts for the emergency room, but most of their work involves pulling inactive records for storage in the warehouse, records for use in the next day's clinics, and records needed for one or another research project. Pressure is intense on the day shift. Everything is about speed. Ella remembers the sorting table, "sometimes so full you feel like dying." And always more charts piling up.

"Every twenty minutes Gerry comes in with the requests and you have to drop filing to pull those charts; and you fall behind. When a patient dies, their chart becomes inactive. But it seems as soon as you send it to the warehouse, some doctor wants to do research on it, and you've got to get it back."

Gerry guessed that about half the charts requested are not in their proper section, and for half of those, there is no record of where they might be. The sign-out guide is less than perfect. "There is a file in the out guide," Ella recalled, "from 1967 to a doctor who's not even here anymore."

On the telephones, in trouble-shooting, tracking, and delivery, the day has a rhythm: before 8:30 and after 4:00 things slow down, and there is time to breathe. In filing, you can never breathe. There are always piles to remind you that there is still more work.

Thin and very high strung, Gerry Richardson is really involved in his job—at least in the perpetual motion part of it. Every twenty minutes he makes a delivery round to all ten clinics. Although several clinics share a single space, the clusters themselves are scattered throughout the hospital on the main floor and several levels of basement. Before the clinics open, Gerry fills a cart with perhaps five hundred inactive charts destined for shipment to the warehouse. These were pulled and stacked on the floor by the night shift. Then he fills another cart with charts for the day's clinic appointments, also pulled by the second and third shifts, and checks with the telephone receptionist for the first round of telephone requests of the day.

"I tried to figure how many miles I did. When I first started, I went every fifteen minutes; now its every twenty minutes. I do about twenty-four, twenty-five trips a day and each trip's a mile. When I come back I

sit down. Every chance I get I sit down. If I've got a little change I eat.
I get out. That's one of the benefits; I'm cruising all the time. Management
to labor contact gets slacker as you go up."

On the other hand, Gerry is a flak-catcher. "Sometimes the clerks hate
me, because I'm one of the priority people." They have to drop what they
are doing and fill the clinic requests that Gerry brings. Likewise, when
a chart is not where it is supposed to be, and Gerry doesn't bring it, he
gets blamed by the clinic staff. There is extra confusion because people
outside the medical records department do not understand the department's routine. People request charts a month before they are needed, or
they make many requests at once for things that are needed at very
different times.

In part because the work is so thankless, in part because of chronic
problems with the supervisor, there was a vicious circle of low morale,
poor social relations, and high turnover in the filing unit. The supervisor
"has a lot of pressure on her; no one's ever satisfied with filing or how it's
done." Clerks felt she made the problem worse by playing favorites and
treating most workers with no respect. This lowered morale and led to
high turnover and chronic understaffing, which in turn increased the
pressure on those who stayed.

"The supervisor gives you grief for staying out. . . . But if you're sick
you're sick." Despite this conviction, Ella Graham never took any of her
sick days and is somewhat resentful of her supervisor's attitude. Gerry
gave an example of the kind of "grief" Ella spoke about. "If I say I don't
feel well, the supervisor says, 'well I don't feel well either, but I'm here.'"
He felt this method of attendance-by-intimidation and contempt sometimes backfired. Because it was "dread" to get a day off or to telephone
in sick, "some people will just stay out rather than face the supervisor on
the phone." Ella believes they are in the majority: "Just about everyone
has had words" with her. For Gerry and Ella, "Anytime there's a problem,
it's a responsibility game. It's not about solving the problem; it's about
blaming someone." Primarily blame came from the supervisor and some
of the senior clerks who formed a clique. "The four of them huddle and
whisper in front of everybody."

There was also favoritism; some people got to rotate from filing to the
telephones or to trouble-shooting, whereas others never got away from
the files. "Some people can stay out and do what they want and there's
no problem. Others catch grief for asking." There was also a shared recognition that the favorites are up at the front, whereas others were "stuck

away" in the back. Ella, who is white, said that race was the issue, that the previous supervisor was prejudiced and put black women in back. One black woman who transferred out described the unit as "the most prejudiced place—all white women up front and black women in back." The new supervisor is black and is said to be changing that. In 1980, there was only one black senior clerk; by 1983, there were four senior black and seven senior white clerks.

Not all of the clerks' responses were negative. "People help each other out at least to spite her [the supervisor]." Ella has done or helped do work of sick co-workers so they would not be so far behind when they returned. "Pregnant women get no help. You can't sit and the rows of files are narrow. One black women got a hernia and her doctor told her to quit. They finally put her on the phones."

Dottie Clarkson used to feel as Ella and Gerry do, but she's become exasperated at clerks for complaining but not being willing to do anything about it. It all started when she accepted the administration's offer to form a worker committee to meet with the department's administrator over the accumulated grievances. Most grievances were from the filing unit and focused on working conditions, harassment, prejudice, and discrimination. There was only one meeting. Dottie felt that the administrator was more than willing to deal with the problems, that he was "one of the most honest and straightforward directors" she'd met. She welcomed his initiative in having a personnel representative interview each worker about their grievances. Other workers saw it differently and were apparently suspicious; Dottie felt that she was ostracized as a "spy" after she worked on the committee.

Others also recalled the meeting and that workers pulled together in affirming dissatisfacation with the way they were treated. But in their view, it was hard to complain. The most specific complaint that anyone was willing to voice was that "some people get treated different from others." When they were asked for particular instances, no one was willing to supply them. Some workers believed that this was because at one level everyone shared a working pretense that they were all on friendly terms, and they feared the consequences of denying it by bringing up concrete cases. That is, a public discussion of favoritism and prejudice could endanger the picture of friendliness among workers that allowed them to get along to the extent that they did. Workers, especially women, put considerable effort into developing harmonious relations, shared values, and social ties among co-workers. In this case they did so in the face of a very divisive and hostile supervisory situation. For medical records clerks, it seemed safer as well as more tangible to build a shared work culture that appealed to conditions shared across race lines despite, or because of the fact that race was an ever-present reality used to divide them by discriminatory treatment. In some ways, medical records clerks hung together by complaining together about being driven and watched; this helped clerks share a consciousness of common oppression across racial lines. But it was dangerous to express grievances to supervisors, because an important dimension of the grievances was of racial discrimination and personal favoritism. Unless white clerks openly acknowledged and protested the racial discrimination against black clerks, race would remain a powerful issue in turning around and undercutting the oppositional potential of work culture in this unit.

Conclusion: Resistance and Race

Medical records work shared certain unpleasant working conditions with food and cleaning services, just as secretarial work shared others with the work of DTOs. Medical records clerks and secretaries were aware of these conditions and complained about them to one another, but unlike DTOs and service workers, they lacked a public and collective oppositional work culture.

Although the specifics varied, the similarities of complaint turned on the racial definitions of clerical and service work and on the dynamics of racial relations in that context. In medical records, opposition to supervision and speedup were central to the work culture. It was a culture of complaint: It was socially acceptable to grumble and joke about it, and to some extent, to challenge a supervisor about such behavior in a way that might not be so easy for a secretary. Secretaries occupy that strange structural position where they are expected to do the impossible, but where they also have a fair amount of autonomy in shaping their conditions of work. To a certain extent, the combination can encourage a super-woman syndrome in which workers can take pride in doing the impossible, but in which they may also feel inadequate when they cannot carry it off, even as they blame the boss for demanding it. In contrast, dietary, housekeeping, and medical records workers are expected to carry out tasks that they have no responsibility for shaping. Where secretaries and DTOs coordinate because the job falls to no one else, that is not at all the case in these other departments. There, the design and coordination of work has been appropriated from those who do it by managers who have unambiguous authority to direct, but who do not work. As a result, workers in these departments tend correctly to blame unrealistic expectations and heavy workloads on management rather than to take them as negative reflections on their own abilities.

Although there has been plenty to complain about and little in the structure of work and responsibility to inhibit its expression in these departments, this has not meant that people act together on complaints because they have complained about the boss together. In medical records, the public culture of complaining was self-limiting and undercut group resistance. First, to confront management directly threatened to undercut such cooperation and solidarity as clerks had been able to build, because the clerks would have had to raise the issue of the supervisor's racial prejudice, an issue they feared might cause friction between black and white clerks. On the other hand, inability to confront management here reinforced consent to the prevailing practices. Second, resistance was inhibited by the knowledge that medical records clerks often were able to transfer away from this assembly-line to other clerical jobs. Indeed, the prevailing response in medical records seemed to be an individual one: to get out of that job as fast as possible, a response given force by the high turnover in that unit. In contrast, food and cleaning workers and DTOs often complained that they were unable to get out, and their history of collective action emphasizes the point.

DTOs, receptionists, and secretaries constitute a kind of invisible administration of the hospital's wards and clinics. Almost by default, they are the ones saddled with responsibility for putting together the many fragments of treatment and transportation, diagnosis and diet, laboratory and financial workups, to produce some sort of reasonably integrated medical care and to record it for future reference. To varying degrees, all such front-line workers face a common set of structural dilemmas shared by clerical workers everywhere.[15] They are low paid and lack authority to do many of the things they must do in order to make things run smoothly. Yet when foul-ups occur, the workers are the ones blamed.

There seem to be two contradictory sets of expectation about such workers' jobs. One is that their job is to carry out doctors' orders and perform routine hospital functions; this view presumes that doctors and administrators are the creators and decision makers. The other view is that the workers make the impossible possible. Unfortunately, the former view seems to prevail when it comes to determining wages, while the latter is all too often the operational view of doctors and administrators when things do not work. The structural position of DTOs, secretaries, and receptionists contributes to the double bind of their work. They are information keepers and integrators; they are in a central place and cannot easily run away; they are in contact with all parties. In short, they are a captive source of information held responsible for drawing conclusions from it but denied authority to make the decisions that stem from putting two and two together. To a great extent, DTOs and secretaries are aware of the skills they exercise and aggrieved at the lack of acknowledgment and compensation for them. Anger over unacknowledged skills was a source of pro-union sentiment among secretaries.

Among secretaries, but not DTOs, the precariousness of their working conditions was a two-sided coin. Each office was a separate work environment with its own social relations. Much depended on a secretary's maintaining a good relationship with the boss, finding and keeping a good boss, and having a boss who would fight for her raises with the administration. However, the other side of this coin was that a secretary often could remedy a bad situation by acting individually to transfer. In contrast, DTOs found it much more difficult to transfer, had no patronage relationships to serve as buffers in their daily working conditions, and therefore were more clearly channeled into collective activity.

In sum, there were many similarities in the nature of the work and its discontents among predominantly white office secretaries, somewhat integrated clinic receptionists and secretaries, and primarily black DTOs. There were also parallels between the work organization and dissatisfaction of integrated medical records clerks and those that animated black dietary and housekeeping workers in the sixties. In food and cleaning services and among DTOs, all predominantly black departments, there were high profile, pro-union, and militant work-based cultures. Both groups had walkouts and lawsuits over their specific working conditions and were bulwarks of union strength, as we shall see in the next chapter. Secretaries and medical records clerks expressed many of the same dissatisfactions and complaints as DTOs and food service workers, but neither had anything that could be thought of as a visibly identifiable or militant work culture.

In stressing black women's work culture and militancy, one runs the risk of leaving the impression that white workers were antiunion, or worse, that they had no reason to be pro-union. Neither option is true, and it is important to union strength that there were many pro-union white workers. However, the intermediate step of a publicly identifiable presense is an important aspect of mobilization. Although there were pro-union white secretaries and medical records clerks, they did not build a collective occupational identity as a pro-union constituency, nor did they believe that most of their co-workers would join them.

The fact that different work cultures developed from similar work processes suggests a complex relationship among race, work process, work culture, and collective action. There is a growing feminist literature on gender and work culture, but almost nothing about race and work culture, even though the jobs in which women predominate are segregated racially.[16] Secretaries and medical records clerks did complain together and in some sense that was a work culture. However, neither group mobilized around their complaints in a public way. This seems largely to have been because of the way in which race interacted with job definitions. Unlike dietary workers and DTOs, secretaries and clerks have—or seemed to have—individual solutions to some of their grievances; their jobs seem to have been viewed by personnel in such a way that the occupants were deemed competent for a wider range of jobs, and they were thus able to transfer out or up. In addition, and not least, collective action among medical records clerks would have required them to address directly the fact of racial discrimination.

Even though the race and gender-typing of particular jobs changed in the late sixties and early seventies, the *fact* of race and gender-typed jobs did not. Credentialing requirements for white jobs and what black workers widely regarded as racist hiring and transfer practices were part of the edifice that maintained such job segregation. The consequence was that black women experienced their jobs differently than white women did. Indeed, the very typing of a job as "black" or "white" seemed to affect the ways its occupants were viewed (or stereotyped) and treated, and may have made it much harder for black women to transfer out of such jobs. This would apply to emerging clerical jobs like DTO, as well as to the older service jobs like food and cleaning services. As a result, work-based militancy and its absence centered on the different ways workers were treated occupationally as black or white women because the job was "black" or "white." This pattern existed apart from individual discriminatory treatment that black women in "white" jobs often faced. In addition, the very existence of a racially segregated occupational structure meant that racial considerations and stereotypes influenced even jobs that were integrated and shaped the development of work culture there as well, as we saw in examining the work of medical records clerks. These considerations underlay the centrality of black women's initiative and activism in the hospital union drive of 1974–76, which the next three chapters will examine.

NOTES

1. Benson, 1978.

2. U.S. Training and Employment Service 1970.

3. *Fuller* v. *Duke*, Dr. Carl C. Hoffman affidavit, 16.

4. *Caston et al.* v. *Duke University*, "Plaintiffs' Motion for Determination that the Action Should Proceed as a Class Action."

5. Ibid: 7–16.

6. Legal sources indicated that a condition of the settlement was that the nature of the settlement was not to be revealed.

7. *Fuller* v. *Duke*, Dr. Carl C. Hoffman affidavit, 28.

8. Ibid.: 29.

9. My figures for 1976; *Caston et al.* v. *Duke University*, Exhibit B figures: 316 secretaries, 120 medical secretaries, 104 administrative secretaries.

10. My figures; Exhibit B: 6 black administrative secretaries; 5 black medical secretaries, 45 black secretaries, or 10.4 percent.

11. Lockwood, 1958; Kessler-Harris, 1982; Tepperman, 1976.

12. Murphree, 1984; Goldberg, 1983; Tepperman, 1976; Glenn and Feldberg, 1977; Feldberg and Glenn, 1983; Scott, 1982; Gregory and Nussbaum, 1980; Machung, 1984.

13. The medical chart has become even more important with the use of diagnosis related groups (DRGs) in prospective pricing insurance reimbursement since 1983.

14. My figures from 1976 include 8 white and 11 black senior clerks, all women, and 5 white and 8 black male clerks; Exhibit B figures: total 35 white and 59 black clerks.

15. Murphree, 1984; Kahn-Hut, Daniels, and Colvard, 1982; Glenn and Feldberg, 1977; Tepperman, 1976; Goldberg, 1983.

16. Benson, 1978; Feldberg and Glenn, 1979; Goldberg, 1983; Sacks and Remy, 1984.

4

The First Medical Center Drive

Local 77's victory early in 1972 indicated that it was possible to force Duke to recognize a union and to gain significant improvements with it. Still, the victory was incomplete in that many hospital workers were left without the representation they had worked so long to gain. In the fall of 1974, responding to activist initiatives by some of these workers and to changes in the National Labor Relations Act that gave hospital workers the go-ahead to unionize, Local 77 announced that it was beginning a drive to unionize all service workers in the medical center.

The late 1960s and early 1970s were years of rising activism in a generally supportive political climate. Durham had developed a sizeable community of radical and communist activists. White radicals were centered among medical students, professional workers, and housestaff at Duke, in addition to on the campus. Many had been in Students for a Democratic Society and subsequently formed local chapters of the Duke-Durham Medical Committee for Human Rights and of the New American Movement. Black activists from Durham and black college students from North Carolina and northeastern schools also came to the area, primarily to work with Howard Fuller, Durham's most prominent black leader, and the community organizations he founded.[1] Both black and white activists believed in uniting workers across the color line, and initially worked in harmony despite the growing importance of black power and Pan-Africanism in the black student movement and the growth of sectarian groups among white radicals.

The Spread of Hospital Activism

Duke's approximately 150–70 DTOs were a sizeable and cohesive group, and the most visible indication that black women had cracked the racial barrier to clerical jobs, even though their jobs were created to be typed racially. Some DTOs had been high school activists, some had joined the efforts of Local 1199, the national hospital workers' union, in 1970, and many of them were tied together by friendship or family ties. The same antipoverty movement that opened these jobs to black women also taught DTOs the political skills they employed when they found themselves locked into new forms of discrimination. Their walkout in mid-April 1974, and ensuing organization probably provided the spark for hospital unionization.[2]

Before electronic data entry at video data terminals, most DTOs were white women. Black women were hired in the early 1970s at about the same time that Duke began to automate the job. DTOs differ in their recollection of the date when computers were first introduced. The earliest date remembered is December 1972, but some say it was 1974. The most consistent date cited is October 1973.[3] The group of DTOs that went through the electronic changeover was at the center of the 1974 walkout. At one level, their anger was focused on pay and the lack of respect for their skills that low pay implied; at another level, they were angry at the racism they experienced in the hospital administration's treatment.

Computers were the catalyst for the women's feelings. As one of the walkout's organizers put it, "The majority of us felt with all this new training they should offer us more money. Any time you work with a computer they should give you more. If you're lucky enough to get in research you could make much more out there than here." DTOs also believed that they were given a clerical rather than a technical job classification when Duke discovered that a technical labeling might reinforce their claims for better pay. The administration rubbed salt in the workers' wounds by refusing to provide them with any form of certification of their computer skills that might enable them to find better jobs elsewhere. "As they say in the computer room, Duke will teach you all you want, but they won't give you that certificate." Without it DTOs could not move, and Duke was able to pay low wages.

Computers seemed to be a symbol of the invisible skills that DTOs knew they used, but that the administration refused to recognize on payday. For example, DTOs on the cardiac intensive care unit were assigned to watch the heart monitors. It seemed to them clearly patient care of a skilled sort—DTOs had to be trained by a nurse and pass an examination. It was an unwanted and stressful job, hardly compensated by a token 5 to 13 cents an hour additional pay. When DTOs refused to continue this task, Duke assigned the job to nurses, who, although they were paid more than DTOs, were not paid additionally for this task. Scheduling was also a problem on some services; DTOs often worked eight to ten days straight and seldom had weekends off. Abusive treatment by doctors, unauthorized orders from nursing administrators, and lack of support from their own supervisors added to the list of DTOs' grievances.

One DTO telephoned her counterpart in a hospital in Charlotte and discovered that Charlotte DTOs were paid $3.50 an hour, compared to Duke's then $2.22 to 2.82 an hour. The rankling difference was that the other workers were white. "At Duke was the first time I *saw* what they were talking about—whites on top and blacks on the bottom," she said. "DTOs were considered dumb even though we were running things. Even if I hadn't been to Owusu's school I couldn't take not being treated like a human being."[4]

Three DTOs who were friends and normally ate lunch and complained about the work together decided to call others at their homes to see if they were any happier. "Everybody said 'no,'" so they called a meeting at one woman's home. Some thirty DTOs came and drew up a petition that had four demands: better pay; two weekends off each month for all DTOs: more respect and an end to abuse from doctors, nurses, and administrators; and increased hiring of DTOs ("You worked a ward by yourself then").

There were a variety of meetings, including one with an administrator who was reputed to have said that a DTO could be pulled off the street anytime, they were a dime a dozen. "That was supposed to stop us from walking out, but it had the opposite effect." Because Duke promised nothing in response to their petition except to "work on it," DTOs held a second meeting, attended perhaps by seventy-five people, an impressive showing considering that there were probably no more than 150 DTOs at the time by DTO leaders' estimates, and some of these were working during the meeting. The workers decided to call in sick as a safe way of walking out, because they did not have any union protection.

The whole process from first meeting to walkout took only a few days. This was deliberate, so that Duke's administration would not have time to frighten people. There are different recollections of how long—between two and four days—DTOs stayed out. Two participants resolved some of the discrepancies when they pointed out that their major problem was knowing when to stay out, "It was raggedy getting started."

But once they became organized, DTOs staged a very effective walkout, particularly on the largest and busiest services, where supervisors and untrained administrators had a terrible time trying to cover the wards. DTOs felt that both the hospital and the patients suffered as a result of inadequate coverage, but that the walkout was for the patients' benefit as well as their own because it would improve services. Several DTOs indicated strong support from both patients and housestaff, not least from housestaff active in Durham's community health movement, many of whom were radical activists who supported hospital worker unionization. One secretary commented, "They use patients as an excuse to kill you— and they're robbing the patients blind." Another noted that the hospital was "a mess" when the DTOs returned, and that it took a great deal of work to put it back together.

The walkout brought some real changes. "We said the only way we'll come back is if you don't fire anybody." When management hesitated, "we said we'd still be sick—so they gave in. We got uniforms the color we wanted. They wanted us to pay for it. They paid. We got respect. You know how doctors throw charts? Now they can't." DTOs' pay was raised one level the following January and was later raised again to the level of secretaries. They received an immediate 20 cent raise and alternate weekends off. The unpopular administrator somehow disappeared, although problem supervisors remained. Lines of authority were clarified between nursing and DTO administration so that DTOs were no longer expected to serve two masters. Perhaps among the most significant gains was a large increase in the number of DTOs. Nearly sixty, or a 40 percent increase, were hired between the 1974 estimate and 1978, although this increase seems to have been gradual and uneven over time and by unit.[5]

As a result of the walkout, "All of a sudden someone realized our job was important. Any time you have a walkout, it does tell somebody that something's wrong and that you do have the ability to organize." One DTO who was not an active participant nevertheless thought that the walkout gave all DTOs a "sense of accomplishment" at communicating how responsible, skilled, and important their job was, as well as letting Duke know that they were able to do something about their problems.

Finally, about eight months after the walkout, the hospital presented DTOs with computer certificates. "They just gave it to keep us quiet." Even this action seems to have required some additional meetings and organizing. One DTO said that they got the certificates by having a meeting of their unit with supervisors and unit administration. The initiators were DTOs who were central in the walkout. "If they complained, others would follow suit."

On the heels of the walkout, in May 1974, Local 77 hired Howard Fuller as its business agent. He was no stranger to Duke workers or students. May was also the month in which about eleven workers—primarily technicians and technologists—in the microbiology laboratory walked out for two days to protest the lack of action on longstanding grievances about understaffing and dirty and unsafe conditions in the laboratory. When these workers, most of whom were professional, technical, and white, returned to work, they were given thirty-day suspensions. They held a rally to publicize their case, appealed for support, and filed a complaint with the state Department of Labor. They demanded that Duke fill staff vacancies with qualified full-time workers, get rid of faulty and outmoded equipment, "end contamination of the media; institute quality control and proficiency testing."[6] They maintained a picket line for three weeks in order to keep their case before the community.

Two months later, the Duke internal grievance committees found in favor of these workers, awarded them back pay and benefits, and retroactively revoked their suspensions. However, by August, a microbiology spokesperson told the *North Carolina Anvil*, Durham's progressive newspaper, that conditions in the laboratory remained unchanged.[7] A new director was subsequently hired, ostensibly to clean up the laboratory, but from his perspective, to make it more "productive" by conventional industrial standards. He became an outspoken opponent of unionization. Most of the laboratory workers were professionals, and although professionals were active in community health issues, such a group had never before engaged Duke directly and on their own behalf.

Durham events reflected national trends in the development of links between health-care workers and health-care consumers.[8] Interns and residents were unionizing in New York and Chicago, and radical health professionals across the nation were setting up grass-roots health projects to serve farm workers and the poor in urban communities. Duke-trained physicians were among those who formed the Durham Health Collective of the New American Movement and participated in a variety of community health efforts.[9]

In August 1974, workers and community activists formed a coalition to oppose Duke's plans to build what ultimately became Duke North. At a public meeting they used the hospital's own projections and employment memos to argue that construction would be funded in part by significant increases in the cost of hospital rooms (and higher local Blue Cross premiums) and by squeezes on the wages of hourly workers.[10] The four groups sponsoring the anti-expansion meeting represented the breadth of the emerging coalition. The Citizens for Durham County Health Care was composed of long-time white liberal and progressive community activists. The local chapter of the New American Movement represented more campus-associated and younger white student activists, as did the local chapter of the Duke-Durham Medical Committee for Human Rights, made up largely of Duke housestaff and health-care professionals. The Duke DTO Association was the organizational outcome of their successful walkout. By October, this coalition had brought the issue of hospital expansion to the Duke campus and made it a focal point for demands for improved patient care—citing increases of about 50 percent in the emergency room and in outpatient fees in the last year—and for higher pay and union recognition for hospital workers.[11]

At Duke, as across the nation, the 1974 National Labor Relations Board (NLRB) decision concerning workers in voluntary hospitals gave medical center organizing a strong boost[12]. Medical center workers now had the right to petition the NLRB to hold a union election and were assured that management could be legally obligated to accept the results. By November, with Fuller in charge of Local 77, a functioning hospital worker-consumer coalition, and a green light from the NLRB, a hospital organizing committee of Local 77 was a functioning entity. It included some long-time activists who had worked with Oliver Harvey almost from the beginning, including its chair, Rose Gattis.[13] The campaign also involved campus workers from Local 77, university and medical students, housestaff and health-care professionals, and a small number of black students who came south to work with Fuller as organizers in the hospital.

In early November 1974, pro-union workers made their drive visible with a showing of collective strength. The occasion was Duke's attempt to shift paydays for the last two months of the year so that workers would have received 25.5 rather than 26 full paychecks by December 31 (the other half was to be paid in January 1975). Dubbing it "The Great Paycheck Ripoff," Locals 77 and 465 (the maintenance workers' union), the DTO Association, the New American Movement, and the Duke Workers Alliance joined in a protest. Some 250 workers turned out to a meeting at the Durham YWCA, and about 200 picketed the Duke University administration building the following day. Carrying signs with "Save Our Paychecks," they gathered more than one thousand signatures on a petition to return to the original pay schedule. The unions threatened to seek a court injunction against Duke for violating their contracts and to walk out. At this time, too, Duke was attempting to eliminate overtime pay for heating plant workers by rearranging their work schedules. These workers also received a great deal of student and staff support, and petitions with some 1,400 signatures were presented to the administration. These were heartening shows of force. The *North Carolina Anvil* commented, "Not since the 1968 Vigil had so many employees from different sections of the university come together on a single issue."[14] Duke backed down almost immediately, restored the original pay schedule, and returned to the original heating plant work schedule.[15] This clear victory gave the union drive a strong and public boost and put hospital unionization on the map as the issue of the year.

The medical center campaign was organized around two basic principles. The first involved developing and constantly monitoring union strength through personal contacts among workers and between workers and organizing committee members. The second centered around publicly demonstrating the benefits of organizing. Organizing committee members assisted workers who had specific complaints about their treatment and working conditions. To do this, they reactivated and made use of grievance procedures instituted as a result of the housekeeping and kitchen walkouts. Publicity of grievances was central. Leaflets pointed out that people could successfully fight mistreatment, but they also emphasized the limits of having to do so under Duke's rules. Both these tactics for building strength were the bedrock of more public events: wearing buttons and holding rallies, demonstrations, and social events that mobilized support and presented a mass showing to the hospital and to other workers. It was a careful strategy, perhaps necessarily so, but it was also feisty and often militant in the content of leaflets, in rallies in front of the hospital, and in the way grievances were conducted.[16]

Evelyn Beasley thought that the "Paycheck Ripoff" seemed to be the main demonstration. "I don't remember but one large demonstration, and you didn't have to mobilize to get everybody out; they just came out. [On this issue] we just passed out leaflets to discuss and everyone came." There were rallies in front of the hospital, but how frequent they were is not clear. Rose Gattis recalled many lunch-hour rallies in front of the hospital. People used their staggered lunches to carry signs stating their demands for an end to harassment and better working conditions, and Howard Fuller and other men spoke. Both administrators and workers came to listen. Rose also said that *lots* of people were mobilized when the bargaining unit was first announced: LPNs were angry because they were excluded; others had questions about whether they were in or out. And throughout the campaign, people distributed leaflets in all kinds of weather.

Perhaps the stickiest issue that the organizers had to deal with was that of striking. Different organizers remember handling the issue differently. Most agreed that strikes could be necessary, were very helpful, and that workers should be prepared to use them. Rose Gattis, however, never raised the issue herself. "Let Duke bring it up,"—as they certainly did— "but be prepared to back it up." Her approach was to stress—as she did about all issues—that the union was "the people," and would not strike unless its members voted to do it. Rose thought that people's main worry about strikes was that they could not go long without a paycheck. She certainly understood that, but believed that they had to be willing to strike "if things get bad." Beverly Jones, another organizing committee member, was much less reticent and took on the issue directly, telling people, "We'd strike certainly, as a last resort. We'd talk about how effective it was. We're not going to run away from it. Our main objective was good patient care, but Duke Hospital had to go along with it. [The issue of] strikes is not too bad if people understood it." Both women cited the successful environmental services walkout over mopping in 1973 to indicate why workers needed a strike weapon.

There was widespread agreement that personal contact and an excellent network among workers was the key to success. It allowed those who were publicly identified as union to know their sources of support and strength, whom to watch out for, and whom to rely on, and gave them an up-to-the-minute count of union votes. Organizing Committee members were responsible for building links between public union supporters and workplace networks of nonpublic but pro-union workers. For example Beverly Jones, a DTO herself, concentrated only on DTOs. Barbara Flowers and Shirley Rice focused their efforts on kitchen workers. Rose Gattis, chair of the Organizing Committee, took responsibility for all service workers in her part of the hospital. Edward Berry, a union spokesman, worked as a messenger, a job that took him all over the hospital. As a result, he was in a position to talk to a wide variety of people in all areas. Each of these workers would try to find key people in each area and on each shift and to meet regularly with them to figure out how to proceed.

To some activists, Rose Gattis personified the key to the campaign's strength. "Rose is never scared of anything, but Rose is very, very careful. Rose knows a lot of people at Duke. A lot of workers are her neighbors, are her church members or friends of her neighbors and church members." She talked with them about their jobs, the high cost of living, and what a union could do to give workers more of a voice. She stressed the need for a real grievance procedure rather than the one they had, where "Duke now has the last word." When a person indicated they liked the idea and signed a card, their names were kept secret unless they wanted to work openly. Rose would ask what improvements they'd like to see and get their opinion about lunch-time demonstrations and the leaflets the union distributed. She'd keep a record of Duke's promises and, once the union had support, it would publicly challenge Duke on them. People had to be careful, Gattis pointed out, because all the administrators were walking the halls. It was illegal to be organizing on the job, and organizers were sure to have trouble if they were caught. If workers were willing to be public, they were invited to organizing committee meetings and demonstrations.

Because the campaign was waged without help from the international union, funds were a perennial problem. People on the organizing committee worked around the clock, substituting labor for cash at all possible places. Still, paper costs money, and the union held fundraisers like cake sales and a large social at the Elks' Lodge. Although these took work, people described them as fun—certainly more so than writing and handing out leaflets. Although some people were circumspect about being seen at union socials, the food sale and social at the Elks' Lodge was a financial success. Service workers came in large numbers, although there were fewer clerical workers, perhaps because they "didn't want to be seen" by "Duke finks."

Duke's Antiunion Campaign

Duke was no friendlier to unions in 1974 than it had been in 1968 or 1971. It once again contested Local 77's petition with the NLRB and wrote letters and leafletted workers about the alleged evils of unionism in contrast with Duke's benevolence. Duke waged its campaign on two fronts. First, it attempted to encourage supervisory and administrative personnel to take an actively antiunion role. Supervisors did not seem to have had an option of favoring unionization among workers.[17] They were encouraged to tell workers that although workers "are free to support the union or not, . . . you hope they vote against it."[18] Second, Duke spoke directly to workers. The head of hospital personnel, in a letter addressed "Dear Fellow Employee," credited Duke with voluntarily giving the improvements in pay and working conditions of the previous few years.[19] Most workers, even some antiunion workers as well as some supervisors and administrators, recognized that most improvements in pay and working conditions were either direct results of worker agitation or of Duke's efforts to make enough improvements to avoid unionization.

Duke emerges from its own materials as a powerful parent or benevolent despot: If workers "chose" to relate to Duke as individuals by refusing to organize, they could expect great improvements in wages and working conditions. However, Duke would interpret a union vote as ingratitude and lack of faith and would deal harshly with workers. An effective aspect of this presentation was to represent unions as powerful outside forces in relation to workers—the image of the "union businessman" interested mainly in workers' dues money—but nevertheless a weak businessman compared to Duke.[20] Duke's leaflets sometimes stressed management power and union weakness in an overtly threatening way. For example, "It is Duke University Hospital which furnishes your job and your pay check—not the union. The union will never furnish you a day's work nor a cent of pay. . . . There is no way for the union to force Duke University Hospital to fulfill the promises that the union has made to you."[21]

Unions were also presented as a far-off force that posed a threat to workers' wages and freedom: "If you don't work, you won't get paid. The Hospital won't pay your wages and neither will the union. Sometimes unions pay a few dollars to strikers who carry picket signs. If you want to earn a couple of dollars during the strike, you can carry a picket sign and march up and down the sidewalk."[22]

Just before the election was to take place, workers found the following notice with their paychecks: "NOTICE: NO UNION DUES have been deducted from this pay check!! Don't share your Pay Check with a Union!! VOTE 'NO' No Union-No Dues-No Fines-No Assessments."[23]

The Role of the NLRB

By June 1975, Local 77 had enough signed show-of-interest cards to petition the National Labor Relations Board for a union election. On June

2, they filed their petition for a bargaining unit of between 900 and 1,000 service workers. The petition reflected the growing division of labor in hospital work. The unionists sought to represent all food service workers, patient care assistants, physical therapy assistants, psychiatry attendants, surgical attendants, physical therapy aides, laboratory assistants, unit service aides, central supply room aides, DTOs, messengers, clinic assistants, delivery men, medical supply assemblers, EKG technicians, laboratory research assistants, patient escorts, equipment room clerks, parking lot attendants, bus drivers, chauffeurs, pharmacy aides, autopsy technicians, and electronmicroscopy technicians.[24] Many of these workers had hoped in 1971 to be included in Local 77 but were kept out by the NLRB decision that then excluded all hospital workers with any patient care responsibilities. This petition included most of the same people who had been trying to unionize for the last decade, although it excluded LPNs and included several clerical and technical job titles. It specifically excluded "office clerical workers," by far the largest category of whom were secretaries.

Duke urged the NLRB to dismiss the union's petition on the grounds that the unit excluded many workers who should be considered service workers and excluded workers on the campus. If the NLRB were to approve any unit, Duke argued that it should be one that included office clerical workers and technical workers as well as service workers.

The NLRB regional director held hearings with both parties and in November 1975, ruled that a bargaining unit of medical center workers was valid. But he also agreed with Duke that some 900–1,000 technical and clerical workers, most of whom where white, should be added to the bargaining unit, more than doubling its size. The ruling applied a mixture of criteria—schooling, alleged skill or lack of it, with whom one worked—inconsistently and in an apparently ad hoc manner. At one level, the lack of clarity in the ruling highlights the complexities of the division of health-care labor. Many of the added job categories amounted to a handful of workers each. That so many jobs were contested can be taken as an indication that neither side expected that the march of specialization and finely divided labor had affected all workers the same way.

At another level, this ruling, perhaps reflecting a changing political climate, was an about-face from the NLRB ruling four years earlier, when it granted campus service workers their own bargaining unit independent of clerical workers. The 1975 decision argued that virtually all office clerical workers and technical workers—secretaries and hourly professionals excluding nursing staff—in the medical center were really no different from service workers and should be included in the service unit.[25] Inclusion of several large groups of nonservice workers—notably 560 office clerical workers, 44 pharmacy technicians, 52 laboratory technicians, an indeterminate number of uncertified among the 117 medical technologists, and 58 medical technicians—fundamentally changed the nature of the unit. The NLRB decision had a major antiunion impact. It added to the bargaining unit a large number of workers who had not evidenced any interest in unionization, and whose "community of interest" at the time was doubtful, particularly because it also defined "a unit of clerical employees of fewer than 150 and a technical unit not much larger."[26]

At least as important, because the decision was totally unexpected, it delayed the final determination of the bargaining unit for another year, thus stalling a drive that was accelerating during 1975. The union had spent considerable energy organizing among the approximately nine hundred service workers who constituted a historic unity—a valid criterion for defiining a bargaining unit—as well as a logical one; they immediately requested a review by the Washington office and a postponement of the December 11 election date in light of the fact that decision "more than double[d] the size of the unit requested, from less than 1,000 to nearly 2,000 workers." Like the NLRB, the union presented detailed arguments about the skill, training, education, and working conditions of workers in contested jobs. For example, they argued that secretaries functioned as private secretaries rather than as hospital clericals and that many technical workers who were included were really professionals, whereas some who had been excluded were more like service workers.[27]

Although most of the union particulars were persuasive, the argument was a narrow one in that it relied on a very circumscribed notion of commonality of interest, one that began and ended in formal supervisory lines, formal duties, and formal job qualifications. It was a set of concepts shared by union lawyers, medical center administration, and the NLRB. But it was not an accurate notion of what had historically defined this bargaining unit whose real basis lay in the history of shared efforts—shared within the workplace and within Durham's black community—of the petitioners to form a union. The NLRB decision noted that this shared experience is a legally valid criterion for determining a bargaining unit, although for unspecified reasons, the director did not apply it. More surprising, the union did not build on what would seem to have been one of its strongest arguments, suggesting that their implicit model may have been more the narrow notions of bureaucratic trade unionism than the dynamism of unified class and racial struggle.

It is worth noting too in this connection that there was much debate about the skills and education of technical personnel, who were both men and women, but none about that of the largely female clerical personnel. As we have seen, many clerical jobs demanded a wide range of skills. These seem to have been as invisible to union lawyers as they were to hospital administration.

As a result of the NLRB's decision, people were in motion with nowhere to go. The election was postponed pending an NLRB decision on whether to take up the union's request for review of the regional NLRB ruling. After a year of intensive and very successful organizing, Local 77 and hospital service workers found themselves suddenly put in limbo. Because the differences between the NLRB's unit and the union's unit were so great with regard to number and categories of worker to be included, organizers faced an extremely difficult decision: Should they focus on their pro-union constituency, or should they begin the huge—and problematic—task of organizing among an even greater number of workers who had shown no movement of their own in a union direction and who, once the dust settled, might not even be included in the unit? The NLRB made matters worse by delaying some four months before deciding whether or not it would even review the regional director's decision. Not until March 10, 1976, did the union learn that Washington was willing to review. However, at the end of June 1976, Local 77 was still hanging fire waiting for the decision itself. The election was finally scheduled for November 16, 1976.[28]

Faction-Fighting

In the middle of this enforced wait, political factions developed in the organizing committee, and fighting began. From the beginning of the drive, there had been two somewhat distinct but overlapping and complementing political networks of workers, nonworker organizers, and supporters. Each centered on a group of political activists who, over the course of the campaign, affiliated and became increasingly involved in the national left and communist party politics that dominated much of the mid- to late-1970s activist scene.

Marxist perspectives on American capitalism and Marxist-Leninist party-building grew rapidly throughout the United States in the late 1960s and early 1970s, as student, community, and civil rights activists grew frustrated at systematic opposition to their efforts for social and economic reform. The movement in Durham was no exception. There, the black communist movement and subsequent party-building had its roots in a network of community activists who moved toward Marxism through nationalism. The loose network of black student and community leaders and militants built by Howard Fuller and others in the mid-sixties had generated a variety of local organizations such as Malcolm X Liberation University and the Student Organization for Black Unity by the early seventies. The analyses of imperialism that grew from support for African liberation throughout the country helped stimulate Marxist and Pan-Africanist study groups and perspectives that jelled on a national level into the African Liberation Support Committee (ALSC) in about 1972. Durham's leaders were influential in the national leadership of this organization, as well as active in creating a local black communist movement.

The Revolutionary Workers League (RWL), a national black Communist party with a strong Durham chapter, grew out of the ALSC through a long period of black Marxist study groups and pre-party organizing among activists who had worked together in a variety of contexts. Many black student activists were drawn to North Carolina in general, and Durham in particular, by the vitality of the grass-roots movement that the been built there.

The white student movement was also moving toward more radical and Marxist politics at the same time. In Durham during 1972–73, white activists formed two collectives, a health collective and a socialist feminist collective, both of which affiliated with the New American Movement (NAM). The health collective formed part of a left-wing effort in NAM and part of a larger movement among white radicals to create a new communist movement. This led to the formation of local activist and study groups, which ultimately coalesced into several national Marxist-Leninist parties. In 1973, the Durham health collective became the Durham Organizing Committee (DOC). A year or two later, they left NAM but split internally. One part (which remained DOC) began studying Marxism-Leninism intensely, while the other, critical of a lack of democracy, ultimately formed the People's Alliance.

By 1975, black activists of RWL, and white activists in DOC, were moving in parallel but cooperative paths toward Marxist-Leninist party formation in Durham, and at the same time were also becoming involved in the union drive. Although white activists had their own group, Howard

Fuller stood out as a leader from whom they took inspiration and whose charisma transcended organizational lines. The two groups formed a joint study group and worked out a shared strategy for the union drive. Both groups agreed on the importance of building unity between black and white workers, and both groups had individuals who acted as public leaders in the union drive.

Both Durham groups became involved in the same national network of groups attempting to build a unified communist movement. By late 1975 or early 1976, while the drive was stalled, DOC became the Communist Workers Collective (CWC) and began exploring national affiliation with other communist groups, notably the Workers' Viewpoint Organization (WVO). At a national level, the WVO, the Puerto Rican Revolutionary Workers' Organization (PRRWO), the August 29th Movement (ATM), and the RWL were all heavily minority communist groups that worked closely together and hoped to move toward national unity. The national leaderships of RWL and WVO after long discussions agreed to merge their organizations, but the RWL leadership changed its mind and decided instead to merge with the Puerto Rican Revolutionary Workers Movement, setting in motion a great deal of national antagonism between RWL and WVO/CWC that had fateful consequences for the Duke drive.

Meanwhile in Durham, local differences were developing independently between the CWC and RWL over how to conduct the union drive and how to work together as communists. Some were cultural and class differences between black and white activists; others had to do with differences in how to deal with racism as an issue in organizing; and still others had to do with tactics. Especially after the CWC joined the WVO, the national leaderships of the RWL and the WVO insisted on treating differences like antagonisms and in so doing fanned local disagreements into flames. Although both groups had initially agreed that party politics were to stay out of the drive, they became a more and more pervasive part of it. The CWC accused the RWL of trying to disrupt organizing meetings, and the RWL tried to vote the CWC out of the drive.

After its decision not to merge with WVO, the national RWL was rocked by internal conflict and purges that destroyed it. Some believe that police agents were involved, but in any event, the organization ceased to be active outside of Durham and was very rapidly consumed by its own inner battles. Some North Carolina activists in RWL split off, formed their own group, and joined with WVO. But in Durham, the local RWL was opposed to the purges and conflicts, resisted being drawn into them, and tried to focus its energies on the union drive. Some members ultimately left RWL in disgust, but they were nevertheless drawn into the fighting.

By the summer of 1976, the RWL and the CWC each had its own newsletter. These came to reflect some of the internal changes and changes in the groups' relationships with each other. *Tell It Like It Is* was initially *The Newsletter of Durham Health Workers and Patients*; *The Union Organizer* was the newsletter of Local 77. Both papers focused on the hospital drive. But by August 1976, *Tell It* became a publication of the Communist Workers Committee and criticized the Revolutionary Workers League, whose members were key activists on the *Union Organizer*, for, among other things, trying to exclude CWC people and supporters from the organizing committee. The local substance of the conflict seems to have been that the CWC felt it was important to explain the inadequacy of reform struggles in general and unionization in particular for lasting improvement in workers' lives. They accused the RWL of fostering illusions that unionization was enough. For their part, the RWL accused the CWC of using the drive to build their party and not contributing to the drive itself; they do not seem to have used their newsletter to publicize the dispute.

The Union Organizer charged that Duke was having a field day, using their quarrels to feed racist and anticommunist sentiment. Several hospital workers told organizers that their supervisor gave them the same line, "There are two factions in the union. One is Communist and one is Socialist Workers Party. The two constantly fight among themselves. And the president of the union is a third shift floor finisher."[29] The last months of what many activists later saw as sectarian mud-slinging was widely regarded as the cause of union defeat. It frightened some workers, angered others, and weakened or destroyed a major part of the worker-activist networks that had been the heart of the union drive.

When the union election was finally held in November 1976, it was for the expanded clerical, technical, and service bargaining unit of some 2,025 workers. Given the circumstances, organizers were right in seeing a narrow loss as an impressive showing of the breadth of pro-union sentiment. After two years of intensive organizing, the union was defeated by a scant 59 votes (743–684), where 189 votes of 1,616 were challenged, most by the union.[30] Local 77 claimed that supervisors and administrative secretaries voted, and Duke claimed irregularities and that part-time workers voted. The NLRB agent challenged all names that did not appear on the voting list, although the union claimed that many eligible workers did not have their names on the list, and that Duke changed people's job titles just before the election and did not notify them of the changes. Local 77 listed some fourteen job titles that were excluded from the voting list that should have been included. They filed for a hearing with the NLRB on the challenged ballots and filed objections to Duke's antiunion campaign.[31]

What transpired next is not clear. A hearing scheduled for February 16, 1977, was "postponed indefinitely" on February 15 in a letter from the NLRB regional director to Duke's attorney and to Local 77's attorney. "This action is taken as the result of the resolutions of the outstanding issues in the above-styled case." Duke withdrew its objections, and the results of the election were certified on the basis of a revised and final tally of ballots. The fate of 65 challenged ballots and the nature of an agreement between Duke and AFSCME about them remain unclear in the absence of the documents that were sent as attachments to the letter in Local 77's files.[32] No local unionists with whom I spoke knew what happened, nor did they seem to know of this correspondence; some were still asking in 1978. Pro-union workers felt robbed, and many were demoralized, but enough were encouraged to try again and to correct their mistakes.

Most of the participants saw three related factors as responsible for their defeat: the NLRB's role in putting secretaries, including those with supervisory responsibilities, in the bargaining unit, and the board's slowness in making a decision; a bargaining unit that added (at the last minute) a white majority or near-majority with no previous initiative to unionize to service workers, most of whom were black, who had been actively organizing for a decade; and a fight between two groups of self-defined communist activists, central participants in organizing, that scared away many people who were on the fence.

People did not credit Duke with defeating them. Indeed, they saw most of Duke's harassment and antiunion propaganda as backfiring because the union was able to expose and publicize the hospital's injustices, because they were able to defend some workers effectively in individual cases, and because they showed the strength that can come with unity when they prevented a change in paycheck schedules. Duke's key victory—the expanded bargaining unit— was credited to the NLRB, without whose help they would not have won.

Union activists, both black and white, focused on the 460 secretaries in the bargaining unit, compared to some 900 service workers. Organizers saw the secretaries as antiunion for the most part, who felt that they were higher status than service workers. Duke's practice of separating clerical from service workers on its employee councils would have cultivated any such feelings. Some activists felt that the mixture of racism and status was less a problem among nonsecretarial white clerical workers and virtually absent among white service workers, who faced the same rigid structure and pressure as black service workers but lacked the "one on one" and flexible atmosphere of secretarial work. Whether the unionists' assessment of secretaries was accurate at the time is not clear. It did play a significant role in shaping the strategy of the next attempt to hold a union election, one in which clerical workers in general and secretaries in particular were to figure prominently. In addition, white workers may have been more frightened by red-baiting and the fact that there were communists among the union activists than were black workers, who had worked with both groups in a variety of contexts, and who experienced red-baiting as a tactic for defending racist practices against civil rights efforts to change them.

Union forces were demoralized and angry at the November defeat. Some of the most active, nonpublic people were bitter, and both groups of activists were privately criticized, accused of selling out or of irresponsibility. Charges of sellout were even leveled at Fuller, who became demoralized, ill, and left town just before the election, as well as at some of the prominent activists who were promoted to better jobs or supervisory positions after the election. Other political activists were accused of wrecking the drive to build their party and scaring workers with inflamatory rhetoric. In retrospect, people on both sides regretted what happened and were self-critical about being drawn into those kinds of activities. People who were RWL activists in the first campaign worked to keep CWC people involved in the organizing committee on the second, largely for fear they would disrupt if they were excluded; and the CWC people in the second campaign "kept it strictly union" but felt that they were being excluded from the inner circle of decision making and meetings.

Still, the damage had been done among what seemed to be a fairly large number of activist black workers who were the core of the in-hospital networks in the first drive. They simply refused to participate in the second. Many I think felt pulled in two directions and did not want a repeat. They did not become antiunion by any means, but they did become inactive, and that was a critical loss.

The next chapter will move from history to daily life to explain the anatomy of women's informal social networks and work culture at the hospital. It will show why faction-fighting was so destructive to the activism of the black women who sustained the union drive as a social movement. Chapter 5 suggests that the structure of movement leadership was a complex one, that women activists and their social networks were a hidden but important half of the leadership for unionization.

NOTES

1. See Wise, 1980, for an extended discussion of black activism in Durham in the late 1960s and early 1970s.

2. With the exception of one newspaper story in the *Durham Morning Herald* (April 14, 1974), this walkout received almost no campus or press coverage, although it was a very successful job action and an important link between subsequent community support and worker organizing.

3. Some of the discrepancy may be because of the fact that training classes were spread over two years. Those who began when computers were first introduced took some classes but were primarily trained on the ward by the first group.

4. Malcom X Liberation University; Howard Fuller had changed his name to Owusu Sadauki.

5. Between 1974 and 1978, the number of beds grew by less than 9 percent, from 823 to 895, and the number of admissions increased by about 11 percent (AHA: *Guide to the Health Care Field*, 1974, 1978).

6. *Duke Chronicle*, June 17, 1974.

7. Local 77 Newsletter V, no. 1, May 24, 1974; *North Carolina Anvil*, June 1, 8, 15, July 6, 27, Aug. 3, 1974; *Duke Chronicle*, May 27, June 3, 10, 17, 1974.

8. Ehrenreich and Ehrenreich, 1970; Kotelchuck, 1976.

9. Bermanzohn and McGloin, 1976.

10. *North Carolina Anvil*, Aug. 17, 24, Sept. 14, 1974.

11. Ibid., Oct. 5, 1974.

12. Denton, 1976; Becker, Sloan, and Steinwald, 1982.

13. Local 77 *Duke Employee News*, Nov. 1974.

14. *North Carolina Anvil*, Nov. 9, 1974.

15. Ibid., Nov. 16, 1974; *Duke Chronicle*, Nov. 7, 1974.

16. *The Union Organizer*, March 23, April 13, June 30, July 14, 1976.

17. O'Connell memo, April 29, 1975, author's possession.

18. "What the Supervisor Can Do and Say in a Union Campaign," undated leaflet, author's possession.

19. Jackson letter, Dec. 5, 1975, author's possession.

20. O'Connell memo.

21. Undated fact sheet, author's possession.

22. Fact sheet.

23. Photocopy, author's possession.

24. Local 77 files, folder "June 2, 1975 Petition for Election Case No. 11-RC-4041," June 2, 1975; and "Decision and Direction of Election Case No. 11-RC-4041," Nov. 14, 1975, 3.

25. Local 77 files, "Decision and Direction."

26. Local 77 files, "Request for Review, Case No. 11-RC-4041," Nov. 25, 1975.

27. Local 77 files, "Request for Review."

28. Local 77 files, folder NLRB 1976, "Rowan to Fuller," Jan. 26, 1976; "Truesdale to Fuller," March 10, 1976; *The Union Organizer*, June 30, 1976, DU Archives, Employee Unions.

29. *The Union Organizer*, Nov. 12, 1976.

30. *Duke Chronicle*, Nov. 17, 1976; *Durham Morning Herald*, Nov. 17, 1976.

31. *The Union Organizer*, Dec. 1, 1976.

32. Local 77 files, folder NLRB 1977, "Johnstone to Counts and Rowan," Feb. 15, 1977.

5

How Women Organized

This chapter is about the ways women organized and exercised leadership in the organizing drive. Unionists did not address gender or women's issues in either hospital drive, but neither the successes nor the ultimate failure of unionization can be fully understood until the visions and voices of the women—specifically black women—are placed at the center of analysis. In chapter 3, we saw how daily work and the structure of jobs shaped women clerical workers' work cultures, but we also saw that black and white women often had different jobs, and hence experienced work differently. Although black women and white women had similar workplace networks, I have very little information indicating public politicization of white women's networks during either union drive. In contrast, much of the first union drive's vitality and strength came from the high-profile, militant work cultures of black women, notably the work cultures identified with dietetics and DTOs; they were points with which other workers could identify and to which they could link. Here we turn from the content of work cultures to the social networks and leadership through which black women transformed their shared dissatisfactions into publicly oppositional work cultures and union organizing, and also discuss the limitations and constraints of these networks and cultures.

Men and women both exercised leadership in the union drive, but they did so in different ways. When I raised the issue of leadership among a group of women activists, both black and white, on the union organizing committee, one woman expressed her view that, "Women are organizers: men are leaders." This was acknowledged by other women in the room.

They suggested that women created the detail, made people feel part of it, and did the menial work upon which most things depended, while men made public pronouncements, confronted, and negotiated with management. The 1974 DTO walkout seemed also to reinforce this notion. Although the actors were overwhelmingly black women, they chose the "lone black male," as one of them put it, to present their petition to hospital management, although they were right behind him. As a feminist activist, this approach made me uncomfortable, and I did my best to promote women's leadership in the union drive.

The result was a methodology best described as leading with my chin. The notion of leadership I carried and acted upon implicitly equated public speakers and negotiators with leaders and accepted the distinction between "organizing" and "leading," although that only became clear in retrospect. The incident that showed me my biases and forced me to rethink this notion of leadership was a situation where I was one of three middle-class feminists (two white and one black) who set up a public forum for hospital workers on the organizing committee to address a sympathetic audience and build community support for their unionizing efforts. We engineered a situation where all five speakers were women workers (two white, three black), and where none of the usual male public speakers were present. The women did beautifully, and I felt I had helped to further a much-needed women's leadership role until the women themselves called me into a fairly sharp criticism meeting. They were angry at being manipulated and pressured into doing something they did not want to do, even though they too thought that they had done well. While I agreed with their criticisms about manipulation and pressure, I could not understand why they were afraid of "saying something wrong," and why they did not want to be public speakers.

In trying to answer that question, I came to believe that the notion of leadership I had inadvertently promoted was a class, gender, and perhaps racially biased one, in that it recognized only one aspect of leadership, that of public and solo speaker, and missed what I think may actually be a more crucial aspect, that of network centers. Women and men both took leadership, although in different ways. Almost all the public speakers and confrontational negotiators were men (I tend to merge these activities, and to refer to those who do them as spokespersons or spokesmen), women were centers and sustainers of workplace networks—centerwomen or centerpersons—as well as the large majority of the union organizing committee. By equating leading with speaking, I recognized only spokesmen and missed women's key leadership role as centerwomen. I think this is a significant omission for understanding leadership in grass-roots movements, for the structure of these movements seems more complex than individuals following a popular orator. At Duke, leadership in the union drive involved mobilizing *already existing* hospital-based social networks, rather than individuals, around class and race-conscious, or at least job-conscious activities and values. Those I call centerwomen were key actors in network formation and consciousness-shaping. Leadership resided not in either person, but in the interaction of spokesmen and centerwomen.

The gender division in leadership gave men and women somewhat different perspectives on the union drive. Men and women highlighted different things in their analyses of the drive. For the most part, men who were public spokespeople stressed rallies and taking grievances through the hospital's grievance committee structure. They viewed fighting individual cases and publicizing the unfair treatment of workers by Duke's internal grievance procedure as central for showing people what they could gain by organizing themselves into a union. Women leaders stressed talking to people with whom they worked, usually one-to-one, signing them up, and asking them to organize others. They discussed setting up a well-organized, large, nonpublic network of supporters throughout the hospital. Women and men agreed that there were many people "who were not visible [who] were doing *a lot of* work": and that women workers were the core of these activities. One of the leading men was particularly insistent on the point.

Participants often recognized this aspect of leadership even when conventional language did not make it easy to express. "Women don't lead . . . but they *do* lead!" was how an official of Local 77 tried to answer my question. He described a typical union meeting that he chaired, and at which he could speak freely and make any suggestions he chose, but where "nobody had anything to say" until one or more of five or six well-respected women (whom I would call centerwomen) commented either for or against something he said. Then and only then did people move. If these women were silent, so was everyone else, and nothing happened. These were women who had been active in organizing Local 77, and who were as much leaders as was the official. It was their *interaction* that made things happen.

The roots of unionization in particular and of resistance in general lie in Duke workers' everyday social ties and networks, and in the efforts of the women at their centers in maintaining and mobilizing these networks. Workplace networks contain a tension between accepting working conditions and medical center relations as they are and making organized efforts to improve them. Most workers probably spend most of their time using social ties to try to make the best of a bad (or less than ideal) situation. Even these efforts seem to be two-sided, though. On the one hand, they generate social pressure to live with poor pay, insulting work relations, and occupationally based race and gender segregation. On the other hand, they provide the infrastructure and shared understandings by which people also resist these things and express that resistance.

The first part of this chapter will deal with the daily life and language of social networks at Duke Hospital. The second will examine some of the ways that women used familistic rhetoric and symbols in social networks and work cultures that animated both the DTO walkout and the union drive, in particular the role of centerwomen in sustaining these networks. The third part of the chapter will deal with some of the limitations inherent in social networks that compromise and accept on the one hand, and resist and confront on the other. Centerwomen in the union drive were simultaneously thrust forward and held back by their support from and commitments to co-workers. Their strength lies in consensus, which was considerably weakened by faction-fighting, and therefore so too was network mobilization.

Daily Life: Friends and Family at Work

Mary regularly brings her lunch from the cafeteria to eat in the office where her mother works as a secretary. Dotty met her best friend Sandra when she worked in the clinic. Even though she has gotten so fed up with her job there that she's transferred out twice, she's come back because the clinic is "my home," and she misses seeing Sandra. Another Dottie, when she discovered a group of friends in her workmates, found a home in Medical Records after moving through several jobs in a few years. Beverly Jones came South to Duke a decade ago as a political organizer, found friends, and settled in. Robert is an artist, felt somewhat silly working a "nothing" job, figured it was temporary until he went back to his university, but began to realize that all his friends were at the hospital and he wanted to stay. Paulette and Patricia are sisters and DTOs. Evelyn, her sister-in-law Felicia, Denise, whom Evelyn has known from high school, and Denise's husband's cousin Nancy are all DTOs on the same service as well as friends who hang out together outside of the hospital.

Much of what seems to keep workers at Duke is each other. Because it is the largest employer in a fairly small city, it would be strange indeed if many families did *not* have several members working in the hospital. Predictably, many workers I came to know had several immediate and not-so-immediate kin and in-laws scattered throughout the medical center. For some, the hospital was the place where they met their closest friends and was a center of much of their social lives. Many workers, both black and white, were born and raised in Durham and have ties of kinship, marriage, school, community, and church all interwoven.[1] As a result, there are many workers in the hospital with whom they share at least one set of ties, and often more.

Workplace socializing, social networks, and family ties are complex. People referred to the hospital as a hotbed of gossip; "a little Peyton Place," where everybody knew each other and their business and was probably related. This wasn't entirely true, because race and class were dividing lines for socializing outside work—although not completely. The union was certainly an important place where black and white workers socialized together.

Social ties operated in varied and sometimes contradictory ways. On the one hand, they were sometimes so important that workers seemed almost willing to endure miserable working conditions for them. On the other hand, they were sometimes a sort of worker telegraph carrying a collective message of protest against unfairness. However, not everybody was connected, and networks seldom, if ever, were always in harmony. While some supervisors were like sisters or "play mothers," (a fictive kin relationship), others seemed to be positive sociopaths, fostering an atmosphere that put workers at each other's throats. Some departments seemed fairly anomic, places where the safest course seemed to be to do your job and keep to yourself.

While much of hospital social life is informal, there is also an institutionalized aspect to it in the covered-dish lunches, breakfasts, and dinners that are organized for holidays, wedding and baby showers, goodbyes (to a patient, staff member, or rotating crew of housestaff), or for no special reason. Such events and occasions are also characteristic of offices and factories in which women are concentrated.[2] Everybody in a unit is invited and expected to make some contribution in food. Some of these events, especially those around holidays, are initiated—or sponsored—

"from above" by the head nurse or the attending physician in charge of the unit. But birthdays, showers, and good-byes are usually set in motion by a close co-worker, although they involve the unit authorities in planning and permission for time to arrange things, and they become an all-unit event.

The size and elaborateness of a luncheon—how many people come and what they bring—are indications of closeness to the person and closeness of the unit. Clearly, in-hospital parties have constraints on their form and how long they can go on, but there is a fair amount of variation on the pattern. The spring I spent in Mrs. Beecham's clinic seemed especially sociable. Harriet made a birthday breakfast for her closest friend; Pauline, who often organizes parties, gave a breakfast for a secretary who'd only worked a short time before her job was phased out.

Mrs. Beecham's goodbye party was one of the more elaborate ones. After years in the clinic, she was leaving to become a float nurse, working both wards and clinics as needed. She'd trained Mary Pearce when Mary came to the clinic from the wards and, as Mary said, "taught me things I wouldn't have learned otherwise." The two women often worked together, and Mary organized the surprise luncheon. Mrs. Beecham's daughter who worked in the medical library came. Alice came in on her day off and brought her two grandchildren (who spent part of the afternoon in the clinic with Eleanor, Alice's daughter who also works there). It was a major feat of human engineering to hide the entire clinic staff, including the doctors, in the conference room to surprise Mrs. Beecham, but it was done during the break between morning and afternoon clinics. While in theory nothing happens in the clinic between noon and 1 p.m., people had to come and go during the hour to attend patients, and it was impressive to see how closely patients were attended to during the luncheon. Those closest to Grace Beecham stayed longest, as did most of the nurses. Harriet and Barbara were on the desk, so they just fixed their plates and went back to work. Carol, the head nurse, spent most of her time with a patient whose doctor could not be found, but then she joined Grace and the other nurses. The food was spectacular; there were huge quantities of cornbread, green beans, potato and macaroni salad, as well as a table full of cakes and pies. The women brought the cooked food, and Dr. Farnsworth contributed money for fried chicken as the medical staff's contribution. Everyone chipped in for Mrs. Beecham's present, a stethoscope, and several people also gave individual presents. As 1 p.m. approached, people began to return to their stations.

Even though all hospital parties take much the same form, they are not at all identical. Mary, a DTO on a not-so-close unit, was furious when an unpopular supervisor organized the obligatory Christmas party to be held at night, in the hospital with bought food. Mary said that she'd "be damned" if she'd pay for night parking to go to "the thing." What made the supervisor's plan wrong was that it took the form of a party for people on a single shift, and added the insult of involving no one in bringing food. To make matters worse, Christmas was usually the occasion for the biggest all-staff party for all shifts. Mary saw the supervisor's party as a cheap excuse for what should have been a party at someone's (either a social organizer or a person with some administrative authority) house, with everyone contributing, and where alcohol could be served.

Much socializing outside the hospital is informal, but as Mary indicated, many unit parties and cookouts take place outside of work. The ground rules for these events are similar to those inside the hospital: Everyone is invited and brings something. The difference is that people can really party, and the events are often scheduled so people from different shifts can attend.

In-hospital parties usually joined black and white, professional, clerical, service workers, and technicians reasonably comfortably. But when parties, even quasi-official unit Christmas parties, were held in someone's home, class and race lines were not always so easy to cross. Most people felt easier crossing one line or the other.

Crossing both class and race lines at once was considerably harder. On one hospital ward, all the DTOs were black and all the RNs were white. The nurses tended to be organizers of parties and dinners for the ward. Some were held in the hospital, others in people's homes. DTOs praised the good relations between black and white workers on their ward. But they also said that the black workers—DTOs, messingers, housekeeping staff—didn't go to the parties outside the hospital, even though "they [doctors and nurses] all get after us the next day for not coming." The Christmas party posed a special problem. Every year the black workers talked among themselves and resolved, "If you go, I'll go," but they never did.

When I asked why, one woman said that they were all afraid that they wouldn't fit in outside the hospital, and that discovering that they were not welcome would jeopardize the good work relations they had. Another contrasted house parties with parties and showers in the hospital, where everyone comes and brings gifts "because everyone's here"; they belong and don't have to explain themselves. Both these women also indicated that the root of this lay in the hospital's segregated hiring patterns. One said that if there were more black nurses, DTOs would be more comfortable going, for they would not have to jump the class and race barriers at once.

Some white workers have a difficult time crossing the color line because of their own prejudice even when class is not the issue. In Becky's department, the centerperson for organizing the potlucks and showers is a black woman. For Becky, who is white, "race is usually a delicate kind of subject." Although the staff is fairly well integrated and works together comfortably, Becky feels she and her best friend Ellie (also white) don't really belong. "Oh we're *invited*, but they [black workers] usually stick together. If they plan it, they set the time and just tell us." On the other hand, Becky is forthcoming about her racist attitudes. She says that she does not like to be with black people, and both she and Ellie usually don't socialize; they say they have to get back to their work.

The general feeling was that doctors socialized separately. Most workers indicated that doctors did not attend events workers organized outside the hospital except, Sandra thought, "maybe the female ones but not the males." "We don't go to their parties; they know each other and we don't know them. They get together with their families and wives," seemed to be a consensus. In some places, the gulf was between doctors and RNs on one side, and everyone else on the other. The doctors whom people generally spoke about were housestaff. Attending physicians and upper administrators were not part of the social scene except when they made a brief appearance at a holiday party. On the other hand, the housestaff was very much a part of most ward and clinic working communities— although not as equals. Several clinics and wards have parties when the housestaff rotates out. "We bring food for the doctors to show we miss them; we don't eat it; it's for them." But at parties for co-workers, everyone eats.

Although there is a fair amount of variation in the actual amount of in-and out-of-hospital socializing that is quasi-official, these are forms recognized by all workers at Duke, probably by all other hospital and office workers as well. The potluck for everybody who works in a particular place seems to be a standard event in American workplaces wherever women are concentrated. The family-related occasions for having them are also standard. Events that are associated with family and "non-work" are brought into the workplace to join workers together, to overcome (or deny) the things that divided them, and to establish a familistic language or framework for workplace unity.

In some ways, punctuating the work week or month with parties seemed to undercut supervisors' control over the work and the work pace. Lower-ranking aides, secretaries, clerks, and LPNs seemed to initiate social events and to receive the go-ahead from higher-ranking head nurses, doctors, and supervisors for a break in the routine. Doctors and RNs seemed less inclined to organize these events. Actually, I never knew doctors or housestaff to do so; their events were professional and peer group oriented. On the other hand, LPNs and clericals often gave parties for them. Were these handy occasions to assert control, to take a break from the routine, or were they traditional expressions of deference to doctors or supervisors? I suspect they were all three simultaneously, and that the weighting of perceptions varied with the person and the particular event.

Family Values, Networks and Resistance

Familistic symbols and values seem to be the antithesis of the confrontational or the radical, even when they are used to challenge the established order. Part of their strength lies in their multiple meanings and their ability to bridge racial, gender, and occupational divisions. Thus, contradictory meanings can be embedded in work-time potlucks and baby showers without causing any conflict: They can reinforce deference or patronage behaviors in the workplace hierarchy, but they can also steal back a little social time and invert (at least for the event) the hierarchy of decision-making when hourly workers plan the parties and how they will handle their work.

Familistic notions of work, adulthood, and responsibility also formed a basis for a working-class-conscious culture and networks among Duke workers. These networks provided the structure of the successful DTO walkout, and perhaps of the earlier kitchen and housekeeping ones, all of which helped catalyze the subsequent union drive. Underlying the particular values is an awareness and valuation of interpersonal skills, a central part of the "invisible skills" discussed in chapter 3 and exemplified particularly by centerwomen, who are central to forming and sustaining work-based networks and linking them to union organizing.

Women workers discussed being a good worker in the hospital in many of the same ways that they discussed becoming a good adult in their family. Indeed, women seemed to stress the continuities between family and waged work. As housekeeper Dee Stebbins, a Local 77 member, sees it, holding a paid job is a necessary part of being a mother and an independent person. "I have six kids and I'm thirty-six years old. I'm a mom. I'm a housekeeper . . . I'm everything. I just do the things that's natural for my children. And working is one of them . . . working is a part of my job."

Women workers often expressed their rules of behavior at work in family terms and concepts. The links were particularly clear with regard to work, adulthood, respect, and conflict mediation.

Work. Women whom I interviewed discussed their hospital and household work, child care, and the part-time waged jobs they performed while still in school in qualitatively similar terms. Neither housework nor hospital work was described as lists of tasks, although that is how job descriptions most often read. Instead, women workers focused on the responsibility and initiative they took for knowing what needed to be done. The mental and organizational aspects of work were central in their descriptions. When they discussed childhood household responsibilities, several women indicated that these skills were rewarded by praise, and also by them being given more responsibility. One woman's father told her that she released him from having to worry about whether the house was clean, "If you're around I know everything's taken care of." She described how she arranged her part-time job, school, and housework, and how she threw her brothers and sisters out of the house on Saturday mornings so she could get the cleaning done when she had time. Women focused less on the tasks themselves than on the fact that they took responsibility and initiative for knowing and keeping mental track of what needed doing, and for arranging their lives so they could do all they had to do and wanted to do.

In this sense, work, especially the responsibility and decision-making involved in its mental organization, is an important part of adulthood. At the hospital, women workers—housekeepers, lab technicians, secretaries, and clerks as well as DTOs—stressed the "importance of setting your priorities," of arranging how you were going to accomplish all the goals you set (within the constraints of the job). They indicated that they were taught in their families that housework and work for wages share a key similarity in the mental organization (coordinating things, setting priorities of time and effort) required, and that this was a significant source of pride and sign of adulthood.

Adulthood. An adult is someone who can take responsibility for meeting commitments and obligations, for making decisions, and for arranging her own life to do what she has to do. In families, however, the relations among work, responsibility, and adulthood were not always smooth, especially when parents tried to retain responsibility for their children's non-housework decisions. Several women as teenagers began to fear that their parents were coming to depend on them too much in terms of work responsibilities, but were unwilling to allow them to make the decisions about their lives that they felt they had demonstrated the capacity to make. Several women felt that if they did not leave home, they were going to be given the major responsibility for running the house, but that their parents would continue to make decisions *for* them about their hours, social time, and friends. Both black and white women gave these considerations as the main reasons they moved away from home as soon as they could get a job to support themselves. Their job was a means to, but not a definition of, adulthood.

As I see it, these women learned in their families that work in the house and for wages are not qualitativley different, and that the mental organization—coordinating things, setting time and effort priorities—of both is a most significant source of pride and of adulthood. The rub came when parents were were reluctant to yield that autonomy in nonwork aspects of their children's lives, and when parents tried to retain responsibility for their children's decisions.

All the women who spoke of this conflict resolved it by moving away from home. Significantly, they all said that there was no bitterness about the move, no break in the family relationship, rather that it made for a positive change. Interviews with mothers of two of these women confirmed the daughters' perceptions: The mothers noted that children were grown when they were able to take responsibility for living on their own. Parents then recognized and reinforced their daughters' claims to increased adult autonomy. Daughters then went to their mothers for advice—adult to adult—instead of having their minds made up for them. Adulthood was gained as a process rather than a single event.

These meanings of work, respect, and adulthood are at loggerheads with job classifications and descriptions that distinguish mental from manual labor, and almost deny that service and clerical workers need to use their heads. Women's familistic interpretations counter management notions of work with a sophisticated understanding of the invisible mental planning and coordinating needed to carry out waged work and housework

alike. Not surprisingly, many workers regard close supervision and assembly-line pacing as demeaning as well as exploitative in that it robs
them of adult priority-setting prerogatives. Here too, familistic values
challenge management notions of economic rationality, and in that respect
operate as a language used by women for creating an oppositional worker
consciousness.

Adulthood and respect are concepts tightly interrelated and even used
interchangeably in many conversations. One becomes an adult by an active process of learning a variety of things, from basic skills to how to
make a decision and how to create and sustain a variety of interpersonal
relations. Women stressed the experiential process more than they did
major events such as parenthood, and jobs. Being an adult means achieving competence in making decisions for oneself, and being accorded the
right to make such decisions. Those rights need to be respected. Indeed,
that seems to be the central meaning of respect: to be accorded the right
to make up one's own mind, to plan one's own activities, and to have and
express one's own feelings and not to have feelings, decisions, or beliefs
denied, appropriated, or subsumed by a dominant other.

Respect, Equality and Hierarchy. Black and white women alike described respect in their families as simultaneously egalitarian and hier-
archical: "I never talked back to my father. I did disagree and brought my
point up, but not to the point of impudence." "Part of black family teaching is to give respect to elders in your behavior." "I would never walk into
my mother's house with so much as a beer." Because of their social relationship, parents and elders have certain rights to establish ground rules
and to command services and some deference from their children. At the
normative level, it has nothing to do with their personal abilities. There
is also an egalitarian or reciprocal aspect in that all adults are to be accorded respect (by all other adults as well as by children) regardless of
their social position, and children are also to be accorded respect in particular areas of their lives as they grow toward being able to take responsibilities and fulfill commitments. "Children are expected to make
decisions, rather than parents imposing them." One woman explained
how yelling at a child was not good. She pointed out that her son says
yelling is part of child abuse. He is "disappointed more than scared. It
makes him mad—maybe the same way as being yelled at on the job—it's
demeaning."

At work, DTOs, secretaries, clerks, laboratory technicians, and house-keepers were all prepared to work for and to grant people prerogatives they felt were due to their place in the job hierarchy, but they were equally insistent on their rights as adults, which were quite independent of occupational hierarchies. Part of these rights is the expectation that they will organize their work on their own, will "assign their own priorities" (a phrase that crops up often), and not be watched and directed. In this reciprocal sense, respect is a recognition of adulthood and the competence it connotes.[3]

When workers (male and female) complained that they were not treated with respect on the job, they were insisting on their right to make decisions about how they will work and about the part that their work will play in their lives—basic adult prerogatives. In the walkouts as in the union drive, workers placed this familistic and reciprocal demand for respect high on their list.

Conflict Mediation. DTOs and other front-line clericals have a particularly difficult job in that they need to coordinate the activities of people who are above them in the hospital's status pecking order. Some of those people—notably doctors—seem to operate by an informal code that it is acceptable for a superior to criticize a subordinate publicly (but not vice versa). This contradicts the reciprocal notion of respect shared among workers that sees such behavior as demeaning the doctor as an adult and embarrassing the worker, also as an adult. One DTO described difficulties she had with a nurse who spoke to her "like dirt" when she first arrived. This DTO responded to the nurse's public criticism by insisting on discussing it with her in the back room, together with another DTO. She emphasized that a public fight or criticism was both embarrassing and demeaning.

Another DTO analyzed several situations in which she learned the difference between the right and the wrong way to speak up. When she was new, there was a doctor with whom she could not get along. Their daily arguments upset her and resolved nothing. Looking back, she realized that the doctor was wrong to pick a fight in public, but that instead of responding in kind, she should have taught him how to behave. To do that, you "take them in the back room and argue it out one on one." She stressed how important it was to insist, calmly, on correct and considerate behavior even in small things and to have a sense of humor. She illustrated her meaning by describing another doctor who was in the habit of dumping a mixture of charts with and without written orders in her in-box. This created extra work for her because she had to search all the charts for orders. When she told him this, he grudgingly separated them and said, "You want anything else?" She answered, "Yes, I'd like a cup of coffee." In this case, she explained the consequences of the doctor's actions for her work load and did so without anger. The doctor's response was ambivalent: He accepted the correction but resisted being criticized by someone below him. The woman then used humor to upset the status relationship and to reinforce the positive, co-worker aspect of the doctor's response with humor. That gave him both reason and reinforcement to act as a co-worker. He got the coffee.

DTOs were particularly eloquent on their need to teach doctors and nurses to treat them as adults. "I'm an adult; I'm grown. If you can't speak to me without yelling, don't speak to me at all." This approach cuts through hierarchy and authority. Holding fast to status prerogatives can make it almost impossible to solve problems and resolve conflicts such that people can continue working together. Almost all DTOs as well as many other clerical and service workers related some version of, "when I first came I really had trouble with doctors (or supervisors, administrators or nurses), and I had to set them straight. Now they know their limits and we get along fine."

Centerwomen and Interpersonal Skills. Probably the most palpable family-rooted values are these interpersonal skills of mediating, resolving conflicts by reconciliation so that relationships are maintained, and providing emotional supportiveness and advice. They are the key to success not only in the jobs of DTOs, but also in those of secretaries, nurses, and other front-line workers. Some women are better at it than others. Some women seem to have developed these skills in their families, while others learned a great deal from their co-workers and from the informal work-culture that affirms and teaches them.

Centerwomen seem to be key in sustaining work-based social networks and seem also to embody and to reinforce many of these familistic skills and values by their behavior and actions. Most of the women who were centers in workplace networks also seemed to be centerpeople (or to have been trained for such a role) in their family networks. As I see it, the role involves keeping people together, ensuring that obligations are fulfilled, and acting to express the group consensus. From family interviews and participation among DTOs and union activist families, it seemed to me that workplace centerpeople were also trained to be centerpeople in their families, but that they often first practiced the role at work. Most described a particularly close relationship in their childhoods with the family center—sometimes a grandmother, aunt, or mother—and in one case a father.[4]

For example, I asked Alice Dixon, a DTO and centerwoman, whom she saw as the center of her family. She said that it is clearly her grandmother, who lives in town and whom everybody visits on Sundays and holidays. "She loves to cook. If you want to find out something you call her." The grandmother keeps up with what everyone's doing, "and what you shouldn't do." For the most part, people listen to her advice. She is also likely to enlist the aid of her children in helping one another. Alice is the center of a workplace network that joins pairs and small groups of very close friends. When I spoke with her, she saw herself as closer to a few real friends than to her family. "A real friend is willing to help whenever you're in need." She distinguished real friends from "the others I just be with." There is a certain fit between her value on a few close people and on the way she is organizing a birthday club—on linking good friends to other good friends—a chain of small, strong links of trust. As we will see, this is also a group and part of a larger community. At least that is the hope for the birthday club.

Where does Alice's family fit in her learning to bring people together and to seek and give support? Do people in Alice's workplace network share her values, have they laid their expectations on her? Alice was raised by her mother's parents. Her grandparents had twelve children, and Alice was raised with her aunts and uncles—they were really more like brothers and sisters—on a farm near a small town north of Durham. Recently, one of her aunts, Jody, who is about Alice's age, has been coming to Alice for advice and has been sending other cousins to talk with her about their personal health and marital problems. Not long ago, Alice's younger half-sister stayed with her when she was having problems with her husband. Alice says that she is having responsibility put on her and that she feels good about it. People seek her out for personal advice because they know that she had a hard time with her first husband, knows about personal adversity, and has come through it stronger and wiser. Other people reinforce Alice's own sense that she has grown from the experience. She is a center in a large family, but, as with her friendships from work, her family relations are two-way; she goes mainly to her Aunt Jody for advice.

Beverly Jones, a center of a large social network of DTOs, stresses mediation and initiative in smoothing interpersonal family and work relations and in collective action. Although she does not see any role model in her family, she does see critical events in the context of her family relations, particularly peace-keeper. That role developed from Beverly's initiatives as a teenager in a very large family. "Respecting parents is the utmost. That was my God." But when she graduated from high school, Beverly decided that she had to move into her own apartment if she was going to grow independently and without argument. From her description, it appears that her move created a family role that was needed but not really there as long as she stayed at home and therefore remained a child in her parents' eyes. The role was one of adult mediator: Beverly's mother calls on her for advice. Her parents' expectations and treatment of her have been taken up by her brothers and sisters, who also call on Beverly for advice, mediation, and help with interpersonal problems, even though she lives a long distance from them.

Church and work experience may have been learning contexts as well. Beverly describes herself throughout high school as "a sheltered kid," quiet, not allowed to go out after school, and therefore not part of high school socializing. But her mother was secretary of her church for twenty-five years, and very much involved as an organizer in church affairs and social networks, and Beverly went to church every week until she moved into her own apartment. When she was in high school, she began working as a hospital messenger during her work study program. Her mother worked as a nurse's aide in another hospital, and, for her mother as for Beverly, workplace friendships and networks played an important role in life.

Acceptance and reinforcement of her personal initiative transformed Beverly's respect for her parents into the social role of a family center. Beverly's personal discomfort and her attempts to deal with it apparently helped others in the family to see a need for a mediator. As long as she remained at home, her parents were responsible for resolving conflicts. Beverly resolved part of the family's contradiction as well as her own by moving out. She created a new and needed role, and family members reinforced and helped give it shape. Even though Beverly seems to have modeled her own role, she is now a role model for her nineteen-year-old sister.

Beverly Jones and Alice Dixon are both centerwomen in ward-based networks of DTOs and LPNs. Both were active in the union drive, and Alice was an active participant in the DTO walkout. Many of the DTOs involved in that walkout were already part of a high school cohort. As we have seen, many of Durham's black students in these years had a significant fund of political movement experience. Likewise, many of the DTOs from Durham's black community shared ties of school, church, neighborhood, and kinship with other hospital workers. By the same token, work organization shaped which of the many potential ties were developed and deepened, and which were not. Many DTOs have made their closest friends at the hospital, from among other DTOs, aides, and LPNs with whom they work. People tend to tell friends and relatives about job openings and to recommend them, so that ties of kinship, work, and friendship reinforce one another. Most workers agreed that friendships came from or were deepened at work. In short, one brings family and family values *to* work, and one creates family and re-creates family values *at* work.

In 1974, the organization of work "from above" established close contact between DTOs within a unit or between paired wards, so that those on all shifts within a unit were in daily communication. Informal social networks reinforced these lines of communication, with DTOs and nurses (mainly LPNs, but also RNs) on a ward or pair of wards getting together for holiday parties, informal cookouts, picnics, and dinners throughout the year. Unit lines seemed more important than physical proximity in the hospital. Indeed, DTOs on a ward of one service next to a ward on another could not think of any DTOs they knew there. Likewise, adjacent wards of the same service under different unit supervision have little day-to-day contact.

Until about 1979, most training of new DTOs was done on the wards and was the direct responsibility of senior DTOs. As these women taught new workers their definition of the job and its worth, they also created new ties of trainer and trainee. Along these ties too was transmitted a mind-set that was both class-conscious and familistic, a consciousness of themselves as responsible adults, of their right to insist on decent pay and adult treatment and to stress cooperation over domination and subordination.

Organization "from below" among DTOs who knew each other from nonhospital contexts brought together different units and services. The core network in 1974 seemed to be the cohort hired between 1968 and 1971. They were concentrated in the two largest services, medicine and surgery. This network included almost weekly out-of-hospital socializing among primarily single DTOs, messengers, aides, and nurses on several wards of both services.

Each of these DTOs was also part of some kind of network on her unit. Thus, two surgery DTOs from this core group, together with several others on their unit, acted as centerwomen for holding meetings and informing those on their wards of events. Those who missed meetings checked in with the two core network DTOs. Another DTO from the core network who worked nights tried to bring the news to people on that shift.

Services other than medicine and surgery were less involved in the walkout. To the extent that people from these services joined it, they seem to have been connected to people in the core by ties of kinship, friendship, or neighborhood. Some from one small service stayed out not only because of the general issues, but also because their friends from the core group expected them to. On the services where friendship and social networks were densest, the bases of trust and communication most secure, participation in the walkout was highest and fear of retribution was lowest.

Most DTOs who were subsequently active in the union drive described the political cohesiveness, pro-union strength, and intense social networks that sustained them as having their roots in the walkout. As networks in the kitchen, in outpatient, and other areas mobilized politically in the course of the drive, the social density and political intensity of each increased, particularly where key people were members of the organizing committee.

In the early 1970s, Beverly Jones became active in the black liberation movement and spent some three years working at a hospital job in the North, recruiting for the movement and speaking on East Coast college campuses. She moved to Durham specifically to work with Howard Fuller on the Duke union drive. Beverly applied for a job as a DTO at Duke several months after the walkout to help organize the union. As soon as she finished her probationary period, she publicly identified herself to management as well as to her co-workers as a union organizer. She became a member of the organizing committee and a centerwoman, the latter in part from personal and political predilections, and in part because the male political leadership of the drive did not assign her public speaking.

As Beverly analyzed it, being a political activist and an organizer encouraged her to think in group terms. Her assignment, to sign people up for the union, meant "I talked to everybody. That was fun work!" As an activist, she gravitated toward the group of militant DTOs from Durham's Hillside High School, who had been at the center of the walkout. Even today, some of this group include Beverly when they think of their high school cohort.

Beverly Jones's network-building and union organizing also came from more traditional hospital activities: She gave a good-bye party at her house for a DTO who was leaving Duke. From that point on, DTOs began getting together regularly for dinner every two weeks, and Beverly has been instrumental in keeping them going. Dinners and other social events have kept the group together for some five years. This particular network joined DTOs on all four wards of a unit, has expanded from time to time to cover larger numbers of DTOs and nurses, and has managed to persevere through the political in-fighting of the mid-seventies and through the years of political inactivity afterward. In the aftermath of the second and very demoralizing union defeat in 1979, that group held together and maintained its DTO identity. As a social club, they collected dues all year long to rent a hall for a big Christmas party for hospital workers. The party was called, appropriately enough, "*Dance To Our Songs.*"

Constraints on Mobilization and Militance

Beverly Jones and Alice Dixon were centerwomen who exemplified family values and reinforced them by their actions. Their initiatives in setting up social groups and activities were important parts of the processes by which co-workers became family and were able to teach and enforce familistic values in the workplace. Centerwomen are structurally important for sustaining perspectives and behaviors that are simultaneously working-class-conscious and familistic, that affirm the worth of women workers and the work they do, and that provide an oppositional idiom to hospital management and support for militant activities.

Centerwomen in particular do so in a way that is not commonly perceived as leadership: They have a great deal of responsibility but little authority. Beverly Jones put it succinctly, "I'm usually the one to initiate anything. People say, 'Jones, why don't we do this?' And they wait for me to do it." But it is a dialectical relationship: If you take initiatives, people check in with you to find out what you and others think, to find out what is happening. Part of checking in then involves suggestions and expectations placed on centerpeople, but also given by them. Because they are at the center, they are at once repositories of others' opinions and keepers and shapers of the consensus. While this gives them a certain latitude, they are also constrained by the limits of consensus.

The ability to mediate and resolve conflicts by reconciliation, and to provide emotional support and advice, were skills that the women I interviewed brought up frequently and valued highly. To be able to do these things was a reflection of being able to demand and give respect in its reciprocal meaning. The ability was learned in families and in informal on-the-job training. Centerpeople were particularly adept and called upon to mediate either directly or indirectly. The skill involved being able to resolve a conflict in a way that did not demean either party. A key element in doing so was to be able to take the person or persons away and to deal with them individually.

The particular mind-set and values embodied in reconciliation and sustaining cordial relations conflict with the demands of confrontation. Yet, as we have seen, this did not deter workers from confronting Duke management. Quite the reverse. It was DTO solidarity that underlay their militance and their ability to confront hospital administrators directly. This was also the case in union rallies, wearing buttons and distributing leaflets. However, when conflicts among workers led to confrontations within the ranks of pro-union workers, the consensus upon which worker militancy rested was severely threatened.

This is what seems to have happened in 1976 when the RWL and the CWP began to attack each other publicly. Several centerwomen and union activists I interviewed described the fighting as something they did not want to deal with, either at the time or in retrospect. Faction lines cut across networks, confronting centerwomen with conflicting expectations and demands from friends on different sides of the fence, each of whom wanted harmony on their terms. Because their role stressed finding and expressing a consensus, some of the most activist women found themselves immobilized and furious at the situation. This was to have profound repercussions for the subsequent union drive of 1976–79.

Conclusion: Centerwomen and Spokesmen

The leadership of the first union drive came from black workers. Men and women tended to play different roles as activists at Duke for a a combination of reasons that are not fully clear. Prominent on the union organizing committee were women who were known and respected hospital workers, some of whom were centers of work-based social networks. Men on the committee were also well-known and respected workers, but do not seem to have been centers of networks in the way women were. Also, the roles of men and women activists seem to have been divided by gender, with men acting as official spokesmen in interviews, at rallies, and in negotiating the lion's share of workers' grievances with hospital management. In part this may have been due to the backgrounds of the men who filled these roles. The most prominent were political activists who came to Duke to help organize a union.

It also seemed partly because of women's and men's shared assumptions about gender-appropriate roles. Beverly Jones, for example, despite her previous speaking experience in the black student movement, did not become a public spokesperson in the union drive. There were also four or five women, some of whom were centers of ward-based networks, instrumental in initiating and organizing the DTO walkout, as we saw in the last chapter. The walkout demands and petitions were drawn up at meetings with a large group of DTOs present and were presented to hospital administrators, also in a group. However, these women chose the only male DTO among the activists to be their spokesman in presenting their demands. As I have described, I was criticized strongly by women for manipulating them into speaking publicly during the second union drive.

The way in which hospital jobs were allocated by gender, and perhaps by race as well, also seems to have reinforced the gender differences in how men and women exercised leadership. Women made up almost all of the "invisible administrators"—the office secretaries, DTOs receptionists, and nurses—whose work, like that of centerwomen, depended heavily on their skills in smoothing conflicts, coordinating, and compromising, and whose jobs fixed them firmly in one locale. Men tended to have jobs that took them all over the medical center, transporting patients and supplies. Two leading spokesmen chose such jobs precisely for their organizing potential. The men's mobility put them in contact with many workers, but also made them less embedded in a fixed, face-to-face work group.

Not surprisingly under the circumstances, as the vast majority of workers, women were also the vast majority of the network centers. Both as invisible administrators and as network centers, women were encouraged to develop skills and strategies for conflict resolution and "smooth relations," which were incompatible with the goals and tactics of adversarial confrontation. Both strategies are needed in different contexts. Centerwomen do negotiate with supervisors and administrators with and on behalf of co-workers, but if they do not succeed in reconciliation, confrontational negotiation may be necessary, and they tended to seek out spokesmen. This is not to suggest that Duke centerwomen cannot be confrontational or militant. Quite the contrary, but they are at their best in a group. Solo performances seem to be particularly risky.

It seems that to be a centerwoman is to be firmly empowered by the resistance aspect of shared work culture and values. Thus, when one DTO analyzed whether or when they might mobilize around a particular grievance, she named several centerwomen and and said, "If they complained others would follow suit." On the other hand, centerwomen seem also to be constrained to stay in hearing distance of network opinions and to stay within limits of a manageable consensus because their authority lies in expressing that consensus. One ex-centerwoman, in explaining why she opted out of activism after the faction-fighting, noted, "This way I don't need to entertain, to see that no one's feathers get ruffled, to keep the relationship going." Her complaint about the role was, "I find myself always in the middle of ten thousand different people who don't like one another pulling at me." She, as well as Beverly and Alice, found the faction-fighting very destructive. The image of being pulled in different directions captures their sense of immobilization.

Spokesmen, in contrast, seem to need a certain degree of independence from the reciprocal values that constrain individual confrontational strategies. After all, part of confrontation is precisely to intimidate and delegitimize an adversary. This role also had its risks, as spokesmen could become co-opted, or could become brokers between workers and administrators. Duke regularly attempted to co-opt visible centerwomen as well as spokespeople by offering them promotions to supervisory positions. By speaking out publicly, one becomes visible to management. Workers were aware that these promotions were divide-and-rule strategies on management's part, just as they were aware that job qualifications were structured such that becoming management was often the only avenue for promotion. Opinions were divided among workers about who was co-opted or who sold out, and about how successfully Duke employed this strategy. Perhaps more common were situations where visible people were persuaded to broker. Rose Gattis was particularly consistent in her opposition to workers agreeing to "straddle the fence," as she put it.

Women activists seemed less fearful of punishment than of becoming conspicuous to other workers and perhaps vulnerable to management bribes, perhaps vulnerable to the danger of becoming a broker between groups rather than a representative of one's own. People who are firmly embedded in workplace networks face more peer constraint. Fear of saying something wrong may have derived from a lack of experience with walking the tightrope of confrontational negotiation and fear of contextual pressure to speak like a broker.

Despite these gender differences and the murky and perhaps contradictory bases for them, it is important to recognize that there were two complementary forms of leadership in this grass-roots movement: centerwomen and spokesmen. To recognize this structure of leadership and to expand the term is to make visible some of the ways in which women have been leaders, and to get beyond equating orators with leaders. Analytically, it is important to recognize that centers and speakers are functions or dimensions of leadership, separate issues from who carries them out. Experiences in the Duke drives raise, but do not answer, whether or not one person can be both a spokesperson and a centerperson: Do these functions necessarily pull an individual in opposite directions? Also, are these roles necessarily gender-linked—spokes*man* and center*woman*? One ought not assume that either role must be gender-specific or that they require different people. After all, neither organizers nor analysts yet know very much about the structures and dynamics of informal work organization. Different work situations may foster different allocations, but sexist attitudes and practices may also exert a homogenizing effect.

In the Duke drive though, the strength of hospital worker organizing lay in the fact that spokesmen articulated shared views, while networks and their centers mobilized around an oppositional work culture expressed through a consensus language of familistic values. When ties between spokesmen and centers broke down, and when that consensus language was not so clearly articulated by centerwomen as happened during and after 1976 in the second drive, unionization efforts came to take a very different form. The next chapter will examine the difficulties of sustaining that drive in an increasingly hostile economic climate and without the vitality of a visible and shared workplace culture of resistance that political mobilization of women's networks gave to the first drive.

NOTES

1. Unfortunately, I did not explore church membership and ties, a weakness that I acknowledge.

2. Lamphere, 1984, 1986; Westwood, 1985; Sacks, 1983.

3. See Barrow, 1976, for a similar discussion of respect in Barbados.

4. Although the *functions of* centerperson and spokesperson are tied to gender here, I do not believe that they are necessarily gender-specific. However, we need analyses of work group structures that are sensitive to links between family and work in primarily male workplaces to determine this.

6

The Second Drive
1977–79

The second drive to unionize the medical center got under way in the summer of 1977, almost immediately on the heels of the first, as union activists of various political persuasions regrouped. Although participants saw it as a continuation of their earlier work, this union drive was to take place in a much more difficult national and local context from that of 1974–76. While it is clearer in retrospect than it was at the time, hospitals had begun to face growing financial pressures after the mid-1970s. Too, the federal government and the political climate became much less supportive of popular movements. Therefore, as the decade wore on, the hospital administration seemed to have an increasingly congenial climate, whereas the workers' obstacles were multiplied. In addition, many workers who had been central to the previous drive tried to distance themselves from the ugliness of political infighting, and in the process, from the drive as well. As a consequence, the 1977–79 union campaign had a significantly less grass-roots character than previous ones, a tendency heightened by the prominence in it of AFSCME's Washington office. The combination of events worked against success.

The central issues of this campaign were still low wages; poor health, sickness, and vacation benefits; lack of an impartial grievance procedure; favoritism, discrimination, and capriciousness in raises, promotions, and transfers; and Duke's hostility to unions. The existing grievance panel, empowered to adjudicate the last step of any grievance, was composed of administrators, supervisors, and faculty; nine of its twelve members were thus medical center management. Parking was another irritant. Workers

paid for it but were assigned to lots far from the medical center and forced
to depend on an unreliable bus service. When they were late because of
this, they were docked pay. Rising cafeteria prices were also a widespread
bone of contention, especially because prices rose considerably faster
than workers' wages.

In 1978 many full-time kitchen workers earned less than $7,600 a year,
some less than $6,000. The vast majority of workers who would be in-
cluded in the bargaining unit earned under $10,000. These wages were
inadequate to sustain a family of four on the federal government's "low
budget" of $10,928 in September 1978. As union leaflets pointed out,
there were dietetics workers who qualified for food stamps.[1]

The Changing Political Economy of Health Care

During the early and middle years of the 1970s, Duke workers had
pursued their first union drive with the support of community activists
concerned with the quality and accessibility of health care to all citizens
of Durham. It was an alliance of workers and consumers that came together to protest Duke's expansion. Durham was not unusual. In the
mid-1970s, Duke and Durham health activists were part of a national
health-care movement with its own organizations, networks, and publications.[2] That movement took hospitals to task for extravagance in construction, purchase of expensive equipment, inflated staffs, and corrupt
business practices.[3] Grass-roots activists protested the degrading, sexist,
racist, frequently harmful, and sometimes life-threatening conditions
under which medical care was given. "Nonprofit" medical centers, especially "medical empires" like Duke, were also criticized for their role in
generating extraordinary profits through hospitals to a medical-industrial
complex, whose representatives were the bankers, builders, and drug and
hospital supply company executives who dominated hospital boards
of trustees.[4]

The second drive took place in a context that pitted hospital administrations and hospital-based doctors in large nonprofit medical centers against
private corporations who found themselves footing skyrocketing employee
health-care benefits. As the economic boom of the postwar years ended,
as U.S. industry's markets and profits shrank and the economy began its
long recession in the early 1970s, America's largest industrial corporations
became an unlikely ally in the battle against the medical-industrial
complex.[5]

At the same time that corporate influence grew, popular voices weakened, and this transformed the battle away from its goal of service reform to a goal of cost containment. As a result, the struggle became increasingly one among sectors of big business. Some capitalists, doctors, and administrators were getting rich from the health-care goose, while other capitalists—major industrial corporations—were paying an increasing share of that wealth, especially as part of negotiated benefits. Clearly the partnership between big business and big doctors was on the wane, as the former tried to reduce these free-wheeling and independent professional entrepreneurs to salaried employees accountable to management for productivity and cost control. Hospital administrations and hospital-based doctors in large nonprofit medical centers like Duke found their treatment policies at loggerheads with private corporations footing sky-rocketing employee health-care benefits. By the latter years of the decade, the largest and most powerful corporations in the country—those whose unionized workers initiated the struggle for the right to health benefits—became the most influential group in shaping federal responses to runaway medical costs.

Thus, as Duke workers tried once again to unionize, they confronted corporate and federal pressures to contain health-care costs that in turn encouraged Duke administrators to seek out ways of holding down wages and workers as well as implementing factorylike methods of increasing productivity.[6] Hospital workers also faced a situation in which the enemy was no longer just the administration of a particular hospital, but increasingly the major corporations of the nation in concert with the federal government. These pressures have worked against hospital unionization throughout the nation, as indicated by the decline in successful union elections after 1975.[7]

The Second Drive

At Duke, after the electoral defeat late in 1976, both political factions seemed to continue working independently, although often in barely muted antagonism. The Duke Organizing Committee (the Communist Workers party group) remained together through the spring and summer of 1977, and worked with Local 77. They distributed a variety of leaflets and held a rally in June demanding an across-the-board wage increase and recognition of hospital workers as part of Local 77.[8]

During the summer of 1977, Rose Gattis began pulling together hospital activists, both those who had been in the Revolutionary Workers League (RWL), which was no longer functioning, and others with no affiliation, to move more quickly in gathering show-of-interest cards and to prepare for a union election. Among the concerns of some in this group was to disassociate their efforts from those of the CWP, because they felt that white workers were afraid of communism and would stay away from a CWP-linked union. Their strategy was to go to workers they already knew to be pro-union, amass enough cards to demonstrate that union sentiment was alive and well, and to gain AFSCME's support for a new drive. They gathered about three hundred cards in a very short time and persuaded the International to send staff. AFSCME sent a regional representative to Durham in August 1977. Donna Hughes, a novice to unions at the time, remembers the AFSCME staff as being "like a takeover with professionalism": they intimidated people, spent lots of money, and "talked big." They rented an office for the hospital drive separate from Local 77's office because the CWP was influential in Local 77, but the hospital office was larger and nicer. Unionists remember that AFSCME staffers remained in Durham for about six months.

In late August 1977, *The Union Organizer* reappeared, published from the hospital office and separate from Local 77. It announced that medical center workers were seeking a new election, that they were the official organizing committee and were not affiliated with the Communist Workers party, and that they urged workers to sign the enclosed show-of-interest card for a new election. Wilth Rose Gattis as chairperson, the organizing committee included many of the activists from the previous drive: Edward Berry, Shirley Rice, Beverly Jones, Barbara Flowers, Percy James, and some new people such as Donna Hughes.

For the most part, the fall and winter were devoted to card signing efforts and to distributing professionally designed leaflets on local issues such as the high price of parking and the low wages of nonunionized hospital workers and on more general union issues such as strikes, dignity, and paid holidays. In time, CWP activists were incorporated into the new AFSCME-backed organizing committee. Although it was not an easy alliance, both groups were determined to avoid a repeat of 1976.

In December 1977, as a result of charges filed with the Labor Department, dietetics workers were awarded up to two years of back pay for hours worked without proper compensation from Duke.[9] This seemingly major success seems to have received relatively little publicity and does not stand out in participants' minds. Indeed, no one mentioned it during the drive or in subsequent interviews. There were also a number of spirited leaflet battles with Duke in 1977 over a variety of issues and grievances that the organizing committee pursued through the Duke grievance structure.

AFSCME pulled out its staff, apparently early in 1978, believing that it was still too early to file for another NLRB election. But by August, when the organizing committee reported that they had more than nine hundred signed cards, AFSCME sent Harold Sloan down from Washington to investigate the situation. On the basis of his positive report, he was assigned to be the AFSCME representative and to direct the campaign.

Duke's Response. Duke's objective during this "Pre-Petition Period," was to "Impede and if possible, defeat union efforts to obtain a showing of interest (signed authorization cards from 30% of the employees in an appropriate unit)," while also preparing for a union election.[10] Duke and/or Modern Management Methods (3M) of Chicago, its antiunion consultants and one of the nation's largest union-busting specialists, relied on four techniques in their campaign. The first, which was called "counterpunching," was "to create doubt in the minds of employees about the union's credibility and to remove doubts, if any, about the employer's temerity." Duke titled the leaflets by which they attempted to do this *The Facts*.

The second technique was to raise antiunion issues: "it would probably by advantageous to propagandize the way in which employees can legally withdraw their union authorizations. If the impression can be created that some employees actually want to withdraw, then doubts in the minds of others may be raised about the solidarity of existing union support." A sample leaflet was included. Hospital memos also suggested bringing up the issue of strikes, especially information on AFSCME strikes, which were also detailed.

The third technique was to make management "integral" to the antiunion campaign. Supervisors were given instruction on how to convey an antiunion message legally to workers they supervised. For example, they seem to have been instructed on the difference between a statement that could be legally construed as intimidation: "I personally feel this union would not be any good for you. A union has no place in our Medical Center," and a legal version of the same message: "In my opinion, I don't feel we need a union," or, "We sincerely believe that the introduction of a union into the Medical Center is not necessary or beneficial to your welfare and growth with us."[11]

The final "responsibility of the management team is to identify issues relevant to the campaign," "in light of the ultimate objective of blunting the union drive." Although Duke's information to its management counsels "fairness and firmness," it also suggests a less than honest opportunism: "Answers which in another time might seem appropriate (and might well lead to unionization) may not now be worthwhile and indeed could be very detrimental." Management was cautioned that they were in for a long "war of attrition."[12]

The Union Strategy. The union's strategy was to petition for an election as quickly as possible. To do this, they filed on October 31, 1978, for the same bargaining unit that the NLRB had certified for the 1976 election. In his careful way, Harold Sloan indicated that he was very concerned that the union drive not be politicized. He criticized past practices of having "too many unofficial spokespeople," so that the press could get opposing views from different members of the organizing committee. Sloan paid a great deal of attention to image, including having a logo designed for stationery, and was therefore determined that union leaflets be well-designed. As he saw it, art and design were to reflect a more professional image that was more representative of the union itself. Content was as important as design, and Sloan was critical of many of the previous leaflets for what he referred to as their "gossip column" content, but that could also be seen as local, specific, and spirited critiques of Duke's practices.

Behind these specifics was Sloan's more fundamental role: to wage a campaign that would have no communist politics or fighting among various political groups, and that would accomplish this by the participation of all disputing parties acting in accord with the rules of the drive. Those rules were to wage a campaign that dealt only with wages, working conditions, and promotions.

This campaign would be fought with many of the same handicaps as the first one. First, and probably most important, was the composition of the bargaining unit. Service workers and some clerical workers had a clear and longstanding pro-union position. Secretaries and higher level technical workers were more divided, and no one really knew where they stood. Most were not well-integrated in networks of pro-union workers.

However, there was a small but solid social network of pro-union secretaries and skilled trades workers in Local 465 who formed a visible core of union strength among white workers in this second drive. Some local activists, both white and black, wanted to change the composition of the bargaining unit for this election so that those who had been fighting for a union would not be saddled with neutralizing what they feared were an antiunion group of occupations in order to win. It was never fully clear why this was not attempted. Sloan seemed to favor moving quickly, and from past experience it was clear that any move to change the unit would assuredly slow things down significantly. To make matters worse, and to stall, Duke moved to add 33 staff assistants and between 110 and 115 administrative secretaries, both of which had clear supervisory roles, to the bargaining unit.[13] The NLRB regional director ruled, apparently on the basis of a hospital administrator's testimony of what these workers did, that neither group had supervisory duties and included them in the unit. AFSCME's counterargument against inclusion of administrative secretaries did not deal with the supervisory aspect of their jobs, but only argued that they had not been included in the bargaining unit for the previous election.[14]

From past experience, workers believed that a union victory with this bargaining unit would require overcoming a great deal of racism, elitism, and the fear of radicals among a large number of voters. This time, there was never any uncertainty about whether or not it was important to organize among secretaries and technical workers. It was very important; and there were even more of them in 1978 than in 1976. Still, the organizing committee had to deal with the old contradictions: How much effort should they make appealing to secretaries and higher-paid technical workers, most of whom were scattered in ones and twos throughout the whole medical center complex, and to what extent did they need to reorganize and re-involve their strong supporters in dietary services and the laboratories—the DTOs, messengers, aides, and other service workers? Were they still strongly pro-union after all the political in-fighting? Would they remain so?

The International's strategy was to take the first tack, to focus on the secretaries. Indeed, "secretaries" became a symbol, union stereotype, and shorthand for a strategy that presented unions in a middle-class image—being "nice" and "sweet," as several activists retrospectively characterized it—showing unionism as being no different than what doctors and lawyers do to protect their interests. Or as Harold Sloan put it, giving the union a professional image. Sloan practiced what he preached; he never raised his voice and was the model of a professional administrator. As a black man, he was very concerned to balance the organizing committee and staff, which meant recruiting more white women to convince the secretaries that the union was for white as well as black workers.

All parties agreed that in-fighting had to be avoided. Local activists agreed with Sloan's strategy that the way to prevent it was to incorporate everyone—so no one would publicize unofficial and left-wing analyses or critiques—and to keep all activity focused only on union issues. Still, part of this agenda was to depoliticize the drive and, ironically, to play down even conflicts between Duke and its workers, as in the lack of publicity after 1977 surrounding workers' grievances and unionists' efforts to fight for them.

Unfortunately, this strategy all but ignored the black women who had been the animating force for a union all along. Those who might have worked had very little role to play in such a campaign, for there was no place for one of the most important public tactics of the first drive, taking workers' grievances. In this campaign, it was acceptable to publicize categorical unfairness, but to fight against a particular instance, rather than simply to state that collective bargaining would eliminate it, was associated with politics and believed to be frightening to the secretaries. For this reason too, there were no rallies or demonstrations, for these also did not fit the image that AFSCME thought would appeal to white clerical workers. This strategy ignored all the lessons of the old union movement of the 1930s, and those of the more recent black, women's, and poor people's movements. Indeed, service workers were taken for granted, and this was a bad mistake.

Local organizers were ambivalent about assistance from the International. They hoped it would help resolve some internal weaknesses and provide some badly needed legal help. But they also had serious misgivings, based on past relations, about who was going to make decisions. The dynamic set up was to invest authority in Harold Sloan. He was well-liked, not heavyhanded, and seemed willing to play the role of arbiter among different interest groups. Sloan's approach was to do a complete about-face in the tactics and strategy of the first drive. The mass-produced word was emphasized over face-to-face contact and over winning and publicizing workers' grievances. The International hosted professionally planned meetings in motel conference rooms and held press conferences instead of bake sales and public rallies. The culture of this union drive was distinctly Washington-style, nevertheless, it was accepted gratefully by the organizing committee at the time. Not only did it mean less exhaustion for those who had been through a do-it-yourself drive, but it also seemed to be a sensible way to appeal to those who were thought to have been antiunion in the last drive.

As the drive wore on, the contradictions inherent in this approach began to surface. The strategy took the strongest and most politically sophisticated supporters of unionization for granted and appealed on a dubious basis to a less politically experienced group of workers. The first group, primarily black service workers, DTOS, back-office clerical workers, and technical workers who learned their craft on the job, saw unionization as a way of organizing *themselves* by using an ambivalent legal apparatus to help them win improvements from Duke. They had learned the value of united action from movement experience. The second group, primarily white, mid-level clerical, and college-trained technical workers, lacked these experiences, worked in small, scattered groups without intense contact with other workers, and had not developed visible work cultures by which these lessons could be shared. Their relative job mobility and the flexibility in their work encouraged opting for individual solutions to their problems. Although many were less than happy with their working conditions, many were also uneasy in 1976–79 about joining black service workers to solve problems together. The structure of this campaign did not demonstrate the effectiveness of unity to this group. Although several members of the organizing committee pursued grievances for individuals, including white clerical and technical workers who had been treated unfairly, these were not publicized. For most workers not already convinced, it was "the union's" word against Duke's, with no way to know whom to believe. This was exactly what Duke hoped to foster by its counterpunching strategy.

Picket lines, rallies, and marches were avoided because it was thought that they would antagonize white clerical and technical workers (but not white service workers). They were also associated with political activism in general, and with the fear of being called communist in particular. The political faction-fighting of the last drive had been exploited to heighten this fear. In previous campaigns, as we have seen, black workers maintained a collective workers' presence, identity, and interests. Walkouts, rallies, pickets, parties, wearing buttons and holding bake sales made pro-union workers visible to each other so they could see their strength. These tactics linked them historically to some twenty years of a very

effective freedom movement. To fight, win, and publicize the grievances
of individual workers was to affirm that the needs of each person were
important parts of the collective struggle. To reject these tactics was to
deny a powerful and effective heritage, and to reject the workers who
developed and identified with it. It was also a rejection of anything that
could be labeled *communist*. It is ironic that self-defined communists (of
both groups) accepted a strategy that was so anticommunist and antimove-
ment. However, the strategy followed from a strategy that simultaneously
viewed white clerical and technical workers as conservative and saw them
as the key to union success.

One palpable consequence of this strategy was that there was little to
do on a day-to-day basis, either for those who had worked on the last
campaign or those who wanted to involve new people. Edward Berry, a
prominent activist in the previous campaign, wrote some of the leaflets
before they were "polished" by the International's public relations man.
Most people on the organizing committee leafletted, but there were not
that many leaflets compared to the weekly distributions for much of the
first drive. Percy Davis and Edward Berry, both of whom had served in
the first campaign as spokesmen, talking at rallies, and more important,
pursuing individual grievances, had a much diminished role in the second. As significant, they were no longer members of the bargaining unit.
Both had married and become involved with family, school, and careers.
The combination of things worked to diminish their activity and to reo-
rient their social ties considerably. CWP activists Macon Villa and Sharon
Stone felt excluded and seemed ambivalent about how active to be, or in
what ways to be active. All of these people were prepared to take public
roles, but there was little they could do in this arena. Without a public
focus, experienced organizers could continue to talk to people they knew
and to sign people up, but there was no next step in which to involve
them, and no way to let people see the scope and effectiveness of their
collective strength. These things also demoralized the organizing
committee.

The lack of activity could not be attributed entirely to the International.
Harold Sloan persistently pushed organizing committee members to pull
together a meeting of "key contacts," his phrase for hospital workers who
wanted to organize but did not want Duke to know they were pro-union
activists. He even sent a "Dear Key Contact" letter to perhaps thirty
people whom organizing committee members had suggested as potential

activists. The letter did not produce results, and committee members joked about bureaucratic culture. Nevertheless, there seemed to be an active and near-universal reluctance on the organizing committee to rebuild the network of in-hospital support that had been the strength of the first drive. People associated with either faction said that the other faction was dragging its feet and not holding up its responsibility. Others claimed that organizing individuals was too hard, and still others that it wasn't necessary and that word got around anyway. At the same time, most participants agreed that the dynamic between mass mobilizations with public spokespeople and a nonpublic, lower risk network of face-to-face support was the mutually reinforcing core of the first campaign. In the second campaign, there was no structured progression of opportunites by which people could involve themselves and show their involvement.

In addition, the stuff of activism and involvement in the past had been occupational and departmental issues, as well as taking grievances on behalf of specific individuals who had been treated unfairly. Most of the union's issues came from things that particular groups of workers were angry about. Without day-to-day political contact between spokesmen and centerwomen, those issues did not reach the organizing committee, so that even if the International had not been reluctant to hold rallies, there might not have been much basis for them.

On the other hand, the attitudes and circumstances of core activists and centerwomen were not the same as they had been a few years earlier. Some who felt badly burned by the in-fighting refused to participate in this drive, dropped out in the early stages, or remained distant and passive. This attitude was particularly conspicuous among DTOs. Others in food services and laboratories, and some secretaries, remained solid members of the organizing committee. Many organizing committee members, even those who were part of, or centers of, dense workplace networks, seemed reluctant to try to mobilize their friends for the drive. The campaign lacked the movement flavor of earlier years, and the feeling prevailed that it was an uphill effort to involve each person on an individual basis. This was heightened by meetings that were fairly intimidating in their office or motel conference room settings. Some, but not many, informal meetings were held at local cafes or worker lunchrooms. One woman on the organizing committee urged house meetings. She said that she would invite her friends to her home, and that they would come because they couldn't insult her by not coming, which they could do at an office meeting. On the other hand, she did not organize the meeting until the eve of the election. Much of the resistance was passive and subtle, but it persisted.

An ironic consequence of a strategy with no mass mobilizations was that there was also no safe space for people to participate in the drive. To stand around at a rally or picket line, to accept a leaflet, even to buy a chicken dinner or pie didn't publicly identify a person to Duke as a union supporter. One could support the union privately, but see and talk with others in a public context who might also do so. These were forms of participation that allowed a person to hedge their bets—to be a supporter, and to let other workers know that they were, but to be able to tell a supervisor that they were just watching or just hungry. Events of this campaign gave fewer opportunities for this. An open house or celebration on union turf— of which there were several—was less ambiguous. There were no forums that one could watch in public space. There was no mass wearing of union buttons as had been done in the previous drive. Accepting a leaflet was the only such activity available, but it was hard to linger long enough to see how many other people were doing likewise.

Inside the hospital, there was at least some depoliticization of networks that had been intensely political a few years earlier. Beverly Jones's large DTO network grew in size and formality to the extent that people met together monthly for dinners and undertook to organize a Christmas party for all hospital workers. Beverly, whose energy had all gone into the earlier drive, now became group treasurer as they turned to creating a DTO-sponsored social event for hospital workers. Alice Dixon focused on forming a a birthday club that seemed to join several smaller networks of DTOs and LPNs together. Alice had worked on her unit for ten years, and this network grew from among the friends made over her years training new DTOs and from among their friends and neighbors. Each person paid an annual membership fee, with the funds to be used to treat each woman on her birthday. Clearly a social agenda: "At least it gives you something to do besides go to church and work. It's something to look forward to . . . especially for single girls from out of town." They also hoped to sponsor a needy family at Christmas and to give a Christmas party.

Denise and Evelyn, who had been initiators of the 1974 DTO walkout, felt that their old network had just disintegrated, that there were fewer organized parties and dinners on their unit and between units. However, they themselves helped bring about the changes. Both indicated in different ways that they wanted to opt out of the responsibilities of being a center—even though they wished someone else would take up the initiative for continuing both the social and political activity. Thus, Denise pointed out that she and another DTO had organized previous unit Christmas parties, but "we didn't want one last year." On the other hand, both women are still very much involved in smaller ward-based social circles, with friends, kin, and "play" (or fictive) sisters. Although Alice, Denise, Evelyn, Beverly (as well as most of the thirty or so DTOs I came to know) were all pro-union, they remained inactive and distant from the drive; their social lives were not politicized in this campaign.

Union Busters. By going counter to the experiences of several decades of movement activity, AFSCME's strategy played into the hands of the union-busting campaign for which Duke hired Modern Management Methods. People on the organizing committee identified four 3M consultants at least three months before the election. The union claimed that each earned $600 a day plus expenses, and that Duke paid 3M about a half million dollars all told. In any event, the hospital's spending and slickness far outshone that of the union. This itself may well have been part of a larger strategy to intimidate workers.

3M's campaign followed what is by now the standard pattern for union busters—interestingly, the same procedure Duke employed in the 1974– 76 drive.[15] They organized more intensively among the supervisors, incorporating them into a "management team" for defeating the union. Supervisors who were pro-union, or unhappy with an antiunion role, were made to feel ostracized, while others were coached on legal (and not-so-legal) ways of persuading their workers to oppose unionization. Workers were suddenly of great interest to top management, who began holding coffee hours for them. As one union leaflet commented: "Q: When was the last time Duke gave you the 'red carpet' treatment? A: The last time there was upcoming union election."

A barrage of Duke's letters hammered home the same themes in virtually the same phrases as were used in the previous campaign: The union doesn't care about you; it only wants your dues money so that union officials can live in urban opulence. The union will take away your free choice and tell you what to do; it will make you go on strike, and you can lose your job. Duke was again presented as benevolent to workers who choose to "represent themselves" as individuals, but more powerful than any union and determined to give nothing to workers who unionize.

Under 3M's guidance, Duke's propaganda was more effectively intimidating than it had been the first time. Duke's *Facts* attacked AFSCME locally as well as nationally. The low pay of Local 77 workers was played up, and Local 77 was accused of not fighting for the rights of those it represented. "Consider this: Eight unionized Duke employees have been discharged from campus and medical center departments in just the past two months—but AFSCME has done *nothing* for them." "If *you* don't want to take a chance on putting your job and your future in AFSCME hands . . . vote 'no' on February 16."[16] Nowhere did Duke indicate whether any of these workers wanted to initiate a grievance.

Duke also represented its treatment of workers—including firing them—as the automatic workings of natural law, while ignoring the gains in pay, benefits, and working conditions Local 77 made for all workers. In addition, Duke circulated the salaries of the leaderships of most AFL-CIO unions, including AFSCME. They were indeed staggering sums compared to what Duke hospital workers, or any worker, earned. In this context, AFSCME's campaign strategy did not look good. Three-piece suits, rented offices and rooms downtown for meetings, printed leaflets, and television spots could be interpreted as a misuse of workers' money. 3M also circulated leaflets on almost every election AFSCME lost, suggesting that workers in these places knew something Duke did not.

Most of the propaganda barrage came in the last months of the campaign, and most of the leaflets came from Duke. Many appear to have been prepared well in advance, with an eye to intimidation. The union did not come close to matching Duke in volume. AFSCME's strategy was to be genteel, actually more so in the important months before the election. Earlier leaflets pointed out specifics with some punch and persuasiveness: Dietetics workers published a petition accusing Duke of trying to buy them out. "It looks like Duke is up to its old tricks again. As you know several weeks ago Duke 'surprised' Dietetic employees with a small raise of about 20¢ an hour. . . . The real question is, *why now?*" "Duke is not much different from some politicians. . . . They figure that when we are handed our ballots, we will remember the raise and forget all the reasons we need a union." "They gave us the raise because they know we're 100 percent behind the union. . . . Thanks for the raise Duke, but: WE'RE STILL STICKING WITH THE UNION."

A fall leaflet, "Duke raises food prices—again" showed that wages had risen just over 27 percent in the last four years, while cafeteria prices went up 84 percent right after raises were announced, putting workers in a

vice. "We think the cafeteria should *service* the workers, not profit from
us. Many hospitals throughout the country have discounts for employees. . . . Being served food at cost is one of the demands that we will take
up in a union contract. This is our only real way to fight to get some justice
at Duke." There were also leaflets on the parking situation and personal
statements about why they were pro-union from a secretary, a radiology
worker, and from dietetics workers.

There was really only one leaflet answering Duke's *Facts*, and although
this exposed some of their distortions, it did not catch them all, nor did
it have the same concreteness that earlier union leaflets had, or that
Duke's flyers did. Thus, the answer to 3M's strike scare was that Duke
had provoked three walkouts without a union, that "Unions help prevent
strikes," by bargaining and negotiating. "The only people who can call a
strike are the members of the local union (by a majority vote of the
membership)." The tone of the campaign combined with a weak answer
to the strike issue implied acceptance of 3M's assertion that striking was
morally wrong. Nowhere did the union discuss strikes in an affirmative
light—as ways that workers force hospitals to improve patient care and
working conditions. AFSCME, along with many local people, knew of
3M's notorious record, but 3M was never exposed publicly until the very
end of the campaign. By that time it was too late to undo the fears they'd
heightened. Union strategy played to weakness and ignored strength,
alienated an indeterminate amount of strong support, and may have
added inadvertently to the persuasiveness of 3M's arguments even among
those the union was trying hardest to win.

In February 1979, the union lost the election by more than two hundred
votes, suggesting less than total support among service workers, but also
suggesting some support among the by now approximately six hundred
secretaries. Because the election was by secret ballot, how people voted
can only be speculated upon. However, some handwriting appeared on
the wall a few weeks before the vote. The kitchen had always been a
bastion of union strength because of years of activism among its workers,
and because of the wide base of support its activist workers had. However,
under 3M's campaign, Duke's promises of raises, and lack of union visibil-
ity, kitchen centerwomen and organizers saw that solidarity being undercut and held a series of last-minute meetings to combat it. DTOs, another
previously leading group, were conspicuous by their absence during this
campaign. Various DTOs had worked with both the RWL and the CWP
in the last drive, and the fight between these groups caused a great deal

of conflict among this group of workers, who had also long been active on
their own and others' behalf. When it was time for the election and the
union sought poll watchers, they pleaded with several of these centerwomen to help. They agreed, although it took a major effort to persuade
them. Much later, Rose Gattis was to claim that both dietetics and DTOs
turned against the union. Although I suspect that the antiunion votes
were a minority, these key departments did not manifest the public and
militant oppositional work culture that gave the past drive its movement
character on a day-to-day basis.

A month after the election, Rose Gattis summed up the reasons for
defeat: "We didn't go to the people with rallies; the leaflets were slick,
but they didn't address the issues in the hospital. Percy and Edward took
grievances, but there was no feedback to workers about what was won.
All that information was sat on by AFSCME. Last time without them was
better because it was in the hospital."

In summary, the ties between the organizing committee and hospital
workers that had been the core of the earlier drives were severed after
1976. Where the first drive had been a movement sustained by a public
workplace culture radiating out from several large departments, this was
an election, largely because the dynamic between centerwomen and
spokesmen was considerably weakened as networks and their centerwomen depoliticized. Still, the organizing committee contained people
who had played and were still able to play both roles. But they seemed
reluctant to try to politicize work-based social ties, perhaps because there
were no concrete issues, as well as little to bring people out to public
rallies and grievances. Although AFSCME sought a professional tone for
its campaign (one characteristic of business unionism), despite the lessons
of grass-roots movement successes, it is also true that economic conditions
and the legacy of political in-fighting made such a movement much harder
to re-create.

NOTES

1. DU Archives, "Employee Union" folders, union leaflet, "We Don't Want
Food Stamps. . . . We Want a Living Wage!"; "Dear Colleague," Feb. 12, 1979,
Jack Preiss and others; "Fact Sheet Concerning Unionization of Non-Academic
Employees at DUMC," Jan. 24. 1979, faculty letter.
2. Kotelchuck, 1976; Ehrenreich and Ehrenreich, 1970; Reverby and Rosner,
1979; Sidel and Sidel, 1984.

3. Kotelchuck, 1976:288–330; Rodberg and Stevenson, 1977:109–10.

4. Bermanzohn and McGloin, 1976.

5. Brown, 1979:208; "Employee Benefits," 1976; Ellwood, 1982:110; Eilers, 1974:1.

6. Yaggy and Anlyan, 1982.

7. Denton, 1976:230–31; Becker, Sloan, and Steinwald, 1982.

8. DU Archives, "Employee Union" folders, *Duke Workers Newsletter* no. 1, April 29, 1977; Duke Workers' Organizing Committee leaflets May and June 1977.

9. "Workers File Charges with Labor Department," leaflet, Dec. 20, 1977.

10. Photocopied paper, "Pre-Petition Period," author's possession.

11. "Employer Freedom of Speech Discussion Guide," author's possession.

12. "Pre-Petition Period."

13. Duke also requested denial of an election until sometime after July 1979, when Duke North opened because some six hundred new employees were to be added. The NLRB denied this petition (Case 11–RC–4607, Jan. 15. 1979).

14. Case 11–RC-4607, Jan. 15, 1979.

15. McDonald and Wilson, 1979; "Modern Management Methods, Inc."

16. *The Facts*, undated, author's possession.

Rollbacks in the Eighties

Parts 1 and 2 have discussed the life-cycle of the Duke hospital workers' movement, from its birth in the 1960s to its demise in the late 1970s. Part 3 focuses on work and working conditions in the late seventies and early eighties, a time of economic cutbacks and no unionization effort. Duke workers were losing some of their earlier gains, and work-force divisions on racial and class lines seemed to be increasing. Still, continued financial pressure on hospitals and the ways they reorganize to cope with it seem to be eroding the relatively good positions that allied health professionals enjoyed in the 1970s, and may diminish racial and class divisions. In any event, future hospital activism will necessarily be shaped by a different set of relations among professional, clerical, and service workers from that of preceding decades.

In the 1960s and 70s, black women gained access to clerical and technical jobs in significant numbers, but they still remained near the bottom of a growing, specializing, and professionalizing female work force in health care. Most hourly jobs at Duke were women's jobs, but few were integrated racially. Hence, gender was not a divisive issue in the same way as race and class. Union organizers grappled with the divisive forces of race exacerbated by differences in occupational statuses, working conditions, and relations. The need to encompass and simultaneously express both the shared and the divergent needs without alienating any group remained an ongoing source of tension in efforts to unite workers.

The nature of health-care funding cuts and organizational changes in the 1980s suggests that future organizing efforts are likely to face a different constellation of work-force divisions. On the one hand, increased emphasis on formal educational credentials has sharpened distinctions between professional and technical workers with college degrees and clerical and service workers without them, and has made mobility more difficult. On the other hand, as health-care funding continues to tighten, professional and technical workers are beginning to face pressures similar to those experienced by service and clerical workers: work intensification, heightened supervision, and loss of job security. Health-care workers, especially as salaries, wages, and working conditions worsen, will become more heavily female in number. Some professionals, particularly registered nurses, have become noticeably militant, combining class and gender consciousnesses, although not a racial one. Thus, even as hospital workers become more occupationally stratified and segregated by race, they may also become less separated in their class and gender-related working conditions and relations. This may generate a new wave of hospital worker activism, although its shapes are far from clear at present. What is particularly problematic is the extent to which one of the largest and potentially most powerful women's industrial work forces will be able to overcome and unite across its racial divisions.

At Duke though, it was the divisive aspects of change that were most visible in the immediate aftermath of the union's defeat. Service and clerical workers feared a return to working conditions of the early sixties. Food and cleaning services experienced a new wave of rationalization and speed-up that reminded older workers of the early 1960s. Secretaries faced a job evaluation that seemed reminiscent of their earlier experiences with Proudfoot. Some thought that computers, which began to be introduced into offices on a wider scale after 1980, would facilitate the process. DTOs saw their control over training new DTOs being undercut by a new management program, which they viewed as an attempt to indoctrinate new workers and undercut their solidarity. Other workers pointed to the shrinking numbers of service workers and to the imposition of new schooling requirements that once again excluded black workers from some of the jobs the movement had opened up. To some activists, it appeared that upgrading or professionalizing the technical and allied health work force was an excuse to replace feisty working-class workers, black and white, with docile middle-class and college educated white ones. There was little visible activity among this latter group, and what appeared to be a widening of class and radical divisions among women workers.

Activism and organizing among Duke hospital workers in the early 1980s was at a twenty-year low. It is likely that pressures on professional and technical workers will heighten, but it remains to be seen whether this will lead to a resurgence of organizing or unity across racial and occupational lines. The next two chapters sketch the changing political economy of health care in the 1980s and how those changes have affected Duke workers. Chapter 7 describes the national picture and discusses its impact on Duke service workers. Chapter 8 discusses the ways that the emphasis on formal educational credentials has further divided black and white women's jobs and opportunities for occupational mobility, as well as limited those of working-class white women.

7

Service Workers

The health-care cost cutting efforts of the 1970s flowered in the 1983 prospective pricing system (PPS) of reimbursement to hospitals for treating Medicare and Medicaid patients.[1] Under PSS, patients are assigned to one of some four hundred diagnosis related groups (DRGs), and hospitals are reimbursed at a fixed rate depending on that diagnosis. Prospective pricing has brought about a major change in the ways in which hospitals operate and a revolution in hospital funding. Earlier forms of insurance reimbursement encouraged doing more for (or to) patients because reimbursement was based on the kind and quantity of treatment. Under PPS, hospitals are encouraged to do less and to discharge faster because reimbursement levels have been detached from treatments and standardized by diagnosis categories.

Even before prospective pricing, other patterns of government funding and private insurance coverage were beginning to undercut the system of hospital-based medicine by encouraging cheaper forms of health-care delivery. Such changes facilitated the rapid growth of profit-making hospital chains, health maintenance organizations (HMOs), private nursing home chains, and home health-care chains. All these institutions preceded prospective pricing in sharing an incentive to cut costs, usually by doing less and paying their workers less (although they do not necessarily lower costs to the patient).[2] As a result, hospitals are having a difficult time filling beds; some are closing, and more are taking to aggressive advertising.[3]

In the 1970s though, profit-taking hospital chains grew rapidly, faster

than the computer industry, primarily by buying out private, usually doc-
tor-controled hospitals that had already been weakened by the rise of
university-based medical complexes. By 1983, one in three hospitals were
members of chains; most were for-profit hospitals. Some predict that
chains will also proliferate among nonprofits.[4] By 1981, three companies
operated almost 75 percent of the beds in the for-profit sector of multihos-
pital chains. The private hospital boom seems over as prospective pricing
causes problems there, too.[5]

Changes in federal insurance reimbursement have also stimulated the
dominance of large profit-making chains in extended care facilities and
home health care. Private nursing homes expanded sharply after 1966
when Medicare first provided the elderly with insurance coverage. Today,
the largest nursing home chain, Beverly Enterprises, has more than seven
hundred facilities.[6] In the mid-1970s, changes in Medicare/Medicaid
guidelines also allowed expanded coverage for home health care. Between
1970 and 1982, the share of costs covered by insurance rose from 27
percent to 43 percent, of which 30 percent was public insurance in 1982.[7]
As a result, home health care also grew rapidly after 1974, both absolutely
and relative to hospitals. Home care increasingly offers high technology
services. Employment in home care grew much faster than in the rest of
the health industry between 1972 and 1982, such that this sector employs
about one in eight health workers (compared to one in eleven in 1970).

Health maintenance organizations (HMOs), are pre-paid medical plans
for both outpatient and hospital care. They were among the earliest alternatives to fee-for-service medicine. Until the last decade, almost all
HMOs were local and nonprofit organizations. Now, national chains dominate this field, too, the largest of which is Kaiser-Permanente. As of 1980,
just under 10 percent of all Americans were HMO members[8] HMOs were
initially attractive to business because of their relatively low costs achieved
largely by avoiding hospitalizations. Thus, Kaiser members spent only
half as many days in the hospital as a similar population of Blue Cross/Blue
Shield users. Critics point out that Kaiser cuts costs by making it difficult
for its members to gain access to the services for which they have paid,
citing waits of several weeks for appointments, impersonal treatment,
difficulty of finding and keeping a personal doctor, and deliberate policies
of hiring too few doctors and other staff, in part to discourage people from
seeking care. Although Kaiser is nonprofit, critics argue that its policies
of cost-cutting at staff and subscriber expense, and increasing enrollment

income and using the difference to pay physicians bonuses and expand to new locations make it hard to distinguish from for-profit ventures.[9] Kaiser opened a branch in Durham in 1985.

HMOs and for-profit hosopital chains are frequently accused of "creaming" or "dumping." HMOs have tended to enroll a younger, more affluent, and generally healthy clientele requiring relatively little in the way of major care. This is creaming. For-profit hospitals specialize in high-profit, low-cost procedures (another kind of creaming). They can and do turn away or transfer out the unprofitable people and cases (dumping), leaving high-risk, expensive, and unprofitable care to underfunded, under-equipped, and understaffed public hospitals

Nonprofit private hospitals, including most of the large teaching hospitals, have been hit by cutbacks in research funds and reimbursement levels, increased competition from HMOs, and most seriously by prospective pricing.[10] Duke responded to prospective pricing by curbing its price increases. In 1984, the hospital's CEO announced that, "Room rates will not change and the average of all prices [for patient services] will not change"; he also indicated that rates increased less than 5 percent in the previous three years. Overall expenditures were expected to rise 3.8 percent for 1984—85, wages to increase 5 percent, and neither an expansion nor a reduction of the work force was projected.[11]

Even at teaching hospitals, businessmen are beginning to challenge doctors for control over the establishment of medical standards, long considered the sole prerogative of physicians. Cost effectiveness (which often becomes simply cost) is pitted against medical effectiveness as business school-trained managers struggle to break physicians' power. The latter have begun to protest that they are being pressured to discharge patients before they are ready and forced into poor medical practices. There is widespread alarm that people are not getting the care they need, that they are being released from hospitals "quicker and sicker."[12] The losers in these battles of course are consumers, especially the poor and the aged, but there is widespread fear of overall deterioration in both the quality of care and the well-being of workers under the constraints imposed by prospective pricing.

The cumulative effect of all these changes is that hospital growth has slowed relative to growth in outpatient and convalescent care facilities, and since about 1982, has all but ceased. Although hospitals employed 62 percent of all health-care workers in 1972, their share dropped to 55 percent a decade later.[13] In contrast, nonhospital employment—especially HMOs, extended care facilities, and the growth of home health care—almost doubled in the 1970s.[14]

Hospital managements and industrial spokesmen tend to blame increased wages for rising hospital costs. One proponent of this view indicated that wages represent 60–70 percent of hospital operating costs, compared to half that in most "industrial activities."[15] If unionization were a major threat to hospitals' future existence, it certainly would explain the industry's hostility to them. However, other analysts dispute this view, noting that there was a drop of more than 10 percent in the "proportion of health spending devoted to labor costs" in the 1970s.[16] Still others show that it is not the wages of hourly workers causing inflation. They found that union growth increased real hospital care spending by about 5 percent, compared to a total increase of 67 percent.[17] Also, to the extent that wages are responsible for cost increases in medical care, they are most likely to be the salaries paid to doctors and administrators; together with the insurance industry, the latter consume one-fourth of all health-care dollars.[18]

More than wage levels may be at stake in hospital hostility to unions. Staffing levels and job duties seem to be central issues. Humana, the most profitable of the private hospital chains in the early eighties, increased its profit margin by some 50 percent in four years by hiring part-time workers and keeping their numbers closely tied to shifting patient loads—in other words, laying workers off when beds were not filled. Likewise, full-time jobs and retention of senior nurses were important issues in the 1984 nurses' strike in Minneapolis. Management insistence on flexibility seems to mean an erosion of hard-won job descriptions, job security, income, and wage levels, all things unions would be expected to protest.[19]

The health-care industry of the 1980s has inherited a work force shaped by the economics and social movements of the 1960s and 70s. For most of that period, thanks largely to the availability of research funding, the dominant trajectory in hospital-based and specialized medicine led to the development of a wide variety of allied health professions and semiprofessions. As economic prosperity combined with popular movements and urban unrest—the carrot and stick behind many progressive domestic policies in the 1960s—the federal government funded training programs in basic nursing and the health professions. These grew in size and numbers of specialties, as well as levels of training, although the distinctions between levels were not always clear or consistent. As the numbers of health professionals grew, they became less the auxiliaries of physicians and more members of a peer group of hospital workers or a peer group of occupational professionals. This ultimately led to a growth of professional associations and some unionization, as new professionals sought to establish control over their training programs and conditions of practice. Although professionalization may have been a welcome counterweight to unionization in some contexts, new and expensive health professionals and new militancy among them are a growing problem for hospitals in the 1980s.[20]

Even if, as some Duke unionists believed, the professionalization of the health-care work force in the late 1970s and early 80s was an antiunion force, it certainly was not a cost-cutting measure. In general, the initiative seems to have come from nursing and other allied health professions, lobbying for licensing laws and battling with the medical profession to upgrade and professionalize their occupations. Although the strategy of professional upgrading has improved pay somewhat, it has not won the full professional status its proponents want. More recently, even the economic benefits are threatened as hospitals begin to make new demands on nurses.

The new corporate entrepreneurs of the health industry's proprietary hospitals, extended care facilities, and home health care sales companies seem to be of two minds about RNs and other allied health professionals. On the one hand, they are more expensive than LPNs and technicians, but they are also cheaper and less powerful substitutes for physicians in many tasks; and they also may well be allies against physician control of health-care institutions. On the other hand, hospital administrators also want to cut the costs of RNs and allied health professionals. For such workers to rely on hospital administrators as allies is dangerous indeed, for what a nurse clinician or registered technologist can now do more cheaply than a physician, someone else may soon do cheaper still. Nurses increasingly find themselves stretched out doing tasks formerly done by staff as diverse as physicians and nurses' aides. Although the changing dynamics of health professsional organizing and alliances are beyond the scope of this work, hospitals and other emerging health-care institutions seem to be finding ways to turn some of the recent RN victories back against nurses and to their own economic advantage.[21]

In the late seventies, when Duke was opposing unionization, it was also increasing the number of RNs and technologists at the expense of LPNs and hospital-trained technicians. Activist black workers interpreted the racial and class aspects of these changes as, at least in part, forms of social control. Even if Duke was reluctant to hire more schooled and costly workers, by seeking to include them in the bargaining unit the medical center may well have hoped to decrease its reliance on black and working-class employees, and hence restrict the scope of support for unionization efforts in the future. That the hospital might subsequently attempt to intensify the work of professionals, or that professionals themselves might subsequently moved toward union-style militancy, does not undercut the validity of black workers' interpretation for the late 1970s and early 80s, a period when service workers especially were being subjected to a new wave of work intensification on familiar industrial lines. These were especially visible in housekeeping and dietary services.

Housekeeping Services: New Handle on the Old Broom

Margaret Sims remembers that cleaning workers initiated unionization efforts at Duke in response to the university's first attempt at "scientific management" in the mid-sixties. Both she and Mrs. Hattie Bagley, who is her contemporary, also remember their 1973 walkout over the addition of wet mopping to housekeepers' jobs. In the last three or four years, they and other housekeepers once again have had wet mopping and other duties added to their workloads. Looking back in 1983, she must have felt a little like Sisyphus, the ancient Greek who was condemned for eternity to push a boulder to the top of a hill, only to have it roll to the bottom each time. To workers in housekeeping, it seems as if each time their efforts bear fruit, Duke finds a new way to rob them of their gains. With unionization in the early seventies, it seemed that paternalism, with its low pay, poor benefits, and capricious work demands by white supervisors, had been beaten. Some years later, Duke subcontracted out management of the housekeeping services department to American Hospital Supply, a giant health supply firm that also sells cleaning supplies to the medical center and whose president, Carl Bays, was a member of Duke's Board of Trustees.[22] Housekeepers believe that there have been consistent increases in the pace and quantity of their work, cutbacks in the number of employees, and closer monitoring and more punitivness by supervisors since the early eighties after Duke North opened. In addition, they point to heavy assaults by Duke and American Hospital Supply on some of their hard-won sickness and vacation benefits.

However, unlike Sisyphus, the pushing done by Mrs. Sims's generation has not been undone, even if it is held precariously. Part of the union legacy is the message to younger workers embodied in the organization of Local 77 that they too will need to keep pushing against oppression that is simultaneously race-based and class-based.

Caroline Walters is in her mid-thirties. Although she only started working at Duke when the new hospital opened, she is part of the late sixties-early seventies cohort of Durham high school graduates, has a variety of ties with some of the second generation activists in that group, and is herself active in Local 77. She works the day shift (harder than the night shift) in Duke North, which is acknowledged to be the hardest place to work. She is supposed to have sixteen patient rooms, including discharges (rooms vacated by people going home), that she is responsible for cleaning. She told me that there are supposed to be two housekeepers on a unit of thirty-two rooms, but there is usually only one. Cleaning here is done on all seven days, two shifts, with a third shift for "stat" (hospital jargon for something to be done immediately) discharges. Discharges are the heaviest cleaning, and no one is supposed to have more than five a day. More than that are taken care of by the special discharge crew or by other housekeepers. When a patient is discharged, everything in the room has to be washed down with disinfectant before the room can be assigned to a new patient. Housekeepers have to strip and clean the bed, disinfect the trash cans, and clean inside the drawers, sills, and counters. Carolyn Walters knows about the 1973 walkout, and that janitors used to mop the floors; she also knows that now housekeepers do it, as well as washing walls. Of course every room has its own bathroom, and this too needs to be thoroughly cleaned and disinfected.

Elizabeth Simmons, also an active unionist and Carolyn Walters's contemporary, also began to work at North shortly after it opened. She has since transferred to a non-ward part of South. At one point Mrs. Simmons used to be a steward, but quit because it involved too much work and conflict. She was always being pulled off her job to deal with one grievance or another. Because the number of grievances was growing, and because there was no one to relieve her and help out with her workload, she ran herself ragged.

The planners claimed that Duke North would be easier to clean than the old hospital, in part because of built-in cleaning devices, and in part because they felt its design would catch less dirt, and hence they expected to be able to do with fewer housekeepers.[23] Nevertheless, planners foresaw a need for some increase in staff when Duke North opened. Indeed, there is a built-in vacuum system throughout North, and there are vacuum trash and linen chutes on each floor. Housekeepers don't find them particularly helpful, though. They find vacuum hoses heavy and cumbersome, and most of the new cleaning aides, especially the linen chutes, "always broken." Then too, as Margaret Sims pointed out with respect to the new buildings in general, they are easier to clean because they are new, but if let slide, they are difficult to get back into shape. If that happens, a housekeeper's job becomes a real "bear."

Mrs. Bagley described her workload in the hospital years back as hard, but compared it favorably to current workloads at North. Then, each ward had a regular team and a relief team, each with a maid and janitor. She remembers arguments with the nursing staff when they tried to get the housekeepers to fill ice pitchers and perform other services that were not part of their jobs. But housekeeping supervisors backed up their workers and kept their jobs from getting too undefined. In a sense, such conflict is the other side of invisible administration when people try to coordinate those over whom they have no authority. Such conflicts are likely to become more acute when supervisors push workers to do their tasks more intensely, and tasks that are needed but not clearly assigned sometimes become straws that break the camel's back.

The total number of housekeepers responsible for cleaning Duke Medical Center does not seem to have kept pace with medical center growth. By my calculations, the approximately 285 housekeepers in 1976 grew to 390 with the opening of North in 1980, an increase of a little under 37 percent. However, between 1980 and 1983, the total number of housekeepers fell to 341, a decrease of some 12 percent. Housekeepers and their union do not have the statistics, but they know firsthand that they are working harder and that there are fewer of them. Older and younger workers shared a strong feeling that working conditions deteriorated seriously all over the medical center since the opening of Duke North, and that they have become especially bad in North. A Local 77 officer indicated that there were only 157 housekeeping people in Duke North, which has the vast majority of patient beds, whereas there were 180 in South with far fewer beds and much less intensive use.

Heavy workloads and intense surveillance—worst at North—are the primary grievances in housekeeping. However, in some ways housekeepers working North's inpatient units may have a more sociable job because they are in close contact with many workers and patients. There are more shifts of housekeepers, both day and evenings and weekends as well as weekdays, as well as a special crew that does heavy discharge cleaning. Sometimes, too, housekeepers become friendly with patients and console, comfort, and cheer many patients. The reverse of this familiarity however is housekeepers' concern about contagion and carrying sickness home to children and family.

The advantages of working in office and research areas seem to lie in much more autonomy and looser supervision, and those seem to be attractive to housekeepers with enough seniority to transfer. Margaret Sims works in one of the research buildings; before they were built, she worked in the hospital for eleven years. She has a great deal of seniority: "That's how I got away from the hospital." The work in the outlying buildings is easier, not least, according to Hattie Bagley, because "there's nobody behind you rushing you." A supervisor "can't afford to, he has eight buildings to cover!"

Both women like the autonomy they have in their work. Mrs. Sims commented that the people in the laboratories and offices she cleans deal directly with her when they want something instead of going to her supervisor. This helps her control the pace and rhythm of her work. Mrs. Bagley's daily round involves sweeping the floors, dusting, and emptying the trash baskets in all the laboratories and offices. Unionization has helped eliminate some of the job's occupational hazards. The dangers from broken glass and needles in the trash have been mitigated since the housekeepers and their union brought the matter to the attention of the health inspectors. Now, these things have to be put in sealed containers. Housekeepers also asked for and got radiation badges, which they turn in to be read every month. I asked both Mrs. Sims and Mrs. Bagley whether they had ever seen a printout of their readings; both said they had not.

Still, Mrs. Bagley, who is close to retirement, and Mrs. Sims, who has retired since I met her, have both seen their workloads increase a great deal since the late seventies, and they don't like it at all. Mrs. Sims worked in one of the newer, shinier, government-funded research laboratories, while Mrs. Bagley handles an entire floor of one of the oldest places in the medical center. Her area is crowded with a jumble of laboratories and offices and is filled with the dirt of almost constant reconstruction and renovation. All the research buildings have one cleaning shift, from 7 a.m. to 3:30 p.m., five days a week. No one cleans at night or on the weekends. If someone is sick, the others have to do their work

for them. There are no floaters or relief crew. Sometimes, if one building
is very short-staffed, someone can be pulled from another building to
spread the work around.

In her building, Mrs. Bagley remembers, there used to be a maid and
a janitor on each floor until about four or five years ago, when American
Hospital Supply arrived. They fired some workers, did not replace others
when they left, and soon had the work force reduced so that one person
alone cleans a whole floor. Mrs. Sims saw the staff of nine housekeepers
in her building shrink to six. "The work is much harder than it was then."
She and one man clean a whole floor, as well as a small adjoining laboratory building. The relief person who used to fill in when people took their
vacations is long gone. In two other large research buildings, there are
five housekeepers each, and Mrs. Bagley's estimate is that there are about
seventy-five rooms plus bathrooms on each floor.

The Work. Housekeepers distinguish between their work and their
working conditions. They take pride in the work, or at least would like
to. Family and waged work are part of the same category for Dee Stebbins.
"I clean offices, treatments rooms, bathrooms. It's pretty good . . . it's
work. Pretty good money; supports my babies and keeps me busy. . . . "
Dee learned the housekeeping skills she uses at home and at Duke from
her mother, and these fuse planning , decision making, and execution.
"When I was growing up, my mom taught me how to wash. . . . on my
hand. I did that for a long time before I got a washing machine. She
taught me how to clean a house. . . . I guess that came naturally cause I
don't like a nasty house. And I'll take this house apart, and when I get to
moving furniture and slinging things, everybody say. . . . she's cleaning
up, get out of her way. I learned to clean my house from my mom. See,
I use to sit down and see my mom take her house apart and clean it
up. . . . She'd take furniture off the walls, pull out everything. She'd have
my father take everything out of her living room if she wanted to mop it,
or if she was going to clean the carpet on her floor or something."

As in her work at home, Mrs. Stebbins takes responsibility for her
assigned rooms—they are *her* rooms. "My daily routine [at the hospital]
is pulling trash [emptying trash containers]. I pull trash every day; I do
my bathrooms everyday and my sinks everyday. . . . and my treatment
rooms. I do the sinks and the footstools in there every day [in the treatment rooms]. I do my offices once a week because they don't be as bad.
But my treatment rooms and bathrooms, I really have to get them every-

day. I high dust [around the doorframes, cabinet tops, and near the air ducts] sometimes twice a week, maybe three times. If I see it needs three times, I'll go three time, but if I see it just needs two a week, I'll do it twice a week. It's just like your house only it's bigger. You just do the routine things that you normally do, like your high dust.

"Tomorrow I won't have to come and work this hard on my sinks . . . . Today is Monday . . . we just coming back from the weekend, everything is a little hectic right now. Do all my general cleaning that I regularly do and tomorrow I'll take time. . . . I don't high dust tonight; I'll do that tomorrow."

Because she takes responsibility for keeping her area of the hospital clean, her work is also a source of pride, "The week that I was out of work. . . . they asked everybody, say, where is that lady at that keep everything so nice and shiny and clean?" Part of what allows Mrs. Stebbins to take pleasure in a job well done is that "I get a chance to work at my own pace." Her supervisor respects that autonomy. "She feel like if she have to be checking on her ladies all the time. . . . she won't get no work done."

Still, there are differences in specifics between one's home and the hospital. Dee's co-worker and her supervisor indicated the hospital priorities to her when she first started working. "When I came over here to work, they gave me the basic things that they knew that they would be fussing about like my stools and my sinks and keeping my outer bathrooms clean. . . . These sinks in these treatment rooms they are fussy about."

"The people over here are a team." Cynthia and Robert, Dee's co-workers on the floor, all work together. Robert usually works between the two women so "he can see me and her." Workers tell of assaults, rapes, and even murder that have happened in the hospital. Physical safety is a matter of some concern to Dee, much more so than caustic or dangerous chemicals. The two women are responsible for about twelve treatment rooms each; and each woman has fifteen or sixteen bathrooms to clean. Because these, unlike offices, need daily cleaning, this is a fairly heavy load if someone gets behind. "They not hard to clean when you do them every day like I do them. If you don't do them every day you run a strain of putting yourself in a strain."

When everyone is there, the working conditions are fine and allow for a good job. But people are sick, and everyone takes vacations. If Cynthia is out, Dee does the most pressing parts of her work, and Robert helps her. Or if both women are out, Robert does the work of all three. "If we didn't team together and help each other. . . . when we really need to help each other, things wouldn't be as nice as they are." Still, there is no real backup, and things are difficult when someone is on vacation. As a result, Dee Stebbins finds it hard to always do the kind of job that gives her (and those whose areas she cleans) satisfaction.

Factory or Plantation? Housekeeping workers are vocally unhappy about staffing levels throughout the medical center. Older workers remember "the plantation," and younger ones seem to be concentrated where work is heaviest. In Duke North, short-staffing is combined with what an efficiency expert might think of as close supervision, but what cleaning service workers see as harassment and constant surveillance, both to extract more work and to intimidate workers so they will not protest. Of late, for example, management has been accused of writing up workers in a variety of locations for "excessive absence," "abuse of sick leave," and for being away from their work area. Workers complain that they are written up even when they have doctors' notes or other legitimate reasons for being out.

To deal with the intimidating effects as well as to hold the line on staffing and hence workloads, Local 77 has been filing an increased number of grievances on behalf of workers for discipline without just cause. In all of 1983 they filed about 125 grievances, but in the first four and a half months alone of 1984, they filed 70. Union officers see Duke as deliberately forcing the union to go to arbitration (by refusing to resolve grievances at lower levels) on cases dealing with paid benefits, such as sick days and personal days. In 1983, Local 77 paid a high price for a more equitable pay distribution when they gave up pay for the first day of *each* sick leave, effectively wiping out compensation for short-term illness.[24]

The union regards such pressure as part of an overall management strategy to renege on past benefits and to curtail them in the future. As part of this attempt, Duke has pushed for workers to be contractually required to have a doctor's note in order to take any of their sick days. The union successfully resisted this attempt. Such a practice would make it difficult and expensive for a worker to exercise her contractual rights. It is also degrading: As Mrs. Sims noted, "A grown person *knows* when they sick." Still, such behavior is certainly in tune with businesses' attack on workers' benefits on a national scale. Duke's change in when they pay housekeeping service workers may also be seen as part of this trend. Pay checks used to be distributed in the morning so that workers could deposit or cash them on their lunch or break times. Duke claimed that workers were "abusing the privilege" of taking time to go to the bank and began holding their checks until the end of the shift. But, as both Hattie Bagley and Margaret Sims argue, people's lunches and breaks are their own time, and you can't be accused of abusing your own time.

By the 1980's, many senior housekeepers and Local 77 activists saw the gains, for which they had fought so hard, under serious attack. It seemed racist as well as plain mean to them for Duke to come down hardest on those at the bottom. But the institution has long practiced giving the smallest percentage raises to those at the lowest levels. In the mid-eighties, with no grass-roots movement to sustain activism, service workers hold dearly to the legal protections that collective bargaining and a union grievance procedure affords. This is their channel for resistance. It is not a very public one though, and workers can see its limits. Arbitration is expensive and a fairly private affair when handled as standard union business; the local is small and poor and separated from another large group of workers with whom they share much of their history of resistance: dietary workers.

If You Can't Take the Heat

There are two kitchens in New South Medical Center, each with its own cafeteria.[25] Today, South serves breakfast and lunch to about 2,500 people a day in the cafeteria and prepares food for the two or three hundred inpatients on South's wards. The kitchen at South dates from the days when kitchens were built for cooking real food from scratch. It is hot and steamy, and the floors are often wet and slippery from steamers that always seem to be dripping.

In contrast, the kitchen in the Duke North basement feeds most of the inpatients, most of the employees from the medical center and the nearby affiliated hospitals, and most of the visitors to the medical center. Workers prepare about three thousand servings of each of three meals a day. The Duke North kitchen was designed for state-of-the-art, late-twentieth-century thawing and heating of processed foods. Scrambled eggs, for example, are a "prepackaged egg product" that is purchased frozen. Cooks thaw it, pour it on a griddle, cook it until it is slightly set, and put it in a large storage/serving pan for cold storage until it is to be served the following day. When North opened, the original plan was to cook everything several days ahead, but that plan did not work. Patient food is prepared a day ahead of time now, but food served in the cafeteria is cooked the same day that it is served.

I was prepared to see a mammoth operation, especially at Duke North. Instead, I was baffled at the tiny cooking area I saw in the main production kitchen. I saw only two ovens and not too much more range space than might be found in the homes of wealthy cooking buffs. When I visited, three cooks were working in that tiny area. It was generally acknowledged that it was difficult for them to coordinate their work so they could all use what they needed when necessary.

The kitchen itself is quite large, it's just that the cooking area gets lost in the middle of things. I took space allocation as an indication of the relative importance of cooking compared to food processing and assembly. Most of the space around the kitchen's perimeter is taken up with flash freezers (largely unused), coolers and supply rooms, and offices. The center of the area is filled with long metal preparation tables where salads, desserts, and precooked foods are plated, "assembled," and loaded onto large metal rolling carts for freezing or cold storage.

The Marriott Corporation manages Duke's kitchens, and according to workers, has done so since the early 1970s. Duke North's kitchen is definitely designed for factorylike production of meals. Although most food preparation is done in the production kitchen downstairs, there is a fair amount of cooking in a smaller kitchen upstairs in the cafeteria. There, custom sandwiches are prepared, and grill cooking is done. Some convenience foods, like precooked lasagna and fried chicken, may also be prepared in the cafeteria. There are managers for the cafeteria and the production kitchen in both Duke North and South.

Menus are complex and varied. First, the introduction of so-called convenience foods brought with it an expanded number of choices for both inpatient and cafeteria foods. Second, cooking for a hospital necessarily means cooking for special diets from low or no salt, fat, and starch to more complex modifications of basic dishes, to specific combinations of foods on a tray. Patients in the hospital have an opportunity to choose among two or three meats, maybe four vegtables, and a variety of desserts and salads. Cafeteria customers have greater variety including fast foods like hot dogs, hamburgers, club sandwiches, and a salad bar.

From a traditional management perspective, food production starts with dieticians, who plan meals for a six-week period and give the plans to the managers of each kitchen and each cafeteria.

Managers translate dietitians' menus into numbers of servings they expect to need for each item in each meal based on the popularity of particular menus, and then they make up "production sheets" for their supervisors. The supervisors then break these down into specific tasks to be assigned to specific cooks, salad, or pre-prep workers. Different supervisors are in charge of different parts of the menu and different groups of workers.

Cooks, for example, generally prepare several versions of a variety of dishes at each meal. They may start with a basic dish and prepare one batch with salt and another batch without it, or they may use different sauces. The production sheet for a cook at one lunch gave some indication of the variety of tasks involved; it included responsibility for five pimento cheese sandwiches, fifteen hamburgers, brocolli and cauliflower, slicing ham, slicing cheese to be used in a chef salad, two kinds of soup, steaks, and regular and pureed green beans.

A cook's schedule tells her how many servings she is responsible for preparing; she is expected to know, for example, how many servings she can get from a piece of meat or a pan of vegetables. "If they gave us a slip which said they wanted 400 servings of roast beef or whatever kind of meat we had, but we was there when all the food that they didn't use would come back to the kitchen. We would see that. We were supposed to look at that and check it. Well, the next day when they said they wanted 400 servings, we would give them 350. We'd always have some cut and if they ran out, they would come back to the kitchen."

Pre-prep workers are linked to the cooks. They prepare meats, cut up and pan poultry, grind onions, clean celery, and prepare vegetables for the cooks. They also slice meat or vegetables, slice and grate cheese, weigh these items into servings, and lay each on paper for storage in the cooler or put them into bins that go to women who assemble plates. All foods, including servings for special diets, have their appropriate places in the walk-in coolers.

Patient food is prepared by food service aides who work in the tray unit. They work in the main kitchen at four or five long tables with bins of food down the middle containing the entrees, vegetables, and desserts. Each woman has her schedule of plates to prepare. She puts these into microwave serving dishes. Drinks and dry goods are packaged in another area of the tray unit. Salads are added at another table, where the schedules indicate what is to be put into each salad. These are all loaded onto large rolling trucks (carts actually) for galley technicians to transport upstairs to the units. Each food service aide is responsible for assembling all the parts into the full meal ordered by the patients for whom she is responsible. Every day at breakfast she takes their orders for the next day's meals and passes them on to the manager to begin the process of making the coming day's round of production sheets.

There are a variety of dietary service job titles, from the reassuringly familiar "cook" to the baffling "dietary technicians," with various kinds of dietary aides and technicians in between. The lines between these jobs, or those between cooking and assembly, seem no clearer in kitchen practice than they are in offices, clinics, or wards. One woman's work as a senior dietary service aide fixing patient trays seems to take her all over the map. "I had two trucks to fill up every day and sometimes three, three and a half. And I had to prepare all of the food. . . . well, over half of the food myself. Like cole slaw. If I had 120 servings, I had to go in the box; I had to get a case of cabbage. I had to cut them and put them in the sink to clean them, put them through the grater, grate them, then mix the cole slaw dressing up in them. And that was just one thing. OK, I had. . . . all this other like desserts. . . . I may have to bake cobblers sometimes. . . . I had like these two sheets of paper that had maybe eight things on each page for me to do. And I had that and I had this other sheet of paper that was the breakfast truck. . . . that was just for dinner. The breakfast truck was a different story. I had to get these little boxes of cereals, fix fruit cocktail. . . . it was just details, all them details. . . . I hated them." This woman resented the fragmentation of work into disconnected, therefore meaningless, tasks.

Many food service workers saw their work as the combination of mental and cooking skills involved in creating and serving a meal. It was that sense of their work that motivated them, but all too often they found that the reward system of assembly-line meals was at cross-purposes with their own sense of a good job.

Several women commented that they enjoyed making patients happy, that they took pride in fixing good food and good-looking plates. "You do it for them. Cause they're sick and they can't help themselves and they appreciate things like that. Well people coming through the lines buying their lunch, they appreciate the food tasting good and looking good and how you serve it to them. . . . that makes the person buying it feel good and make you feel good serving them that way. That's the way you have to go along. You have to have pride in your job."

Assembly-Line Management and Deteriorating Conditions. Dietary workers are caught increasingly between their pride in craft and working conditions that deprive them of both the sources of creativity and the time to do a good job. "It's been a lot of pressure and stress since Marriott been there. They believe in you working every second of the minute." "You know Duke is in something now that they say the budget's so low they don't want any overtime." As in environmental services, workers in dietary also report people being disciplined and suspended for lateness of even a few minutes.

Older workers remember when there used to be more staff, when the load was lighter, and when there was more encouragement to help one another. One woman in her mid-thirties, who started work in the late seventies, a few years after Marriott began to run the kitchen, and whose mother-in-law had worked there long ago, talked about the closeness among workers, "That's where all the extended families came from back in that era. Everybody had sisters, play brothers, children. You know that they just had a good time." Now people are discouraged from helping one another on their own initiative.

Mrs. Shirley Rice has worked in the kitchen for long enough to have taken part in the big 1968 walkout. She remembers that walkout and another one, a very short and sweet walkout not long after that when Duke tried to make cooks wash their own pots. Management told Mrs. Rice that the pot man had too much work to do, and that cooks would henceforth have to wash their own pots. Shirley immediately announced to the kitchen, "We supposed to wash the pots y'all; let's go!" And they walked out into the hall. "And that man had to come out there in the hall and apologize and tell us we didn't have to wash our own pots." Today, cooks and diet technicians have been given additional cleaning duties. For years after the "pots and pans" walkout, "The heavy duty cleaning, they had people that did that daily. But now they said it's our jobs. And [my supervisor] was saying if you can't do it in eight hours you just stay nine, but you punch out, but you only get paid for eight." In recent years, there have been fewer relief people throughout dietary, so that when someone is out, others have to somehow share their workload. "People are now doing two and three schedules. When I first went to work there and worked in the same section that I'm working in now, it was three people out there. One person is doing it now."

Top-down management and assembly-line organization mean that workers do not know in advance what their specific daily tasks will be; they get new schedules each day. "But it's nothing to go by because whenever I go in, whoever is not there . . . he [the manager] tries to be tactful with me, 'will you do me a favor?' Sure, what is it? 'Mrs. D.'s not coming in today, could you do her schedule for me; do you think you can handle that?'" "I don't say nothing. . . . It'll be a big confrontation; you're failing to accept your responsibility and this is a major infraction. He'll try to play it by the book so you'll be suspended for three days."

Workers see Marriott managers as trying to take total control over their time and how they use it so that they can make them work as hard as possible. "I can do more in the morning time than I can in the evening time—after lunch. That's the reason why I don't take my lunch. . . . [til] maybe even 1:00. Cause when I come back from lunch it's not going to be that much work out of me. That's just the way I am. I can go in there in the morning and do the whole schedule in three hours. But don't say that I'm not doing an eight-hour job if I'm doing the same thing that it takes somebody else eight and a half hours to do."

"They said if you get through with your work in three hours then you go to do some more. If they scheduled this schedule for eight hours, this is what's supposed to be done in an eight-hour period, and it don't take you but thirty minutes to do it, the work is done if it's done satisfactory. That's it. But [if] they don't think this is an eight-hour block of work, then how the hell do you time what's eight hours?"

Dietary managers, like housekeeping services, seem to be trying to take back some of the key benefits that workers have won in the last decades. Ironically, health benefits are felt to be eroding particularly fast. "Like Blue Cross and Blue Shield. At first they were paying everything. Then they stopped and started charging us $2 every two weeks, and since then it's up to $75 every two weeks. They got the sick time benefits where they're supposed to give you twelve days a year sick leave, five days a year family emergency, and now I've heard recently, I don't know whether it's accurate or not, that unless you have twelve days stored up, you can't get any of the benefits."

Part-time workers get *no* benefits. The cafeteria at South is closed evenings, weekends, and holidays, "Everybody in the cafeteria except four people are part-time at South. They're not open on the weekend nor holidays, so that makes everybody part-time." There are therefore no benefits. "If you out sick, you're just out sick. You can get a vacation, but it'll be on your own expense."

Unacknowledged Knowledge. Kitchen workers exercise a fair amount of planning and trouble-shooting in meal preparation. With some frequency cooks and other dietetics workers are in the position of secretaries and ward secretaries: To do their job, they have to exercise skills for which they are not paid, and for which they might be punished rather than rewarded.

One woman took Barbara Taylor, her interviewer, through her area of the kitchen in the North cafeteria. Explaining that she had to decide what to cook as a backup in the event that there was a shortage of a particular food, she showed Taylor a supply of extra vegetables she could cook if there were not enough of the dish she was assigned. It is her responsibility to come up with a substitute whenever they run out. She said that they were likely to be short on lasagna that day because the management had not taken into account that "lasagna is on special. . . . so we don't have enough of this so I'm going to do some pepper steaks we'll use in place." Both are convenience foods. The pepper steak is constructed from pre-formed hamburger patties to which a sauce, made in the downstairs production kitchen is added. "I can just about judge what we're going to need for tonight."

Shirley Rice created at least one recipe for Marriott when they first started managing at Duke, but she has never been compensated for any recipes. Over the years Mrs. Rice has gotten increasingly disgusted at how workers' knowledge is denigrated. "I used to tell them how many cases I need, cause I know what I needed; but they might give you some and they might not. And they might shoot off their big lip." Now she tells them nothing and takes whatever is given, even if she knows it is the wrong amount for what she needs. "I got enough to worry about besides Duke. We ain't supposed to know nothing." All information is supposed to go from the top down. Cooks are supposed to do only what they're told.

To add insult to injury, food service workeres cannot help but notice the amount of food that is wasted, and who is blamed for it. "They always talking about Duke is in the red. Yet and still, they throw away tons of food. And that's the budget right there. . . . They want to say black people taking the stuff, but white people's taking the stuff. They doing it to their own selves." "Yet they don't want the cooks to eat even a sandwich. . . . One time they weren't supposed to taste the food. . . . They throw away enough food each day to feed everybody in dietetics a sandwich."

Ostensibly, the priorities in dietary place patient food at the head of the list. Cooks are supposed to prepare patient food for the next day before they do the cafeteria food for the current day. Yet, when there are conflicts between getting food to cafeteria patrons and to patients, food service workers are often yelled at by managers in charge of each operation. "Nine times out of ten," said one disenchanted worker, "they say well do the cafeteria, cause the patients can wait. They gon' be there."

Not-So-Convenient Foods. Frozen or otherwise processed items that can be prepared quickly have become necessary to menu planning. "Look like it should be easier. But all together, it's no difference. We work just as hard." Most fresh vegetables appear only in salads and soups. Patients are said to be served considerably less fresh fruits and vegetables than cafeteria customers. Patient vegetables are frozen, as are just about all desserts and dessert mixes. Sauces and fruit salads are generally canned. To one worker's palate, "Well, it's not as good as our home made cooking you know, but. . . . it's not bad either." With the new technology built into the kitchen at North, convenience foods are a necessity. "We have to use that convenience. This place is not equipped with the things that we need to just cook everything from scratch, like we had when we was over at South." The new kitchen was planned to rely heavily on precooked, frozen foods and on throw-away plates, trays, and utensils, consequently the dishwashing area is relatively small.

Patient food used to be prepared several days ahead of time and flash frozen for storage until it was ready to heat in microwave ovens on the wards. The original plan was to have patient foods cooked three days in advance. When that did not work because it was too difficult to plan so far ahead, Marriott management moved to two days, and now cooking is done one day ahead. New patients are coming in constantly, and Marriott found that they had the wrong amounts of all sorts of items and would have to do a great deal of last minute thawing and cooking.

There were also major problems getting food to inpatients at South. Originally, *all* patient food was cooked at North. Meals destined for South patients were loaded onto large carts and taken by galley techs over to South each mealtime. The trays were popped into microwave ovens that had been newly installed on the wards. There were problems with the galleys, and even more serious problems transporting heavy trucks from one building to another three times a day.

"They come up with all these brilliant ideas, and they're white. You can't tell them it's not gon' work, cause we supposed not to have this kind of knowledge, right?. . . . Anybody know you don't be carrying food (if you have to in an emergency situation then yes, but for a daily routine) for three meals, you don't. Trucks turn over. These little carts they turn over; the food be all messed up, and you got a whole ward full of people and they be looking for something to eat and their food is turned over on a truck. . . . But they had to go through this for two, three months before they could realize that this is not going to work." Now South kitchen prepares food for South's inpatients.

There have also been problems with the food itself, and this has caused the kitchen to back away somewhat from processed foods. First, there are problems of supply. Most of the items come from out of town and do not always arrive on time. Second, many of the products are unpalatable; there is no point using them if they must be tinkered with too much.

Given the amount of labor that has gone into finding and preparing processed foods, it hardly seems right to call them convenience foods. Several people pointed to what happened the first time they used a pre-cooked egg product in the wards. It tasted awful and turned green in the microwaves. The dieticians and workers had to do a great deal of shopping to find a decent brand, and even more experimenting to find a workable technique for precooking and microwaving. At present, the staff is experimenting with the processed food market to find new products and techniques. They have to, there is just no room to cook in that kitchen. At present some fifty processed, convenience foods are being used, and kitchen managers are on the lookout for local suppliers.

There have been other problems with the kitchen technology. When the kitchen was built, somehow drains were neglected. There is one in the production area and another near the room's periphery, but the floor was not built to be drained easily. These problems became apparent when a pipe burst late on a Saturday night. The water took many hours to clean up, but, more significantly, it put the freezers out of use temporarily and destroyed many frozen meals.

Convenience cooking is neither easy nor cheap. The hardware, from microwaves to carts and freezers, is a heavy fixed expense, and the products themselves are an ongoing one. The priorities of industrial cooking in the age of monopoly seem to be to put the money into fixed expenses and intense supervision of workers more than into hiring workers to be paid to exercise their skills and experience.

There has indeed been a supervisor explosion with the advent of assembly-line food production. Virtually all the supervisors in dietary have come from the ranks, and this has meant that many more black women are in supervisory positions. The trend seems to have begun in the wake of food service worker organizing and to have had a co-optive aspect as well as a concessionary one. The problem is that supervisor is about the only promotion available to the black women who work in the kitchen. Some simply do not want to be supervisors, and there are senior dietary workers who remain in their position, despite their abilities and desire for more money and responsibility, because they refuse to become management.

There are also said to be more than a few black college graduates stuck in the kitchen despite their mighty efforts to transfer up and out. As we have seen, there is widespread feeling among black workers that they are blocked by discrimination in Duke's employment office and others responsible for hiring. Several women in food service told of having applied repeatedly for clerical and technical positions with no success.

Speedup and Social Control

The use of management subcontracting with its associated factory-like organization and pacing of work has become increasingly common as hospitals face greater financial pressure. Dietary and housekeeping workers complain of increased workloads, more intense supervision, and greater use of punitive measures from Marriott, American Hospital Supply, and Duke to force them to work harder, all things from a factorylike model of how to raise production without raising labor costs. Patterns of work-force growth confirm housekeepers' perceptions of speedup. Between 1976 and 1983, the number of housekeeper and floor finisher jobs increased from about 313 to about 375, an increase of 20 percent. In the interim, a whole new nine-story hospital was built. In 1980, just after Duke North opened, there were about 435 housekeepers and floor finishers. There seems, by my calculations, to have been a 14 percent staffing cut in the next three years. The food service staff, on the other hand, grew by about 19 percent between 1976 and 1983, although workers argue that there are now two kitchens and growth has not kept pace with the greater amount and variety of foods served.

Dietary and housekeeping workers also complain about their managers' encroachments on time over which workers had gained some control. These include efforts to undermine and take back some of the sickness and holiday benefits Local 77 negotiated, use of forced and perhaps uncompensated overtime in the kitchen, and ironically for a hospital, possibly eroding employee health benefits. These measures are relatively new assertions of management rights to extend its scope of decision making to *non*-work time. Two of Local 77's major victories were to establish defined tasks and working hours for nonunion as well as for unionized service workers and to make their boundaries the subject of mutual negotiation in the case of unionized workers. Housekeeping and dietary workers argue that both these gains are being assaulted, and that management is trying to reassert open-ended rights to their labor, a throwback to paternalistic working relationships under advanced industrial conditions and management by monopolies.

The trends in the dietary and housekeeping departments toward intensification of labor through tight and punitive supervision, automation, routinization, and rationalization of tasks are the most visible changes. They seem to reinforce the idea that industrialization and mass production have to follow an assembly-line model of ever more finely divided labor, de-skilling of the work process, and the degradation of labor.[26] Service jobs are decreasing as a proportion of the health-care work force, making black workers especially more vulnerable and weakening the positions of hospital unions. Changes in clerical, technical, and nursing work discussed in the next chapter go in the opposite direction and suggest instead that de-skilling and routinization are neither necessary developments nor linear ones.[27] Here, both up- and down-skilling seem to be taking place simultaneously and in an ad hoc and opportunistic way. Much of the randomness, however, may be the surface appearance of management's efforts to exercise all available opportunities to control and reshape a work force that developed in flush times.

NOTES

1. American Management Assn. 1957; Committee on Economic Development, 1973; Ellwood, 1982; Eilers, 1974; "Employee Benefits," 1976; "Health Costs," 1882; Relman, 1984; Thurow, 1984; "The Upheaval in Health Care," 1983; Yaggy and Anlyan, 1982.

2. Ellwood, 1982; Edmondson, 1985; "The Robust New Business," 1983; Sekscenski, 1984.

3. Cahan, 1985.

4. "The Upheaval in Health Care," 1983:45.

5. Ibid.

6. Ibid.; "A Nursing Home Drive," 1983:46.

7. Sekscenski, 1984:5–8.

8. Davis, 1982:67; Ellwood, 1982:95–102; Carnoy and Koo, 1975:602; Garbarino, 1960:9, 88–95.

9. Carnoy and Koo, 1975; Salmon, 1975.

10. Colloton, 1982; Relman, 1984.

11. "Duke Hospital to Hold the Line on the Rates," *Intercom*, May 11, 1984.

12. Cahan, 1985; Relman, 1984; Thurow, 1984; Cohn, 1985.

13. Madden et al., 1982:167–68, 172; U.S. Department of Health and Human Services, 1982:112; Sekscenski, 1984:2–4.

14. Sekscenski, 1981:1, 5–6, 10.

15. Eilers, 1974:5.

16. Himmelstein and Woolhandler, 1984:24.

17. Becker, Sloan, and Steinwald, 1982:11.

18. Himmelstein and Woolhandler, 1984:24

19. Teitelman, 1984; *The Executive Letter*, 1984.

20. Teitelman, 1984.

21. Sacks, forthcoming; *The Executive Letter*, 1984; Institute of Medicine, 1983.

22. Pachino, 1982:14. My information of subcontracting is incomplete. It is an area that management interviews would no doubt have clarified.

23. American Health Facilities, 1973:55.

24. *Duke Chronicle*, July 6, 1983.

25. Most of the material in this section is from observation and interviews conducted by Barbara Taylor in 1983.

26. Braverman, 1974.

27. Sabel, 1982.

8

Technologists, Nurses and Clericals

Unlike dietary and housekeeping, the number and job titles of RNs, medical technologists, and therapists increased greatly during the lean years after the mid-seventies, suggesting there may be ways for institutions to adapt other than the "Fordist model."[1] This chapter focuses on jobs that seem to have been upgraded, or at least not "Fordized," and explores the consequences for women who have been long-term clerical, technical, and nursing workers at Duke.

Credentialing in Allied Health

Health-care professionals in the medical center seem to be making significant gains against the economic tide. At Duke, activists thought this may have been an unintended consequence of the hospital's efforts to build up a college-educated, white work force to counterbalance black and white union sentiment. Whatever the reason, between 1976 and 1983, there was a drop in the percentage of LPNs, most of whom were black, and a more than compensating expansion of white RNs, a decrease in technicians and technologists trained on the job, and an increase in technologists and therapists with college degrees. There has been an increased emphasis on schooling and credentialing for practice throughout the nursing and allied health professions, making the organized professions the immediate antagonists of nondegreed practitioners.

Nevertheless, the medical center runs a wide variety of allied health programs including ones for physician assistants, health administration, medical technology, and cytotechnology. Since 1975, "increasing emphasis is being given to degree programs."[2] One of the differences between degree and certification programs is that very high regular university tuition is charged in the former, and much lower fees for the latter, no doubt an important economic consideration in tight financial times.

Caroline Bennett administered one of the allied health certificate programs. In her building, there were several such programs with more than one hundred students. Her particular program has two tracks, a basic program with twelve students and an advanced one with eight. Most students were women and all were white, although a recent class had two black men. In contrast, most of the technicians in the hospital who have learned their craft on the job are black. There were black applicants to the program, Bennett told me, but they were rejected because they did not have high enough grade point averages and their English was not to Duke's liking.

As Caroline Bennett sees it, the bias is toward book learning and toward middle-class students even in the certificate programs, which do not involve taking a bachelor's degree. Duke wants to train "supertechs" as it calls them. After completing the basic program, students can take an optional extra year for an advanced certificate. This gives them access to chief technologist and other management positions as well as familiarity with working on modern equipment in medical research. This program is also affiliated with a private, white college, so that students there can be certified at Duke at the same time that they earn a bachelor's degree at their own school. The prevailing attitude among the allied health staff that Caroline sees is that community colleges can train the people who do the work; Duke wants success in training management personnel and academic contributors to the field. "They've got to realize they need people who know their stuff; good solid people who enjoy their work."

Caroline provided an example of the class bias and elitism in her program's orientation. Vocational Rehabilitation, a federal program that provides career counseling and financial assistance to students who do not have regular diplomas, has tried to persuade Duke to accept its students. But Duke, in Caroline's experience, has an unwritten policy that such students will not be able to complete the program. "They hang it on working class people's alleged inability to relate to high class patients and staff." Caroline cited an example of a twenty-three-year-old woman with five children whom Vocational Rehabilitation succeeded in placing in the program. Although Vocational Rehabilitation paid Duke to provide the woman with a tutor from the outset, those in charge of the program did not do so until the woman was clearly failing her work. "Then, when it was too late, they got a tutor." The woman did not succeed in the program.

Lack of money is also a problem for black and poor students. Caroline found that many black students have difficulty getting Basic Educational Opportunity Grants (BEOG) and GI funds. There is no internal financial aid for students in this program.

Many GIs have had training in emergency medical care in the military, and the present working class, primarily black technicians in the hospital, certainly have a great deal of training and practical experience in their fields. According to Caroline, the Duke program assigns no credit for such practical experience. Caroline explained that students can take a challenge examination to bypass some of the work, but this measures book learning rather than the more practical strengths of these potential students.

Caroline was her own clerical support for the program and typed all teaching, program administration, and staff professional materials. She kept the budget, handled the telephone and correspondence, and set up student interviews, visits, and tours. In large part because she was not impressed with allied health's elitist recruiting policies, Caroline created a program for recruiting high school students and students from community and technical schools in the area. She made the contacts and got the program started. Working with her boss, she persuaded the Allied Health Education administration to accept the recruiting program as a way to remedy the high dropout rate and small number of applications they were receiving. "There was a lot of room where you could create things to do." Not least was counseling students, many of whom were fresh from high school. Caroline also did research on sources of financial aid, handled all the campus tours, and set up the lecture program for student orientation.

"It's dangerous to write this into your job description, especially at that salary. I would've stayed there forever and ever if I could have been paid more—much more." Nevertheless, Caroline saw program needs, and she found that creating opportunities to fill them was a rewarding aspect of her job. When she arrived, the program was not staffed to provide for student needs. There was a guidance counsellor on the staff, Caroline explained, but "what she did was give a personality test and went to Health Administration school the rest of the time." When this woman left, several people were interviewed, but none were hired as a replacement. The deans of Allied Health Education wanted someone with an M.A.

degree and experience. Caroline, who has a B. A. degree, was doing the job this woman had been hired to do, but not getting paid for it.

Within the framework of her own program, Caroline's relations with her supervisors were excellent. After she'd been there six months, she asked for a raise and presented a list of "how things were when I found them, and how they are now, and how they got that way." She was at the top of her pay scale, but Caroline fell victim to the credentialing notion of professionalization. Although she did professional and administrative work, Duke did not pay her for it because she had only a B. A. So Caroline left the job to return to the graduate program from which she had taken a leave.

These trends in allied health have affected many long-time workers at Duke in a negative way. Senior technicians like Betty Riggsbee, who learned their craft by apprenticeship, are being displaced by younger technicians and technologists with more formal schooling. To add insult to injury, it is often the older workers who have to train the new ones in daily practice and hospital routines. There are also technicians and LPNs who came to Duke in the sixties and early seventies, who benefited from federally funded, nonbaccalaureate training programs in allied health fields. These workers too find their mobility blocked by the inflation of schooling requirements and the discounting of practical craft experience. To black workers in this position, it seems that all their efforts to break out of the cooking and cleaning straitjacket are being undone. And it doesn't seem very different to white technicians.

Betty Riggsbee, who is white, talked of the problems of uncertified "old-timers" who had trained on the job and who were being uprooted by the changes in laboratory work. "We used to have a supervisor in each lab. Now it's no longer so. The supervisors are not in the lab, so the responsibility's put on you. At Duke North, two supervisors are on call, but they're in their own office. You're responsible for maintenance on your machine, and you do all you can before you call them. Supervisors used to work in the lab. Ours works; she orders supplies, does benchwork, and scheduling. The head supervisor only does benchwork on weekends, and so do the two other supervisors.

"I like all phases of my job. The thing I dislike is working weekends, working the new hospital, and going out on the wards. But you have no choice; you have no choice. There are no labs left with an 8:30–5, five-day week schedule.

"I'm caught between the devil and the deep blue sea. The reason I've stayed is that I'm a local person, married, with a family. You need to build up your benefits, sick leave. The pension's not so good. I can't move; I have one child in college and a fifteen year old. I like the doctors; they're good to me. I like Duke. I wish though I'd been a secretary because of the hours. I don't think I'd really like secretarial work—sitting at a typewriter. If my kids were educated, I'd leave and try to find a part-time job somewhere."

Betty is angry at being trapped by changes in hospital policy, by the emphasis on schooling for advancement, by the emphasis on specialized medicine, and by the hospital's insistence that technicians be moved about to fit the particular needs of high tech medicine. These changes play havoc with the ways she had developed over the years to mesh her home and work lives.

She had a great deal of seniority at Duke, knew her job well, and was not the only person in this position who feels that Duke is taking advantage of their skills by adding responsibilities without adding rewards. Mrs. Riggsbee found herself victimized by what she'd been led to believe were benefits. She was reluctant to leave the small pension Duke provides, and her lack of a college degree and school certification limited her chances for a job or better schedule at another medical facility. "I'd have to leave the field." Betty has since left Duke. She tried a secretarial job and discovered that, as she suspected, she didn't like it. However, she managed to find a job at a smaller hospital where she can work regular hours and practice the craft she enjoys.

Lucille Davis is one of a small group of black women who are medical technologists, "non-certified." One day she received a slip with her new classification; "last year I was a med tech. The only difference between a med tech and a technologist is pay." The pay is about level 8, and is one of the highest paying jobs black women on the hourly payroll hold.

When Lucille started working in her laboratory, it consisted of herself and her boss, the doctor who now heads the unit. They worked side by side, handling all the tests, doing various procedures and x-rays. It was the beginning of a close working relationship that has lasted almost twenty-five years. When her boss had hard times getting grants and had no money to hire researchers, Mrs. Davis worked on the research; when times were flush, she went back to clinical work.

In the last decade or so, the laboratory's clinical work has grown a great deal with the addition of medical fellows, "the more fellows, the more work I get to do. I guess I could've had more help if I pushed for it." There used to be two technicians in the laboratory, but the other woman died and was not replaced. Lucille feels she can handle the work, even

though there is a great deal. Only one of the five or so major tests she
runs needs immediate attention, but these need to be scheduled in advance, so she knows when they will be needed and can plan her work.
She can plan in advance how to pace her week for the rest of the tests.

The biggest requirement for performing smoothly is cooperation from
and with others. Lucille has good relationships with the technicians who
draw blood and good working relations with the DTOs on the wards who
schedule the tests, so when she gets her requests, she can line up the
technicians to do drawing.

Just about everything in her lab is still done manually, not because
Mrs. Davis is old-fashioned—she's asked for new machines—but because
old machines are the type her boss knows how to work. Sometimes this
has been hazardous to Lucille's health. She had to fuss several years ago
to get an electric pipette for dangerous substances. She used to use a
regular pipette—a glass measuring tube that is used like a straw—until
she burned her mouth and refused to use it any more.

To me, her job sounded quite dangerous—working with blood from
people with hepatitis and tuberculosis that was not always labeled as
such. "Maybe a week later you get a slip saying it was hepatitis." Lucille
agreed that there were a fair amount of unnecessary hazards and that she
had to be alert for her own health.

Mrs. Davis likes her job and is less worried about the health hazards
than she is about what Duke is doing to the opportunities of black workers. She feels that all the emphasis on schooling and certification is block-
ing their mobility. She pointed to a new hospital administrator hired
recently specifically to cut costs, noting that his main priority is to get a
more professional staff and to cut back the number of "nonprofessional"
workers, especially noncertified technicians. He was alleged to have said
that they are earning too much. What it adds up to in Lucille's analysis
is that they "want to get rid of the black workers." She sees speed-ups
and layoffs affecting those at the bottom of the pay scale most, and there
is quantitative evidence to support her perception. In her own laboratory,
she is seeing an increase in interpersonal racism on the part of the doctors
and administrative secretaries she encounters. "Things are going back to
the sixties" in behavior.

Mrs. Davis illustrated what she meant by telling me about an ongoing
problem she was trying to resolve. Because of her combinations of skill
and seniority, Lucille Davis has a great deal of autonomy in her work.
She has consistently gotten outstanding evaluations, not only from the
department head, but also from the man who now runs the laboratory.

As the department has grown, so have extra layers of administration including the addition of one administrative assistant whose unpopularity has also grown by leaps and bounds. This woman has been trying to force Lucille to work the assigned hours, but because she is unwilling to talk to her directly, she leaves memos with orders on Lucille's desk, after Lucille has left for the day so she does not have to speak to her. This infuriates Lucille; "I cuss her out." The woman is not her supervisor and is exceeding her authority, and Lucille believes that the woman's avoidance is racist.

The conflict centers on how much control Mrs. Davis has over her work. She and the head of the laboratory agree that she should have the flexibility to schedule her time as she sees fit. When she leaves early, she often comes in evenings and does not request overtime. Lucille puts in her forty hours, often more, and gets her work done. "Duke don't give me anything; I give to Duke." When Lucille goes on vacation, her work accumulates until she returns, "I'm the only one who can do the work." Lucille has fared relatively well in the department, although she recognizes that there is a great deal of unfairness there, and that much of it is directed against black workers.

The head of her department has begun to turn over departmental administration to his second-in-command, who, Lucille says, is another note-writer, but who has someone else write and deliver the notes. Mrs. Davis finds this bureaucratic style a facade for lack of respect and racism. She contrasted it with the old departmental chair, who talked to employees directly and ironed out problems when they occurred by bringing the parties together to deal with them.

Patricia Pendergast, another senior black medical technologist (also noncertified) in a different laboratory, has not fared nearly so well as Mrs. Davis. The racism she described is less subtle. Mrs. Pendergast has worked her way up against many odds. She started work more than twenty years ago in the kitchen, where she became one of the first black cashiers at Duke. From there she moved to the laboratories as an assistant, washing glassware. As she learned about her work, she move up to become a laboratory technician. She has an excellent work record and has received promotions consistently. It has not been easy. Patricia had to go back and finish high school after her child was born, and she has always encouraged women in similar circumstances to do likewise.

The head of her particular laboratory, and her direct boss, believes in scientific management and certification. Since he came to the lab, Patricia explained, he has made her life very difficult; he has told her that she is not qualified to be a technologist, and that she should be looking for another job. She recalled that her boss told her that she is not qualified for the job because she lacks formal schooling, and that she is making too much money for a person who hadn't been to college. Patricia fumed about this, explaining that she didn't go to college because her parents were poor. "I'm working so my son *can* go. You want to move up when you move, and not *lose* money." She feels her boss is also racist; he told her that she should go back to the kitchen because it's more suitable for her. Mrs. Pendergast is particularly exasperated because she has taught other technicians and has had to teach various doctors and interns one thing or another. She likes this part of the job and is good at it. To protect herself, she learned still more. Another black woman who worked with her tutored her nightly in a variety of new procedures.

Several years ago, her boss's harassment and threats to fire her became so severe that she had to take a month's leave for hypertension and nerves. Things got so stressful that Patricia filed a grievance against her supervisor. As a result of her successful action, she kept her job and had all the man's negative write-ups removed from her record.

Both Lucille and Patricia are strong union supporters and identify unambiguously with black workers, both on the basis of their treatment and on their own work histories. Their upward mobility has been part of the successes of collective efforts led by workers with whom they have close ties both in their laboratories and outside of the medical center.

The large majority of RNs, technologists, and therapists at Duke are at the beginnings of their careers; they have the certification but only one or two years' work experience. The situation is very different among LPNs and technicians. Like Mrs. Riggsbee, Mrs. Davis, and Mrs. Pendergast, many of them have been at Duke for many years, often entering Duke right after high school and being trained on the job. Noncertified technologists have somewhat greater seniority, and black women in this classification have a great deal of seniority—a median of fifteen years in 1983—and seem to have come up through the ranks. This avenue is being closed off, though. As Duke requires licensing and schooling programs for more of their technical jobs, the opportunities for in-house training and upward mobility decrease. With the ending of medical center-sponsored programs in employee education, long-term workers' routes to upward mobility have been curtailed still further (Table 4).

It is not always easy to distinguish racial from class discrimination, for both are consequences of the demands that technical workers be schooled

Table 4: Selected Technical and Nursing Workers, 1976 and 1983

Type of Job	1976	1983
Medical technicians	59	29
LPNs	485	517
Radiation and x-ray technologists	51	50
Research technicians	255	274
Medical technologists	171	234
Staff RNs	463	1106

Sources: Calculated from work-force printouts.

formally.[3] Betty is white; her lack of a college degree worked against her as did Patricia's, although Patricia faced some fairly explicit racism as well. There are half as many black women who are noncertified medical technologists as white, and they have many more years' seniority, suggesting that black women started at lower levels, and/or were promoted more slowly and/or had fewer options for lateral mobility. The situation among medical technologists does not seem to be unique. There are very few black women at upper-level allied health professional positions.

Professionalization in Nursing

Between 1976 and 1983, the Duke nursing staff underwent a radical change, as LPNs lost ground to RNs in numbers and in the scope of their responsibilities. Although the absolute number of LPNs increased slightly between 1976 and 1983, from 485 to 517, this growth was dwarfed by the explosion of staff RNs from 463 to 1,106, clearly a major change in their distributions, from approximately equal numbers to a nursing staff where two out of three are RNs. The shift was equally dramatic racially: Both in 1976 and 1983, four out of five LPNs were black, four out of five RNs were white.

Beginning perhaps in the late seventies, there was a strong push at Duke to replace LPNs with RNs. The emergency room, which had been creeping in that direction for years, finally achieved its goal by about 1981. According to one nurse administrator, the medical center administration wished to make the changeover by attrition, but nursing administration did not want to wait that long, particularly because many of the LPNs in the ER were fairly young. A compromise was reached whereby LPNs were transferred to other work sites. RNs seem also to be replacing LPNs in a widening range of acute care situations. One RN explained that their new power was largely a result of RNs finally taking control of the state nursing board away from doctors and hospital administrators. This meant that nurses themselves determined what kinds of jobs could be done by which types of nurses in different types or grades of hospital. As a result, RNs were required to staff more positions in the medical center. I did not explore the issue of hospital accreditation in relation to RN expansion at Duke, but the replacement of LPNs by RNs is consistent with national trends.[4]

There is a great deal of friction between licensed practical nurses and registered nurses nationally. LPNs regard themselves as nursing professionals and resent the attempts of organized nursing to define them as assistants.[5] LPNs have been the ants who get trampled when elephants— in this case MDs and RNs—fight. They have lost considerable ground and numbers of jobs to RNs, as the latter battle to wrest domination of nursing away from doctors. Part of the national RN strategy has been to stress professionalization and increased schooling, and control over LPNs seems to be one of the spoils of the war.

LPNs' position in Duke Hospital reflects their low status. Despite their licensing, they are paid at the level of medical and administrative secretaries, and they work under the direction of RNs. The situation is sharper still because most LPNs are black, and because they have more years of work experience than do the vast majority of RNs, especially the nurse administrators who are their supervisors, and almost all of whom are white.

Still, professionalization also has a down-side that is beginning to surface under hospitals' growing financial pressures. RNs are able to perform some functions traditionally handled by doctors and other allied health professionals, and they may find themselves stretched out performing tasks formerly the responsibilities of people as diverse as laboratory assistants, respiratory therapists, and doctors. Indeed, there have been attempts at Duke to reassign some such jobs to RNs, apparently not because of differences in pay levels, but because those tasks could be added to RNs' then current workload, allowing the hospital to decrease the number of respiratory therapists. In this case, respiratory therapy successfully resisted the transfer, and nursing was reportedly none too happy about the prospect of additional work.

Some respiratory therapists noted a different sort of shift in hiring preferences: In perhaps 1981 or 1982, their department seemed to be pushing out respiratory technicians, workers who had been trained on the job, but by 1983 or 1984 seemed to prefer them to certified technicians. They relate the change to the changing economics of insurance reimbursement. In 1984, however, these contradictory trends seemed to coexist unstably and uneasily. Thus, although hospitals acquiesced to expansion of RNs and allied health professionals, perhaps partly as a counterweight to unionizing employees in the seventies, by the eighties, with even tighter finances and less union activity, hospitals were also pressuring professional workers to increase their workloads.

Between 1976 and 1983, both LPNs and aides have been "upgraded," in the sense that the relative proportions of workers in these jobs shifted from a concentration at the basic level to a concentration at advanced levels. Some see this as an indication that the modern work force needs to be more highly skilled, and that there are more and better job opportunities at middle rather than low levels of pay. In one sense, Duke's hourly work-force profile bears this out: There are more advanced everything: nurses, aides, food service workers, and secretaries than "unadvanced" ones. However, the workers in these positions do not often see this as real upward mobility, or even a significant pay improvement. LPNs to whom I spoke took a dim view of what this sort of "upgrading" meant for them. They did not see any real differences among themselves in terms of skill levels or hierarchy, and saw the certification requirements more as an irritant than as an opportunity for advancement. The requirements were seen as administrative harassment because many felt that they *had* to become certified in order to keep their jobs, but that their pay and recognition of their skill were still adequate. Most hourly workers with whom I spoke said that their jobs were dead-end. Getting a real promotion required moving into a new area and a great deal of initiative. In 1983, I counted eight different LPN job titles (compared to three in 1976), but the difference in starting pay between the lowest trainee and highest paid advanced LPN amounted to 77 cents an hour, or $1,540 annually, on a total salary of $12,520.[6]

Sarah Moore had been a patient care assistant (PCA) for more than a decade when Duke moved to upgrade its nursing staff. Her recollections suggest that title upgrading is not an entirely new phenomenon at Duke. Her head nurse urged Mrs. Moore to become certified as an advanced PCA, which is what her co-worker is. But Mrs. Moore saw no real need to do it, because "we do the same things." Nevertheless, she brushed up on a variety of nursing skills including blood pressures and vision and hearing checks and won her promotion to advanced PCA. "When I was a maid," Mrs. Moore pointed out, "my work was to pick up paper, straighten the weight room, and keep the beds made. I still do that as a PCA. I had to learn the weight room then because I relieved the PCA when she was at lunch and on vacation, and she reciprocated. There was some pay increase, but not much til they sent me to school for eight weeks. As a PCA, I work in the weight room, take the weights, heights, and temps and record them on the sheet. I also restock the supplies."

Clerical Work

Clerical work in the medical center is anything but uniform. It ranges from some of the most repetitious and thankless filing work known to woman (as in the medical records filing unit) to demanding decision-making and trouble-shooting work in many secretarial, DTO, and receptionist jobs. If medical records clerks worked in the trenches, secretaries and DTOs organized people and paperwork on the front lines. Other secretarial, clerk, receptionist, and transcriptionist jobs also require a fair amount of technical and medical knowledge. Many clerical jobs at the medical center presume that workers will pick up and use more knowledge than management is willing to acknowledge in the form of compensation.

In the last decade, clerical workers and researchers have raised alarms about what the subdivision and reorganization of office work are doing to clerical employment and working conditions. The computer has received devastating criticism for its role in enabling management to subdivide, de-skill, monitor, and pace clerical and data entry work, as well as to eliminate or to export jobs to lower-waged areas of the world.[7] Sociologist Anne Machung has summed up many clerical workers' experiences with office automation and the reorganization embedded in it: "the intersection of repetitious typing with repetitious computer work."[8]

Secretaries. The issues of work degradation and job loss were very much on the minds of all secretaries with whom I spoke in the middle of 1979. Duke had just won the NLRB election, and almost immediately the medical center instituted a full-scale evaluation of all clerical jobs. Every secretary I spoke with had been or was scheduled for an interview with someone from Wage and Salary about her work. Beth Porter asked her interviewer if the purpose was to save Duke money. She was neither surprised nor pleased to get an affirmative answer. Faith Harrison said the rumor was that Duke's plan was to fire secretaries and replace them with a typing pool. One department had already tried it, but everyone was quitting. Louise Shields queried her interviewer about this rumor; he told her it was not true. She asked him if they were going to demote people if they were doing less than their job description. He told her that they could not do that, but that the next person in that job would receive a lower classification. Louise has been working at Duke for more than twenty years, and both she and Faith remembered Proudfoot's earlier attempt to monitor service workers and their redesign of medical records so they no longer could be sent by pneumatic tubes, which meant secretaries often had to hand-carry them if no messengers were available. The women were uneasy to say the least, however the wholesale cuts did not happen, nor does there seem to have been any widespread "Fordization" of secretarial work.

Microcomputers and mass-produced word-processing software were not widespread in 1979. Few secretaries at Duke had yet encountered them, and hence their fears focused on typing pools and clerical assembly lines. At that time Beth Porter, an administrative secretary, worked in a department that had just bought its own computer system, making it a pioneer in office automation. There were at least two "computer gurus" as Beth called them, or programmers whose job it was to develop custom software for the department. According to Beth, they worked to meet the requests of the secretarial staff as well as those of professionals. They also gave courses on how to operate the computers. As a result, several years before word-processing software became a mass-produced item, this department had its own word-processing program and was in the process of developing a dictionary appropriate for its needs.

In a department of perhaps twenty-five faculty and many research and postdoctoral fellows, there were only nine secretaries and typists to handle a very large volume of manuscript typing as well as all the other clerical work. Faculty had their own terminals, and the expectation was that they would do their own typing and editing. Beth's boss did most of his own typing. She typed his letters on the computer, and he called them up, edited them on the screen, and Beth printed them. She loved the system at first.

Some of the excitement was anticipatory. When I first met her, much of the work involved data entry—entering all the departmental files and records into the computer, writing programs for doing this, and debugging the programs. "In about a year this place should really swing." Beth had a marvelous time with the computer. It took about a week to learn the basics, and she had a manual and her class notes to refer to as she taught herself. "It's like learning to cook. Once you learn how to use your oven you refer to your recipe book for the subtleties to come up with the end product. Once you get over your fear, it's easy." Because secretaries were also allowed to use the computer for their own use, Beth wrote a small math program for her daughter, who sometimes came to work with Beth when her school was closed. Secretaries, most of whom are scattered in different offices, used the computer to communicate with each other, sending messages back and forth, and occasionally playing some of the games that the departmental programmers acquired.

On the other hand, Beth saw a negative aspect to computers. "It doesn't add anything to our pay. It's considered a bonus for us; you've acquired another skill and it's reduced our work. I had it out with the manager [about not getting paid for learning to use the computer]." This was precisely the catalyst for the ward secretary walkout five years earlier, but it did not become more than an individual issue here. The other source of concern Beth raised, although she did not feel in any danger herself, was in the loss of jobs as faculty did more of their own typing. In approximately the first two years after the computer's advent Beth thought there was a decrease of two secretaries. But in five years, she feared that more jobs might be lost.

Where Beth works in a research and publishing department, Susannah Hughes is a medical secretary for a clinical faculty member—that is, a practicing doctor who also teaches and supervises students and housestaff. Secretarial work in a clinical setting is quite different from that in a research setting, and I wanted to know whether Mrs. Hughes thought her job could be automated. She is one of two secretaries in an office where they are responsible for correspondence, typing clinical notes for entry into the medical records from dictation, making appointments, scheduling hospital admissions, arranging her doctor's schedule—including travel— and typing any papers and reports that he does. In 1979, Mrs. Hughes thought that computers in her department would not be worth the expense because clinical departments do too many different things, many of which cannot be computerized easily or cheaply. She thought that her job was necessarily labor-intensive, in part because much of her typing (especially the discharge and procedure summaries of her doctor and all the residents he supervised) were typed from tapes, and in part because much of their work involved making appointments, scheduling admissions, and doing other nonroutine but necessary tasks (chapter 4).

By 1983, microcomputers and word processors were well on the way to replacing typewriters. Like Beth Porter, Sharon Lester, an administrative secretary, saw them as a way of speeding up secretaries, decreasing their numbers. In her department, the number of secretaries has decreased to the point that there is no one to cover when people are absent. The work is "so boring, people don't like to come to work," and this attitude creates problems, especially for Sharon, who finds that her job is becoming increasingly that of a supervisor, which she dislikes intensely. She is afraid that Duke will bring in word processors to "break the secretary-doctor relationship." Because word processors are so fast, she fears that Duke will be able to make each secretary responsible to more doctors. However, such moves would likely face the opposition of powerful physicians.

Susannah, like almost every other secretary in 1983, had a personal computer and printer in her office; the typewriter sat forlornly in a corner. Her experience couldn't be more different from that of Beth and Sharon. Neither the computer salespeople nor Duke provided any training; everything she learned was on her own. But it is difficult to learn when you have a full day's work to do at the same time. As a result, Susannah told me that only one secretary in her whole area of the hospital used her machine "to its fullest" in 1983. One woman used it like a typewriter because she has not had the time or training to set up formats for things she types regularly. Used as it is, the word processor is a "waste," an "expensive toy," Susannah feels. She, and apparently many other people, would like to learn how to use the computers well, because all the computer courses the university offers to its staff were overflowing, as were virtually all the courses anywhere in town. However, after about a year of intermittent frustration, Susannah and her office-mate had worked out the problems, developed their own system, and were quite comfortable with word processing on microcomputers.

Microcomputers seem to function for medical secretaries like Susannah in a way similar to that in which computerized inpatient information functioned for DTOs about a decade earlier. That is, they are tools that secretaries control and that eliminate some of the more tedious aspects of the job. However, not all secretaries, or even medical secretaries, share that feeling.

Much of the difference in perception may stem from whether secretaries' work centers around clinical practice or research. In the former case, secretaries are key intermediaries in doctor-patient-hospital department relationships, and the computer simplifies recording and communicating aspects of their work. In the latter case, with Beth and Sharon, manuscript and grant typing loom much larger, and the work seems to be vertically divided, with some secretaries confined to keying, re-keying, and printing, while a smaller number handle the interpersonal administration and coordination.

DTOs. In 1979, with assistance from federal funding, Duke revamped its DTO training program so that trainees spent eight hours daily in class for six weeks before they began to train on the wards under senior DTOs. Some senior DTOs were asked to become teachers in the program but refused. DTOs with whom I spoke believed that classroom training was necessarily inadequate, and that they had to do a great deal of actual training, some of it counter to what trainees learned in the classroom. Probably the most important aspect of on-the-job training was the mind-set, or work culture, of the job that senior DTOs passed on to new workers. We have seen that this was quite different from management's notions of what the job entailed both in terms of skills and attitudes. Management control undermined DTOs' abilities to pass along their consciousness of the job and its requirements. One DTO told me that the person in charge of training had only three months' summer experience as a DTO, that the teachers earn far more than DTOs, and that they focus on "attitudes, psychology and other crap. Then these girls hit the wards with no knowledge of how to do anything, and they feel they know more than the DTOs. We have to train people who think they know." DTOs were clear that they had to "tell the new ones to speak up for themselves when you know what you want to say." The new program requires DTOs to spend a great deal of energy in training newcomers, but they do not even get informal recognition from management for doing this. The on-the-job training is one more part of their job that has not been eliminated despite the existence of the so-called training program. In addition, they are angry that trainees earn almost as much as a DTO with seven or more years' experience. Senior DTOs see this as Duke's way of telling them that theirs is an unskilled job, and that experience and ability are worth nothing.

Changes in the Clerical Work Force. According to Duke's EEO statistics, the 1,831 clerical workers in the medical center in 1978 grew to 2,079 in 1981, an increase of 13.5 percent. By 1983, their number fell slightly, to 2,026. However, the percentage of black clerical workers rose from 32 percent to 39 percent during these years.[9]

An examination of changes in clerical jobs suggests that an upgrading similar to that which occurred among LPNs may have taken place (Table 5). For example, there are now three levels of medical records clerk, with

Table 5. Selected Clerical Jobs, 1978 and 1983

Position	Level	Total Number 1978	Total Number 1983	Black Female/Male 1978	Black Female 1983
Clerk typist	3	38	17	20	13
Clerk typist, senior	4	17	5	9	4
Medical laboratory clerk	4	18	51	10	30
Medical records clerk	3	92	9	57	1
Medical records clerk, senior	4	21	47	11	24
Medical records clerk III	5		11		3
Clinic receptionist	4	63	35	25	23
Patient processor	5	47	37	10	16
DTO	5	195	233	168	189
Secretary	5	294	138	61	31
Administrative secretary	6	124	149	13	26
Medical secretary	6	159	243	9	26
Research secretary	6		12		2
Clinical interviewer	6	40	39	15	9

Sources: 1978 data from *Caston* v. *Duke University*, Peterson Affidavit, Exhibit B; 1983 calculated from work-force printout.

most women concentrated in what used to be the senior level. Likewise, there are more secretaries at level 6 than 5, a shift since 1978; the median seems also to have shifted upward in clinic positions. It would seem too, that the numbers of clericals at the lowest levels may have shrunk, although that is not clear.

The other trend suggests that secretaries had reason for concern in 1979, although the changes did not materialize in quite the way they feared. Most striking is the large decrease in the overall number of medical records clerks, from 113 to 67. There was a smaller drop in the total number of secretaries, from 577 to 542. Some of these positions may have been eliminated or downgraded, but some may also have been upgraded to staff assistant. Although there are statistically more black clerical workers, there were exactly as many black secretaries in 1983 as in 1978; black women are still the vast majority of DTOs, and most of the cuts in medical records clerks seem to have been black (there were six male clerks in 1983). From this limited information though, it would appear that black women have made gains both in numbers and percentage of the clerical work force, and in moving up somewhat within it. It is tempting to speculate that the class action suit initiated by black women clerical workers may have helped more than a little bit.

Summary

By 1983, Duke's hourly work force was coming to include two groups of workers who were increasingly differentiated by race and class. The first was made up of white, college-educated hourly professionals; the second was a racially integrated combination of technical, nursing service, and clerical workers, who were nevertheless segregated racially within particular job classifications. Licensed professional and technical workers, primarily medical and research technologists and registered nurses, were at the highest pay levels in the hourly work force. Registered nurses started at $17,740 a year and could earn up to about $25,000 a year; there were a few specialists whose annual earnings could be upward of $25,000. In contrast, the vast majority of working-class jobs ranged from $8,400 starting and $13,000 top for cleaning, kitchen, and patient care workers to top secretarial pay of less than $16,400, top LPN pay of $17,540, and top technologist (noncertified) pay of $19,250. Although the wages of RNs and other hourly professional workers were higher than those of working-class workers, they were nevertheless low in the overall scheme of medical center wages and salaries for professional occupations.[10]

This bifurcation is representative of changes throughout the health-care industry on a national scale. Proponents of work force upgrading and professionalization argue that a greater level of skill and schooling are needed in today's high tech acute care medicine, and that such a work force is more flexible and hence efficient for cost-conscious management. I have suggested that gains made with such arguments in recent years may be increasingly turned against these workers. The flexibility of well-trained "flexible" RNs has been used to advantage by hospital managements to expand the RNs' jobs, and/or to cut their hours as a means of cutting costs.

The march of professionalization looks somewhat different from the vantage point of working-class service and clerical workers, LPN, and technicians at Duke. From their perspective, "occupational gentrification" might be a more resonant term than professionalization. Their job titles and the number of grades have proliferated, for example in the number of LPN, dietary service, secretarial, and medical records clerk titles and pay levels. This has involved promoting the bulk of workers in these classifications to the advanced, or higher-paid level of the job. However these gains are undercut by restrictions on upward and lateral mobility that stem from demands for schooling in place of on-the-job training for many technical and nursing positions, and by the relative, and in some cases the absolute, shrinkage of jobs in clerical, service, and technical classifications. The combined effect is to restrict the real job and promotion opportunities for working-class people at Duke, even though the number of pay mini-grades and job titles seem to grow like cancer.

The class shift affects black and white women and black men unequally because of black workers' concentration in working-class jobs and white workers' dispersal. Cutbacks in housekeeping and lower-level kitchen jobs affect black men and women both. Black women were concentrated in the same jobs in 1983 that they held in 1976, as DTOs and LPNs in addition to food and cleaning work. New credentialing requirements in nursing have their primary impacts on black women, but other allied health credentialing requirements affect both black and white women by class. The clerical work force seems to have stopped growing, but thanks perhaps to the activism of black women clericals, black women seem finally to be achieving promotions to clerical jobs above the level of DTO, an apparent change since 1980. In 1976, almost the only black women above the DTO level were LPNs. Although LPNs were still a large proportion of the black women at these levels, black women seem to have gained ground in a variety of clerical jobs—most notably medical and administrative secretaries—from which they had been all but excluded earlier. Professionalization did not benefit all white women; rather it would seem to have heightened opportunities for white middle-class women at the expense of both black and white working-class women, whose mobility has been restricted by increased schooling requirements. An emphasis on formal education may divide workers along lines of class and race, but heightened pressures and work intensification of professonals may lead to greater unity across that division. Any organization that may develop in the future will be influenced by unionization efforts of the 1960s and 70s as well as helped by their victories.

NOTES

1. Sabel's phrase for the whole complex of assembly lines, unskilled work, and large-scale production that have been synonymous with industrial production.

2. *Bulletin*, Duke University Medical School, 1975:109.

3. Noyelle, 1984.

4. Sekscenski, 1984; Institute of Medicine, 1983.

5. Reverby, 1979; Melosh, 1982; Sacks, forthcoming; Malveaux and Englander, 1985.

6. Calculated from $6.26 an hour for a forty-hour week, fifty weeks a year.

7. Feldberg and Glenn, 1983: Glenn and Feldberg, 1977; Machung, 1984; Murphree, 1984; 1985; Working Women: National Association of Office Workers, 1980; Howard, 1985; Warnecke, 1984.

8. Machung, 1984:132

9. Opportunity Development Center/EEO Office Reports.

10. Calculated from ranges at each pay level on the basis of a forty-hour week, fifty weeks per year.

Retrospect and Conclusion

Battles similar to those at Duke took place across the country in the 1960s and 70s, and were part of much larger economic and social changes. On the one hand, the 1960s were a period of economic growth in general, and growth in the service industries in particular. Health care nationally and in Durham became a major service industry. The health work force grew, subdivided, and specialized, and in the process organized as workers on a class basis. The leadership of this new labor movement came from black and Hispanic workers, especially from women. Their efforts forced the civil rights movement to deal with working-class issues and the labor movement to confront racism, at least for a time. Neither nationally nor at Duke were gender issues or black women's specific contributions to this movement raised publicly. And for its part, the women's movement was almost silent about working-class and black women's issues. Yet, as we have seen, and as recent studies are beginning to confirm elsewhere, women in general and black women in particular were central in the movement's leadership and to its successes. First I will summarize the gains at Duke, and then turn to the ways that black women's networks and work culture gave leadership to the hospital union movement.

Retrospect

In the demoralization that set in among Duke workers after the union defeat, it was easy to forget that their effort brought many lasting improvements. Their major and enduring victory is that black workers,

especially women, took the lead in forcing Duke to treat all of its service
and other nonprofessional workers as a full-time, regular work force as
opposed to casual laborers to whom they had no ongoing responsibilities.
This did not happen in a straightforward way. Such things rarely do.
Duke's initial response to the Benevolent Society's request for improved
pay, benefits, and promotions was to bring in an efficiency expert to make
them work harder. The Benevolent Society responded by fighting harder,
and more significantly, by changing its form from a fraternal order that
relied on petitions and requests to a labor union that relied on the collective strength of its membership to make effective demands for their rights
as workers. Ironically, Proudfoot's efforts at scientific management facilitated this transition, because they too were based on a contractual notion
that workers "sold" their employer a finite amount of labor time in ex-
change for a wage. Even though they may have been out to bleed as much
effort from workers as they could during those hours, Proudfoot's presence
was an indication that Duke was beginning to view food service and
cleaning service workers as workers, and not Durham's poor who were to
be done a favor by being given day work.

This change became manifest in quantitative and specific gains won in
the next decades. Working hours and schedules improved as workers won
the right to have their jobs and hours defined. Kitchen workers and data
terminal operators fought for and won alternate weekends off. Workers
were no longer forced to work more than forty-hour weeks without overtime pay. Split shifts were ended, as were management-determined summer layoffs in campus dining facilities. Duke was no longer able to change
working conditions unilaterally. Housekeepers prevented Duke from adding wet mopping to their jobs. And cooks prevented food service management from making them double as pot washers. DTOs forced Duke to
hire more workers for adequate staffing of ward desks.

Workers no longer accepted capriciousness as a management right and
developed ways of containing it. Not least of these ways was to organize
two unions, Local 77 (AFSCME) and Local 465 (IUOE). They also managed to gain something of a company grievance procedure and appeal
board, albeit one made up almost entirely of administrators and faculty.[1]
Although the grievance board's structure was not impartial, workers were
able to use it to win grievances, most notably reinstatement with back
pay of suspended microbiology workers. The unions have struggled
against paternalism and personal favoritism, especially in wage increases.
They have argued that "merit" increases are thinly disguised forms of

favoritism and divisiveness and have won annual step increases. This victory, however, was limited to unionized workers. Duke has maintained merit increases for nonunion hospital workers, although it did institute performance evaluations to mollify workers' dissatisfaction with what many saw as favoritism and arbitrariness.

Not least of the gains has been significant wage increases, especially for food and cleaning service workers, who were earning well below the minimum wage even in the boom times of the early 1960s. DTOs also improved their wages and relative status as a result of their walkout.

Black women and men gained access to new clerical and technical jobs, and for the first time, significant numbers of black women became clerks and receptionists. A few black women were able to gain secretarial, medical secretarial, and laboratory technologist jobs. Black service workers were no longer supervised (at least directly) by whites only.

Union organizers and some managers shared the feeling that many of the benefits won by active groups of workers were extended to all workers as part of Duke's efforts to avoid unionization and to make unions look ineffective.[2] In particular, during union campaigns, all workers received at least the percentage wage increase that Local 77 workers did.

These gains were substantial, and even more significant, most of them were made, or at least sustained, during the economic downturn that characterized the latter 1970s. Comparison with national trends provides an additional perspective. Between 1961 and 1980, the number of hospitals with any collective bargaining agreements grew from only 3.2 percent to 27.4 percent, with most of that growth by 1975.[3] Given the high turnover in hospital work forces and the high supply of workers for the jobs that have become unionized, it was a considerable achievement. Real wages in hospitals generally comparable to Duke and in many similar jobs peaked in 1972–73 and fell thereafter to below–1970 levels.[4]

Nationally based findings seem to confirm the benefits of unionization. Becker and his co-workers, in their own study and survey of the findings of other studies, estimate that unions have raised pay by perhaps 10 percent for nonprofessional workers, and by 6 percent for nurses. More significant, they found that unions that are militant and willing to strike make more gains than those not willing to do so: "the effects of collective bargaining in hospitals having work stoppages is substantially higher than collective bargaining effects without work stoppages."[5]

Since 1979, there has been almost no organized or widespread worker or worker-community activism at Duke Medical Center. In many ways, people's day-to-day lives in recent years do not have the look of resistance about them. Women who were intensely active politically a few years earlier now focus their energies on their careers, on developing educational programs, and on their families. Although these may have been the prevailing passions in many of the worksites on which I spent any time, they do not mean that workers who were once active will sit passively and allow their hard-won gains to be taken away. Rather, they are alternate means to similar goals.

There has also been collective resistance, although it is limited and low key compared to past years. The class action suit against racial discrimination brought by five black clerical workers came right on the heels of the union defeat, and although it never came to trial, its existence seems to have helped black women's clerical opportunities somewhat. Informal resistance also continues in daily workplace life, and women mobilize their social networks to skirmish, if sporadically. In some of these battles, black and white women, especially clerical workers, are working together more closely, and white women's militancy seems to be growing.

Conclusion

Duke activists grappled with racial divisions and antagonisms. They searched for underlying commonalities that would join all workers together in spite of these barriers. Their efforts were part of a long tradition of attempts to figure out how to build working-class unity. This work is also part of that tradition, and I link it to still more recent efforts to include the particulars of gender as well as race oppression in the context of class. Duke workers presented their movement in different ways at different times. Initially, they saw it as a movement against racism and economic injustice. By the late 1960s and early 1970s, class justice began to emerge as a more prominent issue as organizers generated support among white women clerical workers. Those efforts bore organizational fruit when white maintenance workers unionized and subsequently aided hospital workers' efforts to do likewise (chapter 2). These two themes prevailed throughout the 1970s' efforts at medical center unionization.

When the women's movement added gender to race and class as part of the national agenda for justice, it seemed to most on the hospital organizing committee just too much to juggle, for this issue too had the potential to be divisive. Sexism and economic justice for women were never issues that the Duke movement articulated. This response has its counterpart in the white feminist movement, where race seems usually to be ignored, and where class is all too often ignored. There were several black workers (women and men) on the organizing committee who regarded feminism as a white middle-class women's issue only. They saw it as anti-working class and divisive of black women and men. These beliefs were reinforced by the National Organization for Women's North Carolina campaign to pass the Equal Rights Amendment. NOW relied on persuading liberal political powerholders—prominent among whom was Duke's president Terry Sanford—to support the ERA. When NOW arranged for Sanford to give an ERA cocktail party to be attended by Eleanor Smeal, its national president, unionists protested. They argued that Sanford was no friend of women, that he was obstructing unionization of a primarily women's workplace, and they urged Smeal not to attend the event. Their protest had no effect, and this confirmed a number of workers' views of the class and race with which feminists stood.

Regardless, gender *was* part of the Duke struggle in that it was women's work cultures and women's community, family, and workplace networks, especially those of black women, that were the framework of organization, that gave the drive its movement character, and that gave both language and leadership to all Duke workers' efforts. The dominant paradigms available in political culture nationally during the years of worker activism made it hard to grasp women's roles because they separated and contrasted racial, gender, and class oppression. Indeed, multiple sources of oppression were all too often understood and treated additively and competitively. For example, the dominant views tended to exclude consideration of family life when it came to workplace issues. This in turn reinforced the tendency to contrast work and family as separate and contrasting spheres of experience. Tendencies to interpret men's experiences and consciousness in terms of work and women's in terms of family further distorted the ways workers of both genders saw their lives and made decisions.[6] So too did thinking that work relations were sources of resistance, but that family relations fostered acquiescence.

Black women's very visible community-based activism and individual leadership in the civil rights movement should have shaken such conventional wisdom. Instead, unfortunately, black women's leadership seems to have been written out of subsequent histories. Paula Giddings' and Sarah Evans' important works are among the few studies that emphasize the point at length.[7] Likewise, black workers' attack on racial and economic exploitation in the workplace, and their mobilization of community and family participation to resist, should have undercut notions that work and family, class, and race were somehow necessarily opposed.

Those are certainly central lessons from the Duke and Durham workers' history. It is not fair to say that activists were blind to it at the time; women and men both built strategy and organization around that knowledge. But there was no real language or political legitimacy to express, fix, and credit women's organizing and leadership. How women organized remained a collection of private understandings and informal know-how, necessarily partial because it was not shared publicly and politically.

One result of partial understanding was that the structure of leadership was misunderstood. As long as women's contributions were not seen as leadership, the notion of leadership that was given force and articulation was that of public speakers. This is a class and gender-biased notion—the kind of leadership the media enhances—and as Giddings has pointed out, distorts leadership in the black community. Perhaps even more serious, the solo conception of leadership excludes what I think is a more important dimension of leadership for any grass-roots movement, that of network dynamics. It leaves the impression that people act as individuals following an articulate orator. However, at Duke leadership involved collective action by already existing and already politicized networks. Center-women were crucial in political consciousness- and consensus-shaping. When a consensus was not possible, the networks could not be political, and either disbanded or sought apolitical and social bases of shared values and activities. Union leadership lay in the *interaction* of center and speaker functions in such a way as to go with the consensus.

In the last few years, stimulated by the rise of black feminism as a political force, scholars and activists have moved away from seeing multiple oppressions as competitive or opposed, and toward a recognition that class oppression takes different forms for black women and white women, and black men and white men (as well as other minorities).

Duke workers' history also contributes to understanding the relations among family, work, and community in a working-class-based movement, and the relations of race, work, and work culture to resistance. There is a growing amount of new scholarship that asks how work and family cultures might mutually reinforce activism rather than work against one another. Some of this work highlights working-class kin networks as important resources for coping with economic adversity, shows women as central economic and political actors in these kinship networks, and suggests that these networks create and carry parts of a working-class culture.[8]

At Duke too, continuities and links between areas once thought to be somehow opposed emerge from the shadows. The integration of work-based social networks with women's community-based kin and friendship networks, and the important part that skills learned in families played in forming networks, counters the old contrast of work and family, docility and militancy. Centerwomen were particularly important in shaping familistic values and understandings into cultures of resistance.

In a similar way, on today's clerical and service "assembly lines" women workers employ organizational and interpersonal skills associated with family life to carry out their job and to generate coordinated resistance to management. We are just now beginning to get glimpses of how such networks functioned in mobilizing workplace resistance, both in famous historical strikes by women garment and textile workers and in smaller and everyday forms of resistance.[9] We are also learning that networks and work cultures do not always or automatically lead to the barricades; sometimes they keep people away from them.

At Duke too, the actual connections between women's work grievances and their collective expressions were complex, and the links between complaining and organizing were still more complex because both work and its social relations were powerfully and palpably shaped by race. Black women and white women for the most part had different jobs, but part of what made their jobs different was the fact that jobs were race-typed and people in them were treated differently because of it. These attitudes affected the work cultures that black and white women developed, as well as limited their occupationally based interracial ties. The union context was a visible and significant place where racial boundaries were overcome, and where women and men activists developed somewhat shared views of work and their relationships to hospital management. There was also diversity. Although class is still central to any workers' organizing, workers are not race- or gender-neutral beings. Race and gender shape their lives in obvious and direct ways, and there is no such animal as a worker whose class existence is separable from gender and race. Working-class men and women have different family responsibilities and relationships; black workers and white workers are pretty much segregated in where they live, go to school, and in kinship, churches, and voluntary community organizations. They are almost as segregated at work by rigid patterns of occupational segregation by gender and race. Thus, the dynamics of workers' efforts in and beyond the medical center were shaped by the differences as well as the commonalities facing a racially and sexually differentiated working class.

Although Duke workers did not win the union for which they struggled, their fifteen-year effort and the gains they made depended heavily on the central roles that black workers played—especially black women—in taking leadership to join civil rights and working-class issues and to link workplace and community issues. Women of all races and ethnicities are becoming an ever larger part of the waged labor force and have become increasingly central and visible parts of movements for justice and equity. The daily work lives and struggles by black women and white women at Duke are part of this larger history too, and their experiences have contributed to our understanding of how to bring about change. They point to the importance of women's work culture for generating the ideas and values that are central to any movement's ability to challenge management's evaluation of workers' worth and rights. They point to the contributions of black and white working-class family values to class consciousness. They highlight the indispensibility of black women's workplace networks and the role of their centerwomen in transforming private understandings into a public agenda. All these things indicate that participation in and leadership of a grass-roots movement is a profoundly collective and interactive process among network members, centers, and spokespeople, rather than a simple relation of individual members and individual leaders.

NOTES

1. Duke University Personnel Notice, Grievance Panel Board, R. L. Jackson, Nov. 20, 1978.

2. "Pre-Petition Period;" "When was the Last Time Duke Gave You the 'Red Carpet' Treatment?"; undated Roscoe Robinson to DUMC Employees, "What Would You Get from AFSCME if It Were to Win the Coming Labor Board Election," leaflets in author's possession.

3. Denton, 1976:vi, 3, 229–30; Becker et al., 1982:10.

4. The hospitals surveyed were large, general, nonfederal, short-term hospitals. Workers covered included custodians, aides, clerks, practical nurses, secretaries, physical therapists, EKG technicians, computer programers, and head nurses. Sloan and Steinwald, 1980:106–15.

5. Becker et al., 1982:10.

6. Feldberg and Glenn, 1979.

7. Evans, 1980; Giddings, 1985.

8. Young and Willmott, 1962; Caulfield, 1974; Ladner, 1971; Gutman, 1977; Humphries, 1977; Kessler-Harris, 1982; Tilly and Scott, 1978; Rapp, 1978; Stack, 1974; Bott, 1971; Day, 1982.

9. Hooks, 1981; Hull, et al., 1981; Rollins, 1985; Rodgers-Rose, 1980; Melosh, 1982; Costello, 1985; Cameron, 1985; Kaplan, 1982; Rowbotham, 1973; Tax, 1980; Milkman, 1985; Lamphere et al., 1980; Lamphere, 1984; Sacks, 1983, 1984; Westwood, 1984; Shapiro-Perl, 1984.

References

Abbreviations

AE: *American Ethnologist*
AJPH: *American Journal of Public Health*
AJS: *American Journal of Sociology*
ASR: *American Socological Review*
IJHS: *International Journal of Health Services*
MLR: *Monthly Labor Review*
RRPE: *Review of Radical Political Economics*

American Hospital Association. 1972–85. *Guide to the Health Care Field.* Chicago: American Hospital Association.
American Management Association. 1957. *Controlling Employee Benefit and Pension Costs.* New York: American Management Association.
Anderson, Karen. 1981. *Wartime Women: Sex Roles, Family Relations and the Status of Women During World War II.* Westport, Conn.: Greenwood Press.
Anlyan, William G., and Jane G. Elchlepp. 1982. "The Challenge and Problems of Developing a New Tertiary Care Hospital for the 1980s: Duke University Hospital North." In *The Role of the University Teaching Hospital: an International Perspective*, ed. E. F. Purcell. New York: Josiah Macy, Jr. Foundation.
Aten, Fred, 1971. "Development of Labor Relations at Duke University 1962–1971." Unpublished student paper, Duke University Archives.
Backup, Molly, and John Molinaro. 1984. "New Health Professionals:

Changing the Hierarchy." In *Reforming Medicine*, ed. Victor Sidel and Ruth Sidel. New York: Pantheon.

Barocci, Thomas A. 1981. *Non-Profit Hospitals*. Boston: Auburn House.

Barrow, Christine. 1976. "Reputation and Ranking in a Barbadian Locality." *Social and Economic Studies* 25 (2):106–21.

Becker, Edmund R., Frank A. Sloan, and Bruce Steinwald. 1982. "Union Activity in Hospitals: Past, Present and Future." *Health Care Financing Review* 3 (4):1–13.

Benson, Susan Porter. 1978. "The Clerking Sisterhood: Rationalization and the Work Culture of Sales-Women." *Radical America* 12 (2):41–55.

———. 1984. "Women in Retail Sales Work: The Continuing Dilemma of Service." In *My Troubles Are Going to Have Trouble with Me*, ed. Karen B. Sacks and Dorothy Remy. New Brunswick, N. J.: Rutgers University Press.

Berch, Bettina. 1984. "'The Sphinx in the Household': A New Look at the History of Household Workers." *RRPE* 16 (1):105–21.

Berliner, Howard. 1975. "A Larger Perspective on the Flexner Report." *IJHS* 5 (4):573–92.

Bermanzohn, Paul, and Tim McGloin. 1976. "Southern Empire: Cool Hand Duke." In *Prognosis Negative: Crisis in the Health Care System*, ed. David Kotelchuck. New York: Vintage Books.

Bishop, Owen. 1967. "Decade in Review—Issues Are New Tactics Unchanged." *Durham Sun*, Aug. 14.

Bodenheimer, Thomas, Steven Cummings, and Elizabeth Harding. 1974. "Capitalizing on Illness: The Health Insurance Industry." *IJHS* 4 (4):583–98.

Bornat, Joanna. 1978. "Home and Work: A New Context for Trade Union History." *Radical America* 12 (5):53–69.

Bott, Elizabeth. 1971. *Family and Social Network*. London: Tavistock.

Braverman, Harry. 1974. *Labor and Monopoly Capital*. New York: Monthly Review Press.

Brecher, Jeremy. 1978. "Uncovering the Hidden History of the American Workplace." *RRPE* 10 (4):1–24.

Brisbane, Arthur S. 1984. "Hospital Occupancy Dip Sparks Income Struggle." *Washington Post*, July 30, A1, A8.

Brown, Carol A. 1973. "The Division of Laborers: Allied Health Professions." *IJHS* 3 (3):435–44.

Brown, E. Richard. 1976. "Public Health in Imperialism: Early Rockefeller Programs at Home and Abroad." *AJPH* 66 (9):897–903.

————. 1979. *Rockefeller Medicine Men: Medicine and Capitalism in America*. Berkeley: University of California Press.

Burawoy, Michael. 1979a. "The Anthropology of Industrial Work." *Annual Reviews of Anthropology* 8:231–66.

————. 1979. *Manufacturing Consent*. Chicago: University of Chicago Press.

Cahan, V. et al. 1985. "Health Care Costs: The Fever Breaks." *Business Week*, Oct. 21, 86–88.

Cameron, Ardis. 1985. "Bread and Roses Revisited: Women's Culture and Working-Class Activism in the Lawrence Strike of 1912." In *Women, Work and Protest*, ed. Ruth Milkman. Boston: Routledge & Kegan Paul.

Caplan, Arthur L. 1983. "Our Unhealthy Health Care." *The Nation*, Oct. 1, 277–82.

Carnoy, Judith, and Linda Koo. 1975. "Kaiser Permanente: A Model American Health Maintenance Organization." *IJHS* 4 (4):599–615.

Carter, Luther J. 1968. "Duke University: Students Demand New Deal for Negro Workers." *Science*, May 3, 513–17.

Caulfield, Mina Davis. 1974. "Imperialism, Family and Cultures of Resistance." *Socialist Revolution* 4 (2):67–85.

Chafe, William. 1980. *Civilities and Civil Rights: Greensboro, North Carolina and the Black Struggle for Freedom*. New York: Oxford University Press.

Cohn, Victor. 1985. "Medicine, Inc." *Washington Post Health*, April 3, 12–15.

Colloton, John W. 1982. "Competition: The Threat to Teaching Hospitals." In *Financing Health Care: Competition versus Regulation*, ed. Duncan Yaggy and W. G. Anlyan. Cambridge, Mass.: Ballinger Publishing.

Committee on Economic Development. 1973. *Building a National Health Care System*. New York: Committee on Economic Development.

Costello, Cynthia. 1985. "*WEA're* Worth It: Women's Work Culture and Conflict at the Wisconsin Education Association Insurance Trust." *Feminist Studies* 11 (3):497–518.

Culliton, Barbara J. 1984. "Medical Education Under Fire." *Science*, Oct. 26, 419–20.

Davies, Margery. 1974. "Woman's Place Is at the Typewriter: The Feminization of the Clerical Labor Force." *Radical America* 8 (4):1–18.

Davis, Karen. 1982. "Regulation of Hospital Costs: The Evidence of Performance." In *Financing Health Care: Competition versus Regula-*

tion, ed. Duncan Yaggy and W. G. Anlyan. Cambridge, Mass.: Ballinger Publishing.

Davision, Wilburt C. 1972. "The Duke University School of Medicine." In *Medicine in North Carolina: Essays in the History of Medical Science and Medical Service, 1924–1960*, vol. 2, ed. Dorothy Long, 527—52. Raleigh: North Carolina Medical Society.

Day, Kay Young. 1982. "Kinship in a Changing Economy: A View from the Sea Islands." In *Holding onto the Land and the Lord*, ed. Carol Stack and Robert Hall. Athens: University of Georgia Press.

Denton, David R. 1976. "The Union Movement in American Hospitals, 1946–1976." Ph.D. diss. Boston University.

DeParle, Jason. 1982. "Money Matters." *Tobacco Road* 5 (3). Durham, N.C.: Duke University Publications Board.

Edmondson, Brad. 1985. "The Home Health Care Market." *American Demographics* 7 (12):29–51.

Ehrenreich, Barbara, and John Ehrenreich. 1970. *The American Health Empire*. New York: Vintage Books.

Eilers, Robert D. 1974. *Financing Health Care: Past and Prospects*. Minneapolis: Federal Reserve Bank of Minneapolis.

Ellwood, Paul Jr. 1982. "Competition and Medicine's Creeping Revolution." In *Financing Health Care: Competition versus Regulation*, ed. Duncan Yaggy and W. G. Anlyan. Cambridge, Mass.: Ballinger Publishing.

"Employee Benefits: Now a Third of Payroll Costs." 1976. *Nation's Business*, Oct., 36–37.

Estabrook, Leigh. 1984. "Women's Work in the Library/Information Sector." In *My Troubles Are Going to Have Trouble with Me*, ed. Karen B. Sacks and Dorothy Remy. New Brunswick, N. J.: Rutgers University Press.

Evans, Sarah. 1980. *Personal Politics: The Roots of Women's Liberation in the Civil Rights Movement and the New Left*. New York: Random House.

The Executive Letter. 1984. Hospital Edition, issue no. 512-H, Sept. 15., 1301 W. Moreno St., Pensacola, FL 32501.

Feldberg, Roslyn, and Evelyn Nakano Glenn. 1979. "Male and Female: Job versus Gender Models in the Sociology of Work." *Social Problems* 26 (5):524–38.

———. 1983. "Technology and Work Degradation: Effects of Office Automation on Women Clerical Workers." In *Machina Ex Dea*, ed. Joan Rothchild. New York: Pergamon Press.

Fink, Leon, and Brian Greenberg. 1979. "Organizing Montefiore: Labor Militancy Meets a Progressive Health Care Empire." In *Health Care in America: Essays in Social History,* ed. Susan Reverby and David Rosner. Philadelphia: Temple University Press.

Flexner, Abraham. 1910. *Medical Education in the United States and Canada: A Report to the Carnegie Foundation for the Advancement of Teaching.* New York: The Carnegie Foundation.

Foner, Philip S. 1980. *Women and the American Labor Movement from World War I to the Present.* New York: Free Press.

Fosdick, Raymond B. 1962. *Adventure in Giving: The Story of the General Education Board, a Foundation Established by John D. Rockefeller.* New York: Harper and Row.

Fox, Renee C. 1985. "Reflections and Opportunities in the Sociology of Medicine." *Journal of Health and Social Behavior* 26 (1):6–14.

Freyman, John G. 1977. *The American Health Care System: Its Genesis and Trajectory.* Huntington, N. Y.: Robert E. Krieger.

Garbarino, Joseph. 1960. *Health Plans and Collective Bargaining.* Berkeley: University of California Press.

Giddings, Paula. 1985. *When and Where I Enter: The Impact of Black Women on Race and Sex in America.* New York: Bantam Books.

Gifford, James F. 1972. *The Evolution of a Medical Center: A History of Medicine at Duke University to 1941.* Durham, N.C.: Duke University Press.

Glazer, Nona Y. 1984. "Servants to Capital: Unpaid Domestic Labor and Paid Work." *RRPE* 16 (1):61–88.

Glenn, Evelyn Nakano, and Roslyn Feldberg. 1977. "Degraded and Deskilled: The Proletarianization of Clerical Work." *Social Problems* 25 (1):520–64.

Goldberg, Roberta. 1983. *Organizing Women Office Workers: Dissatisfaction, Consciousness, and Action.* New York: Praeger Publishers.

Greater Durham Chamber of Commerce. 1981. *Economic Summary,* 1–2.

Gregory, Judith, and Karen Nussbaum. 1980. *Race Against Time: Automation of the Office.* Cleveland: Working Women, National Association of Office Workers.

Gutman, Herbert. 1977. *Work Culture and Society in Industrializing America: Essays in America's Working Class and Social History.* New York: Random House.

"Harmful Side Effects Detected in Corporate Health Care Trends." 1984. *AFL-CIO News,* Oct. 6.

"Health Costs Employers Fight Back." 1982. *Enterprise* 6 (9). Washington:

National Association of Manufacturers.

Himmelstein, David U., and Steffi Woohandler. 1984. "Medicine as Industry: The Health Care Sector in the United States." *Monthly Review,* April, 13–25.

Hirshfield, Daniel. 1970. *The Lost Reform: The Campaign For Compulsory Health Insurance in the U.S. From 1932–1943.* Cambridge: Harvard University Press.

Hochchild, Arlie R. 1983. *The Managed Heart: Commercialization of Human Feeling.* Berkeley: University of California Press.

Hoffius, Steve. 1980. "Charleston Hospital Workers' Strike, 1969." In *Working Lives: The Southern Exposure History of Labor in the South,* ed. Mark Miller. New York: Pantheon.

Honey, Maureen. 1984. *Creating Rosie the Riveter: Class, Gender, and Propaganda During World War II.* Amherst: University of Massachusetts Press.

Hooks, Bell. 1981. *Ain't I a Woman? Black Women and Feminism.* Boston: South End Press.

Howard, Robert. 1985. *Brave New Workplace.* New York: Viking Press.

Hull, Gloria et al., eds. 1981. *All the Women Are White, All the Blacks Are Men, but Some of Us Are Brave: Black Women's Studies.* New York: Feminist Press.

Humphries, Jane. 1977. "Class Struggle and the Persistence of the Working Class Family." *Cambridge Journal of Economics* 1 (3):241–58.

Institute of Medicine. 1981. *Health Care in a Context of Civil Rights.* Washington: National Academy Press.

———. Division of Health Care Services. 1983. *Nursing and Nursing Education: Public Policies and Private Actions.* Washington: National Academy Press.

Janiewski, Dolores E. 1985. *Sisterhood Denied: Race, Gender and Class in a New South Community.* Philadelphia: Temple University Press.

Jones, Jacqueline. 1985. *Labor of Love, Labor of Sorrow: Black Women, Work and the Family from Slavery to the Present.* New York: Basic Books.

Kahn-Hut, Rachel, Arlene Kaplan Daniels, and Richard Colvard. 1982. *Women and Work: Problems and Perspectives.* New York: Oxford University Press.

Kaplan, Temma. 1982. "Female Consciousness and Collective Action." *Signs* 7 (3):545–66.

Katzman, David M. 1981. *Seven Days a Week: Women and Domestic Service in Industrializing America.* Urbana: University of Illinois Press.

Kessler-Harris, Alice. 1982. *Out to Work: A History of Wage-Earning Women in the United States*. New York: Oxford University Press.

Kotelchuck, David, ed. 1976. *Prognosis Negative: Crisis in the Health Care System*. New York: Vintage Books.

Krause, Paul. 1982. "Buck Duke's Legacy." *Tobacco Road* 5 (3). Durham, N.C.: Duke University Publications Board.

Ladner, Joyce. 1971. *Tomorrow's Tomorrow: The Black Woman*. New York: Anchor.

Lamphere, Louise. 1986. "From Working Daughters to Working Mothers: Production and Reproduction in an Industrial Community." *American Ethnologist* 13 (1):118–30.

———. 1984. "On the Shop Floor: Multi-Ethnic Unity against the Conglomerate." In *My Troubles Are Going to Have Trouble with Me*, ed. Karen B. Sacks and Dorothy Remy. New Brunswick, N.J.: Rutgers University Press.

Lamphere, Louise, et al. 1980. "The Economic Struggles of Female Factory Workers: A Comparison between Early and recent French, Polish and Portuguese Immigrants." In *Proceedings of a Conference on Educational and Occupational Needs of White Ethnic Women*. Washington: National Institute of Education.

Law, Sylvia. 1976. "Blue Cross: What Went Wrong." In *Prognosis Negative: Crisis in the Health Care System*, ed. David Kotelchuck. New York: Vintage Books.

Lens, Sidney. 1949. *Left, Right and Center*. Hinsdale, Ill.: Henry Regnery.

Lichtenstein, Nelson. 1983. "Defending the No Strike Pledge: CIO Politics During World War II." In *Workers' Struggles, Past and Present*, ed. James R. Green. Philadelphia: Temple University Press.

Lipsitz, George. 1982. *Class and Culture in Cold War America*. South Hadley, Mass.: J. F. Bergin.

Lockwood, David. 1958. *The Blackcoated Worker: A Study in Class Consciousness*. London: George Allen & Unwin.

Machung, Anne. 1984. "Word Processing: Forward for Business, Backward for Women." In *My Troubles Are Going to Have Trouble with Me*, ed. Karen B. Sacks and Dorothy Remy. New Brunswick, N. J.: Rutgers University Press.

McConville, Ed. 1978. "Oliver Harvey 'Got to Take Some Risks.'" *Southern Exposure* 6 (2):24–28.

McDonald, Charles, and Dick Wilson. 1979. "Peddling the 'Union-Free' Guarantee." *The American Federationist*, April, 12–19.

McMahon, J. A. 1982. "Financing Health Care: An Historical Overview." In *Financing Health Care: Competition versus Regulation*, ed. Duncan Yaggy and W. G. Anlyan. Cambridge, Mass.: Ballinger Publishing.

Madden, Thomas A., I. R. Turner, and E. J. Eckenfels. 1982. *The Health Almanac*. New York: Raven Press.

Malveaux, Julianne, and Susan Englander. 1985. "Race and Class in Nursing Occupations." Paper presented at Mid-Atlantic Women's Studies Association meetings, Washington, Oct.

Melosh, Barbara. 1982. *The Physician's Hand*. Philadelphia: Temple University Press.

Milkman, Ruth, ed. 1985. *Women, Work and Protest*. Boston: Routledge & Kegan Paul.

Miller, Arthur M. 1976. "Desegration and Negro Leadership in Durham 1954–1963." M.A. thesis, University of North Carolina.

Miller, Richard U., Brian Becker, and Edward Krinsky. 1979. *The Impact of Collective Bargaining on Hospitals*. New York: Praeger Publishers.

Mills, C. Wright. 1956. *White Collar*. New York: Oxford University Press.

"Modern Managements Methods, Inc." n.d. *R.U.B. Sheet*. National Organizing Coordinating Committee AFL-CIO, no.3.

Munts, Raymond. 1967. *Bargaining for Health: Labor Unions, Health Insurance and Medical Care*. Madison: University of Wisconsin Press.

Murphree, Mary. 1984. "Brave New Office: The Changing World of the Legal Secretary." In *My Troubles Are Going to Have Trouble with Me*, ed. Karen B. Sacks and Dorothy Remy. New Burnswick, N. J.: Rutgers University Press.

———. 1985. *Women and Office Automation: Issues in the Decade Ahead*. Washington: Women's Bureau, U.S. Department of Labor.

Noyelle, Tierry J. 1985. "The New Technology and the New Economy: Implications for Equal Employment Opportunity." Paper presented at Authors' Workshop, National Research Council, National Academy of Sciences, Washington.

"A Nursing Home Drive." 1983. *Wall Street Journal*, Sept. 20.

Pachino, Marcie. 1982. "Equity at Best." *Tobacco Road* 5 (3). Durham, N. C.: Duke University Publications Board.

Palmer, Phyllis. 1984. "Housework and Domestic Labor: Racial and Technological Change." In *My Troubles Are Going to Have Trouble with Me*, ed. Karen B. Sacks and Dorothy Remy. New Brunswick, N. J.: Rutgers University Press.

"Peonage at Duke University." 1959. *Carolina Times*, March 21.

Preiss, Jack. n.d. "Part One," unpublished and manuscript draft.

Rapp, Rayna. 1978. "Family and Class in Contemporary America: Notes Toward an Understanding of Ideology." *Science and Society* 42 (3):278–300.

Redburn, Francis Stevens. 1970. "Protest and Policy in Durham." Ph.D. diss., University of North Carolina.

Reinhart, Uwe E. 1982. "Table Manners at the Health Care Feast." In *Financing Health Care: Competition versus Regulation*, ed. Duncan Yaggy and W. G. Anlyan. Cambridge, Mass.: Ballinger Publishing.

Relman, Arthur S. 1984. "Who Will Pay for Medical Education in Our Teaching Hospitals?" *Science*, Oct. 5, 20–23.

Reverby, Susan. 1975. "Borrowing a Volume from Industry: A Study of Management Reform in American Hospitals," unpublished manuscript.

———. 1976. "Health Is Women's Work." In *America's Working Women*, ed. Rosalyn Baxandall, Linda Gordon, and Susan Reverby. New York: Vintage Books.

———. 1979. *One Strong Voice . . . or an Out of Tune Chorus?* New York: District 1199 Bread and Roses Project.

———, and David Rosner, eds. 1979. *Health Care in America: Essays in Social History.* Philadelphia: Temple University Press.

Rich, Spencer. 1984. "Growth of Health Plan Costs Slowing Down, Survey Finds." *Washington Post*, June 6, A3.

———. 1984a. "Health Cost Inflation Slowing." *Washington Post*, July 15, A5.

———. 1983. "U.S. Study Analyzes Worker Health Plans," *Washington Post*, July 10, A10.

"The Robust New Business in Home Health Care." 1983. *Business Week*, June 13, 96, 100.

Rodberg, Leonard, and Gelvin Stevenson. 1977. "The Health Care Industry in Advanced Capitalism." *RRPE* 9 (1):104–15.

Rodgers-Rose, LaFrances, ed. 1980. *The Black Woman.* Beverly Hills, Calif.: Sage Publications

Rollins, Judith. 1985. *Between Women: Domestics and Their Employers.* Philadelphia: Temple University Press.

Rosner, David. 1982. *A Once Charitable Enterprise, Hospitals and Health*

Care in Brooklyn and New York, 1885–1915. Cambridge: Cambridge University Press.

Rowbotham, Sheila. 1973. *Women, Resistance and Revolution.* New York: Pantheon.

Roy, Donald. 1954. "Efficiency and the Fix: Informal Intergroup Relations in a Piecework Machine Shop." *AJS* 60 (3):255–66.

———. 1953. "Work Satisfaction and Social Reward in Quota Achievement." *ASR* 18:507–14.

Sabel, Charles. 1982. *Work and Politics: The Division of Labor in Industry.* Cambridge: Cambridge University Press.

Sacks, Karen Brodkin. 1984. "Kinship and Class Consciousness: Family Values and Work Experience Among Hospital Workers in an American Southern Town." In *Interst and Emotion,* ed. Hans Medick and David Warren Sabean. Cambridge: Cambridge, University Press.

———. 1983. "Networking—When Potluck Is Political" *MS,* April, 97.

———, and Dorothy Remy, eds. 1984. *My Troubles Are Going to Have Trouble with Me: Everyday Trials and Triumphs of Women Workers.* New Brunswick, N.J.: Rutgers University Press.

———. Forthcoming. *Women, Technology and Health Care.* Washington: Women's Bureau, U.S. Department of Labor.

Salmon, J. Warren. 1975. "The Health Maintenance Organization Strategy: A Corporate Takeover of Health Services Delivery." *IJHS* 5 (4):609–24.

Schwartz, James. 1965. "Early History of Prepaid Medical Care Plans." *Bulletin of the History of Medicine* 39:450–75.

Scott, Joan W. 1982. "The Mechanization of Women's Work" *Scientific American,* Sept., 166–87.

Sekscenski, Edward. 1981. "The Health Services Industry: A Decade of Expansion." *MLR,* May, 9–16.

———. 1984. *The Health Services Industry in the United States, Trends in Employment from 1970 to 1983 with Projections to 1995.* Washington: AFL-CIO Department of Professional Employees.

Sexton, Patricia. 1982. *The New Nightingales: Hospital Workers, Unions, New Women's Issues.* New York: Enquiry Press.

Shapiro-Perl, Nina. 1984. "Resistance Strategies: The Routine Struggle for Bread and Roses." In *My Troubles Are Going to Have Trouble with Me,* ed. Karen B. Sacks and Dorothy Remy. New Brunswick, N.J.: Rutgers University Press.

Shryock, Richard H. 1947. *The Development of Modern Medicine.* New York: Alfred Knopf.

Sidel, Victor, and Ruth Sidel, eds. 1984. *Reforming Medicine.* New York: Pantheon.

Sloan, Frank A., and Bruce Steinwald. 1980. *Hospital Labor Markets.* Lexington, Mass.: D.C. Heath.

Stack, Carol. 1974. *All Our Kin.* New York: Harper Colophon.

Starr, Paul. 1982. *The Social Transformation of American Medicine.* New York: Basic Books.

Starr, Paul, and Theodore Marmor. 1984. "The United States: A Social Forecast." In *The End of an Illusion: The Future of Health Policy in Western Industrialized Nations,* ed. Jean de Kervasdoue, John R. Kimberly, and Victor G. Rodwin. Berkeley: University of California Press.

Tax, Meredith. 1980. *The Rising of the Women: Feminist Solidarity and Class Conflict 1880–1917.* New York: Montly Review Press.

Teitelman, Robert. 1984. "Labor Pains," *Forbes,* July 2, 68.

Tepperman, Jean. 1976. *Not Servants, Not Machines: Office Workers Speak Out.* Boston: Beacon Press.

Thurow, Lester. 1984. "Learning to Say 'No.'" *New England Journal of Medicine,* Dec. 13, 1569–571.

Tilly, Louise, and Joan Scott. 1978. *Women, Work, and Family.* New York: Holt, Rinehart and Winston.

"The Upheaval in Health Care." 1983. *Busines Week,* July 25, 44–56.

U.S. Bureau of the Census. 1972. *General Social and Economic Characteristics.* Washington: U.S. Government Printing Office.

———. 1982. Statistical Abstract of the United States 1982–1983. 103 ed. Washington: U.S. Government Printing Office.

U.S. Department of Health and Human Services. 1982. *Health United States 1982.* Washington: U.S. Government Printing Office.

———. 1984. *Minorities and Women in the Health Fields. 1984 Edition.* Washington: U.S. Government Printing Office.

U.S. Training and Employment Service. 1970. *Job Descriptions and Organizational Analysis for Hospitals and Related Health Services.* Washington: U.S. Government Printing Office.

Vogel, Morris. 1980. *The Invention of the Modern Hospital, Boston 1870–1930.* Chicago: University of Chicago Press.

Warneke, Diane. 1984. *Microelectronics and Working Women: A Literature Summary.* Washington: National Academy Press.

Westwood, Sallie. 1985. *All Day Every Day: Factory and Family in the Making of Women's Lives.* Urbana: University of Illinois Press.

Whitney, Wayne. 1971. "NLRB Gets Hospital Union Case." *Duke Chronicle*, Feb. 18.

Wise, Leah. 1980. "Stirring the Pot: Oliver Harvey's Narrative Account of the Struggle to Organize Duke University." M.A. thesis, Duke University.

Woolhandler, Steffi, David U. Himmelstein, et al. 1983. "Public Money, Private Control: A Case Study of Hospital Financing in Oakland and Berkeley, California." *AJPH* 73 (5):584–87.

Yaggy, Duncan, and William G. Anlyan, eds. 1982. *Financing Health Care: Competition versus Regulation.* Cambridge, Mass: Ballinger Publishing.

Yanigasako, Sylvia. 1977. "Woman-Centered Kin Networks in Urban, Bilateral Kinship." *AE* 4(2):207–26.

Young, Michael, and Peter Willmott. 1962. *Family and Kinship in East London.* Baltimore: Penguin.

Duke Sources

Affirmative Action Reports: EEO–1:1969; EEO–6:1976, 1979, 1981.

American Health Facilities. 1973. *Duke Hospital Modernization and Expansion Project—1973.* Vols. 1 and 2. Durham, N.C.: Duke University Medical Center.

Booz, Allen, and Hamilton. 1961. *Long Range Plan for Physical Plant Development.* Vols. 1 and 2. Durham, N.C.: Duke University Medical Center.

Bulletin of Duke University Allied Health Programs. 1981–82.

Bulletin of the Duke University School of Medicine and Medical Center. 1965–66; 1970–71; 1975–76; 1978–79; 1983–84.

Duke University. 1952. *The First Twenty Years: A History of the Duke University Schools of Medicine, Nursing and Health Services, and Duke Hospital 1930–1950.* Bulletin of Duke University 24 (7a). Durham, N.C.: Duke University.

Duke University Committee on Long Range Planning. 1959, 1972. Duke University Archives.

Duke University Medical Center. 1964. *Development Program 1964–1970.*

———. 1966. *Today's Challenge, Tomorrow's Promise.* Duke's Fifth Decade Program.

———. 1974. *To Heal, to Teach to Discover.* The Epoch Campaign.

Knight, Douglas M. 1970. *A President's Report. In Deeds, Not Years: A Conversation with Douglas Maitland Knight, President of Duke University 1963–1969.*

Opportunity Development Center. *Reports* 1977–78; 1978–79; 1980–81; 1982–83.

President's Report, 1949–60. Duke University, Durham, N.C.

Duke Periodicals

Aeolus
Duke Chronicle
Heartbeat
Intercom

Durham Newspapers

Carolina Times
Durham Morning Herald
Durham Sun
North Carolina Anvil
Duke Workers Newsletter
We the People

Archives, Private Collections

DU Archives: Papers of Local 77; Vigil; 1199; Employee Union; John Strange; Segal, B.A. honors thesis, David Herderson journal (in Vigil Papers); *Local 77 Newsletter*, and *The Union Organizer* (in Employee Union papers).

AFSCME Local 77 Files: NLRB records and correspondence Case Nos. 11–RC–4041 and 11–RC–4607. *Fuller v. Duke University*, U.S. District Court Middle District of North Carolina, Durham Division, File No. C–75–445–D.

North Central Legal Assistance Program: public documents of *Caston, et al. v. Duke University*, Civil Action No. C–80–137–D, United States District Court, Middle District of North Carolina, Durham Division.

Gladys Glenn private collection: Union and Duke leaflets and mailings.

Index

Davis, Percy, 152
Davison, Wilburt, 20–21
Demoralization, of workers, 116, 131, 211
Department of Labor complaints, 103
  rulings on pay, 146–47
Desegregation activities (Durham, N.C.),
  41–42, 57–58
Diagnosis related groups, (DRGs), 165
Dieticians, 178–79
Discrimination in hiring, 44–45, 78–79,
  97–98, 100, 101
Division of labor, 13–14. *See also* Specialization
Dixon, Alice, 133, 135, 154
Doctors
  offensive behavior of, 76–77, 101
  racism of, 194
  separate socializing of, 126
Domestic workers, 38–39. *See also* Food
  service workers;
  Housekeeping workers
Duke DTO Association, 104
Duke-Durham Medical Committee for
  Human Rights, 99, 104
Duke Employees Benevolent Society, 45, 46
Duke Endowment, 17, 20
Duke family, 16–17
Duke Medical Center, 104. *See also* Duke
  North; Duke "South"
  antiunion campaign of, 107–8, 115, 147–
  48, 155–57, 168
  changing work at, 23–24
  competition from HMOs, 167
  expansion of, 19–20, 23–27, 103–4
  history of, 15–23
  internal grievance committees, 103
  liberal face to union opposition, 34, 56
  wage levels, 45–46, 168
Duke North, 25–27
  food service, 177–78
  housekeeping working conditions, 170–73
  workers and community activists' opposition to, 103–4
Duke Organizing Committee, 145
Duke "South," 24–27, 177
Duke Student's Afro-American Society, 52
Duke University Employees Advisory Committee (DUERAC), 53–54
Duke University, faculty role in unionization, 47, 52, 53
  history of, 17–19

Duke Workers Alliance, 104
Durham, N.C., 21–23, 34
  economic and political climate of, 6, 21–
  23, 42–44
Durham Committee on the Affairs of Black
  People, 41
Durham Health Collective of the New
  American Movement, 103
Durham Organizing Committee (DOC), 112

Efficiency experts, 48, 176–77
Efficiency procedures, intimidating effects
  of, 176–77
Elitism, 149, 190–91
Employees Council, segregation of, 53–54
Employer-paid health insurance, 19, 182
Equal Rights Amendment campaign, 213
Evans, Sarah, 213
Extended care facilities, 168, 169

Faction-fighting, 54–56, 111–16, 138, 140,
  143
Factorylike working conditions, at medical
  center, 25, 88–89, 176–77, 181–82,
  186–87
The Facts (Duke leaflet), 147
Family
  as part of social network, 22, 122–27,
  213–15
  structure and centerwomen, 133–34
  values, derived from, 3, 127–37
Favoritism, 92–94, 210
Fear of radicals, 66–67, 116, 149
Feminist consciousness, 87, 212–14
Few, William Preston, 17
Flowers, Barbara, 50–51, 106, 146
Food service workers, 38–39, 177–87
  and second union drive, 158
  convenience foods, experience with,
  184–86
  health benefits of, 182
  job titles of, 178–80
  role in unionization, 50–51, 69, 158
  satisfactions and frustrations, 180–81
  social control of, 186–87
  strike of, 52–53
  wages versus cafeteria costs, 156–57
  walkouts of, 50–51, 181
  working conditions of, 178, 181–82,
  186–87
Formal education, 162, 190, 192. *See*

A Note on the Author

KAREN BRODKIN SACKS is an anthropologist and feminist scholar long active in the women's movement. Author of *Sisters and Wives*, co-editor of *My Troubles Are Going to Have Trouble with Me* and numerous scholarly and popular articles, she is associate professor of anthropology and director of women's studies at the University of California, Los Angeles.